# Day Hike!

# WASHINGTON
# OLYMPIC PENINSULA

5th Edition

Seabury Blair Jr.

SASQUATCH BOOKS

SEATTLE

Printed in China

Published by Sasquatch Books
27 26 25 24 23          6 5 4 3 2 1

Cover photograph: © Greg Vaughn / Alamy Stock Photo | Cover design: Hillary Grant
Interior design: Andrew Fuller/Anna Goldstein
Interior photographs: Seabury Blair Jr. Additional photos by Steve Zugschwerdt
(pages 46, 174, and 216), Marlene Blair (page 149), and Jeanne Lee (page 171)
Interior maps: Marlene Blair

Library of Congress Cataloging-in-Publication Data is available

ISBN: 978-1-63217-465-9

---

**IMPORTANT NOTE:** Please use common sense. No guidebook can act as a substitute for experience, careful planning, the right equipment, and appropriate training. There is inherent danger in all the activities described in this book, and readers must assume full responsibility for their own actions and safety. Changing or unfavorable conditions in weather, roads, trails, snow, waterways, and so forth cannot be anticipated by the author or publisher, but should be considered by any outdoor participants. The author and publisher will not be responsible for the safety of users of this guide, and neither of them shall be liable or responsible for any legal liability, or any loss or damage or physical injury of any kind, allegedly arising from any information herein.

Given the potential for changes to trail accessibility and hiking rules and regulations post-publication, please check ahead for updates on contact information, parking passes, and camping permits.

---

Sasquatch Books | 1325 Fourth Avenue, Suite 1025 | Seattle, WA 98101
SasquatchBooks.com

# CONTENTS

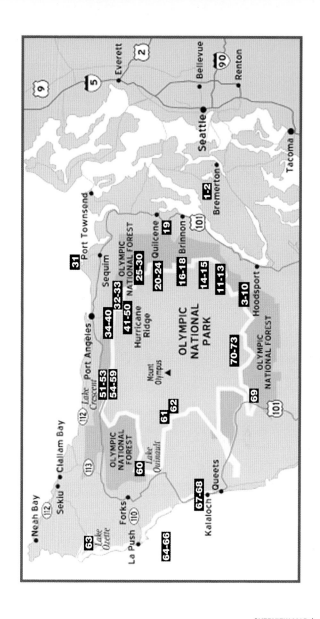

# HIKES AT A GLANCE

## EASY

| NO. | HIKE NAME | RATING | BEST SEASON | KIDS | DOGS |
|---|---|---|---|---|---|
| 3. | Lower Skokomish River | ★★★ | Year-round | ✔ | ✔ |
| 10. | Four Stream | ★★ | Year-round | ✔ | |
| 21. | Lower Big Quilcene Trail | ★★ | Year-round | | ✔ |
| 31. | Dungeness Spit | ★★★★ | Fall/Winter | ✔ | |
| 41. | Olympic Discovery Trail | ★★ | Fall/Winter | | ✔ |
| 44. | Elwha Loop | ★★★★ | Year-round | ✔ | |
| 46. | Aldwell Lakebed | ★★ | Year-round | | |
| 48. | Olympic Hot Springs | ★★★★ | Spring/winter | ✔ | |
| 51. | Spruce Railroad Trail | ★★★ | Year-round | ✔ | |
| 54. | North Fork Sol Duc | ★★★★ | Spring | ✔ | |
| 60. | Bogachiel Ranger Station | ★★ | Spring | ✔ | ✔ |
| 61. | Happy Four Shelter | ★★★★ | Year-round | ✔ | |
| 62. | Big Flat | ★★★★★ | Year-round | ✔ | |
| 64. | Hole-in-the-Wall | ★★★★ | Year-round | ✔ | ✔ |
| 65. | Second Beach | ★★★ | Year-round | ✔ | |
| 66. | Third Beach | ★ | Year-round | ✔ | |
| 67. | Kalaloch North | ★★★★ | Year-round | ✔ | ✔ |
| 68. | Kalaloch South | ★★★★ | Year-round | ✔ | ✔ |
| 71. | Halfway House | ★★★ | Year-round | ✔ | |

## MODERATE

| NO. | HIKE NAME | RATING | BEST SEASON | KIDS | DOGS |
|---|---|---|---|---|---|
| 1. | Green Mountain via Wildcat Trail | ★ | Year-round | | ✔ |
| 2. | Green Mountain via Gold Creek Trail | ★★ | Year-round | | ✔ |
| 4. | Big Creek Loop | ★★ | Year-round | ✔ | ✔ |
| 5. | Dry Creek Trail | ★★ | Year-round | | ✔ |
| 9. | Spike Camp | ★★ | Year-round | ✔ | |

| NO. | HIKE NAME | RATING | BEST SEASON | KIDS | DOGS |
|---|---|---|---|---|---|
| 11. | Lena Lake | ★★★ | Spring/summer/fall | ✔ | ✔ |
| 25. | Gray Wolf Trail | ★ | Spring | ✔ | ✔ |
| 27. | Camp Handy | ★★★★ | Late spring/summer | ✔ | ✔ |
| 40. | Roaring Winds, Obstruction Point | ★★★★★ | Summer | | |
| 45. | Lillian River | ★★★ | Spring | ✔ | |
| 50. | Boulder Falls | ★★ | Summer | | |
| 58. | Upper Sol Duc Campsite | ★★ | Late spring/fall | ✔ | |
| 63. | Cape Alava Loop | ★★★★★ | Year-round | ✔ | |
| 70. | Big Creek | ★★★ | Year-round | ✔ | |
| 72. | Pony Bridge | ★★ | Year-round | ✔ | |

## MODERATELY DIFFICULT

| NO. | HIKE NAME | RATING | BEST SEASON | KIDS | DOGS |
|---|---|---|---|---|---|
| 15. | Big Hump | ★★ | Year-round | | ✔ |
| 18. | Dosewallips Campground | ★★★ | Summer/fall | ✔ | ✔ |
| 26. | Tubal Cain Mine | ★★★ | Summer | | ✔ |
| 32. | Roaring Winds, Deer Park | ★★★★ | Summer/fall | | |
| 36. | Mount Angeles Saddle | ★★★★ | Summer | | |
| 37. | Hurricane Hill | ★★★★★ | Summer/fall | | |
| 38. | PJ Lake | ★ | Summer | | |
| 39. | Moose Lake | ★★★★★ | Summer/fall | | |
| 42. | Mills Lakebed | ★★ | Summer | | |
| 43. | Wolf Creek | ★★ | Summer | | |
| 52. | Pyramid Mountain | ★★★ | Summer | | |
| 55. | Mink Lake Meadows | ★★★ | Spring/summer/fall | ✔ | |

## DIFFICULT

| NO. | HIKE NAME | RATING | BEST SEASON | KIDS | DOGS |
|---|---|---|---|---|---|
| 6. | Mount Ellinor | ★★★★★ | Summer/fall | | ✔ |
| 7. | Mount Rose | ★★ | Summer/fall | | ✔ |
| 8. | Silver Snag Hill, Wagonwheel Lake | ★★★★ | Summer/fall | | |
| 13. | Mildred Lakes | ★★★ | Summer/fall | | ✔ |
| 14. | Jupiter Ridge | ★★ | Late summer/fall | | ✔ |

| No. | Hike Name | Rating | Best Season | Kids | Dogs |
|-----|-----------|--------|-------------|------|------|
| 19. | Mount Walker | ★ ★ ★ | Year-round | | ✔ |
| 20. | Tunnel Creek, Quilcene | ★ ★ ★ | Summer | | ✔ |
| 22. | Marmot Pass | ★ ★ ★ ★ ★ | Summer/fall | | ✔ |
| 23. | Mount Townsend | ★ ★ ★ ★ | Summer/fall | | ✔ |
| 24. | Silver Lakes | ★ ★ ★ ★ | Summer/fall | | ✔ |
| 28. | Royal Lake | ★ ★ ★ ★ | Summer/fall | | ✔ |
| 30. | Lower Dungeness Trail | ★ ★ | Spring/summer/fall | | ✔ |
| 33. | Three Forks | ★ ★ ★ ★ | Summer/fall | | |
| 34. | Heather Park–Lake Angeles Loop | ★ ★ ★ ★ ★ | Summer/fall | | |
| 35. | Klahhane Ridge | ★ ★ ★ ★ | Summer/fall | | |
| 47. | Happy Lake | ★ ★ ★ | Summer/fall | | |
| 49. | Boulder Lake | ★ ★ ★ ★ | Summer/fall | | |
| 53. | Storm King | ★ ★ | Fall | | |
| 56. | Little Divide Loop | ★ ★ ★ ★ | Summer/fall | | |
| 57. | Potholes Meadows | ★ ★ ★ | Fall | | |
| 59. | High Divide Loop | ★ ★ ★ ★ ★ | Summer/fall | | |
| 69. | Colonel Bob | ★ ★ | Summer | ✔ | |

## EXTREME

| NO. | HIKE NAME | RATING | BEST SEASON | KIDS | DOGS |
|-----|-----------|--------|-------------|------|------|
| 12. | Lake of the Angels | ★ ★ ★ ★ | Late summer/fall | | ✔ |
| 16. | Tunnel Creek, Dosewallips | ★ | Summer | | ✔ |
| 17. | Lake Constance | ★ ★ ★ | Summer | | |
| 29. | Maynard Burn | ★ ★ ★ ★ | Late summer | | ✔ |
| 73. | Low Divide–Elwha | ★ ★ ★ ★ | Midsummer | | |

# ACKNOWLEDGMENTS

We all owe our thanks to the trail maintenance crews and volunteers who work every year to keep our wilderness pathways in good condition, making our hiking experience safer and more enjoyable. Organizations such as the Washington Trails Association are key to recruiting and supporting volunteer efforts throughout the state to maintain our wild walkways.

I'm personally grateful to all of the people who made my Olympic adventures so memorable: Eric Cederwall, Jim Drannan, Jeanne Lee, the late Tom Hall, Ron C. Judd, and Steve Zugschwerdt. I wouldn't have seen some of the magical places of the Olympic Mountains without the coaching and tutelage of the instructors of the long-forgotten Olympic College Mountaineering Class. Longtime members and founders of Olympic Mountain Rescue—including Roger Beckett and the late Dave Sicks and Glenn Kelsey—showed me trails I might not otherwise have outlined here.

I've been extremely fortunate to have continued support from the editors of the *Kitsap Sun* since I retired in 1998. They allowed an old guy—me—to keep writing columns and stories about my favorite piece of the outdoors for all these years. I'm especially grateful to Mike Phillips, Chuck Stark, Nathan Joyce, and David Nelson.

Thanks also to Pam McPeek, whose note to me in 2014 reinvigorated this old guy. She told me the first edition of this guide changed her life by getting her back on the trail. Between then and June 2017, Pam and husband Dr. Bill Halligan have hiked 1,916.5 miles (Pam's very fastidious about numbers).

Finally, I thank my wife and mapmaker, Marlene Blair, who gave me inspiration, love, and support—though I must say, little respect.

# PREFACE

Early hiking companions called him "Griz," and Robert L. Wood wrote letters on personalized stationery featuring a growling bear emerging from its cave. On my earliest spring hikes with him, the preeminent Olympic Mountain historian and guidebook author complained about his "hibernation belly"—which rapidly disappeared as vernal outings turned to serious summer backpacks.

Wood wrote *Trail Country: The Olympic Mountains* and *The Olympic Mountains Trail Guide*, which I think are the nation's most lyric and authoritative books about wilderness pathways. He was as much a poet as a guidebook author.

I first met him on the trail in 1974, in the middle of the Olympic Mountains he loved so much. He was leading a group of hikers to the Bailey Range, and I was scrambling from Appleton Pass to High Divide on a one-day marathon trek from Sol Duc Hot Springs. When we passed on the trail, I stopped him and mentioned I was a big fan. We exchanged addresses, and my first hike with him took us to Mount St. Helens, where Wood interviewed an early Lake Cushman pioneer for his book *Men, Mules, and Mountains*.

He was delighted to share his love and knowledge of the mountains at our sunset doorstep. Every year, he guided groups on his traditional climb of Mount Olympus, the summit of the Olympic Peninsula. Wood literally hauled me, a shameless acrophobe, by the hand up the East Peak of that mountain. He knew the Olympics better than anyone: on one of his 28 Olympus pre-GPS outings, we found ourselves in the middle of the Blue Glacier in a whiteout. You couldn't see from one end to the other of the 150-foot rope that connected three climbers.

Nobody had the slightest idea where we were, except Bob Wood, who stopped in the middle of the ice and snow and white nothingness, turned left, and without hesitation, led us directly to camp. How did he know when to turn, I asked?

"I count steps," he replied. He knew how many paces to take from Glacier Pass before he had to turn to Cal Tech Camp; he'd done it so many times before. In years that followed, Wood took me and others to places in the Olympics few people ever go. In researching one of his six books, he retraced the route of the first white man to hike from the source of the Queets River to the Pacific Ocean. Wood was the only person I know who left footprints on the Hubert and White Glaciers, two of Olympus's most remote ice fields.

He died in 2003 from complications resulting from Parkinson's disease, diagnosed 13 years earlier. His close friend Kent Heathershaw—who first scaled Olympus with Bob in 1961—scattered the author's ashes from the summit of Olympus the following year.

I followed Bob Wood's old Danner tracks on and off Olympic trails for nearly a decade, learning his favorite places and scrambling up his favorite peaks. He was my mentor, and I owe him a debt of Olympic hiking, history, and trail knowledge I can never repay. It is my abiding hope that his spirit leads you, as he led me, on the trails outlined in this book.

# INTRODUCTION

Herb Crisler. Chris Morgenroth. Minnie Peterson. They were the lucky ones, the ones who pioneered on the land that is now Olympic National Park and Olympic National Forest.

There were earlier explorers: James Christie and Charles Barnes. They were among the first to see the blue ice of Olympic glaciers; the massive cedar, fir, and spruce cloaking the valleys; the roiling rivers filled with fish. Their tracks were made a scant 85 to 150 years ago, and as far as anyone knows, they were the first human tracks in the interior of the Olympic Mountains.

You may have heard of some of them. Herb Crisler filmed the 1952 *The Olympic Elk* for Walt Disney, and in 1930—8 years before Congress created Olympic National Park—won a $500 bet he could spend 30 days in the Olympics carrying only a pocketknife, 75 pounds of camera gear, and three carrier pigeons for what we might today call "real time" reports.

When he returned from that adventure, Crisler told a reporter in 1977, "I fell in love with the animals, and I vowed that if I ever got out alive, I wasn't going to hunt anymore, only photograph them. The more I photographed, the more I fell in love." Crisler's name and tireless work to establish a national park on the Olympic Peninsula is largely absent from park history.

Chris Morgenroth—some spelled his name "Morganroth"—was a pioneering forest ranger who homesteaded on the Bogachiel River in 1890. Minnie Peterson, whose family settled on the Hoh River in 1888, was a guide and packer in the Olympics for five decades.

James Christie was the leader of the 1889–1990 *Seattle Press* Expedition of the Olympic Mountains. Charles Barnes was among the first explorers who braved one of the worst winters in Olympic history to forge a trail up the Elwha River and out the North Fork of the Quinault, mapping such places as the Bailey Range, which still has no developed trails. In recounting the adventure in the July 16, 1890, edition of the *Press*, entitled "Found in the Olympics: A Resume of the Natural Resources of the Explored Region," he recorded wildlife that the expedition members had seen. There were elk, deer, and bear, he said, and he concluded his report by writing: "One goat was seen by the party."

That was about a quarter of a century before Port Angeles hunters imported a dozen mountain goats to the Olympic Mountains, and a half-century before Congress created the national park. Barnes's journal entry and the *Press* article is largely discounted by Olympic National Park officials, who maintain that mountain goats are not native to the Olympic Mountains.

Imagine what it must have been like to be the first person to walk beside the Elwha River, or clamber across the Catwalk between Cat Peak and Mount Carrie. You'll find trails, both developed and boot-stomped, at those spots today. It would be difficult, if not impossible, to find a single square inch of Olympic National Forest or Olympic National Park that hasn't been stepped upon by a human being. Still, the park and wilderness areas of the forest are as wild as any place you can find in the Lower 48.

When I first hiked to Moose Lake from Obstruction Point in 1969, I saw two other hikers on the trail. Hundreds make that trek on weekends today, campsites are reserved, and park rangers patrol to enforce backcountry rules. During summers, park visitors must often wait in their cars at the Heart O' the Hills entrance station for up to 45 minutes before they are permitted to drive to Hurricane Ridge. Unless you have reserved a site ahead of time at Sol Duc or Kalaloch Campgrounds, you are likely to be sent elsewhere.

Thanks to protections provided by Congress, change walks slowly on this treasured land. However, a million more people visited Olympic National Park in 2019 than five decades before. Despite several notable exceptions in Olympic National Forest, those extra million crowd the same trails that were available 50 years ago. For the most part, the only additional trail miles have been added by roads closed by nature or policy.

Since the park was created in 1938, dozens of miles of roads have disappeared on the Skokomish, North Fork Skokomish, Hamma Hamma, Duckabush, Dosewallips, Elwha, and Quinault Rivers. Day hikes once considered to be of average difficulty, like Boulder Lake in the Elwha drainage or Diamond Meadows on the Dosewallips, have become strenuous for the average hiker to walk in a day. In 1975, you'd climb about 7 miles, out and back, to Boulder; today, it's 12 miles—24 if the Olympic Hot Springs Road isn't fixed yet. Diamond Meadows was a 13-mile walk before the Dose Road washed away 20 years ago; now, it's 25 miles.

I believe the road closures will be good in the long term, once those in my pre-glacial generation have forgotten what it was like to drive to Olympic Hot Springs Campground, then hike 10 miles to Appleton Pass and back before soaking those sore muscles in the hot pools. The 5-mile trek to and from today's trailhead is no longer on paved road and may someday not be recognizable as a former auto route. Nature may reclaim more roads in the Olympics, particularly where they are necessary only to serve hikers—roads such as those leading to Obstruction Point or Deer Park, or the North or South Forks of the Quinault.

Whatever the future holds for these roiling rivers, cloud-clawing peaks, and ancient forests, the certainty is that as long as they remain protected, they'll be there for you and your children. In that sense, you're as lucky as Charles Barnes and the rest.

—Seabury Blair Jr.

# THE OLYMPIC PENINSULA

All but two hikes outlined in this guide are on a lumpy, green, decidedly wet spot of earth called the Olympic Peninsula. It is a unique place of great beauty, a day hiker's dream.

You can walk a pristine ocean beach one day and on the next, stroll to the edge of a living glacier. You can watch orcas playing in the Strait of Juan de Fuca and, with a pair of good binoculars, see them from the tops of 6,000-foot peaks.

Few places anywhere in the Lower 48 are so crowded with wildlife: from seals and gray whales off the Pacific beaches to Roosevelt elk and Columbia blacktail deer of the high country; and from Obstruction Point's radiator hose–chewing marmots to the killer raccoons of Ozette. Rare mountain goats, otters, eagles, ospreys, ravens—critters of every size and shape call the Olympic Peninsula home. There are so many varieties of slugs on the Olympic Peninsula that the whole place turns to slime during big rains. (You can check my research on that point if you want.)

And don't get me started on trees and plants. Take nearly any one of the hikes in this book and you're certain to see some Really Big Trees. In fact, seven of them are documented, world heavyweight champions. Wildflowers and green things are everywhere, from rare orchids to multiple varieties of ferns.

As interesting as the variety of Olympic plants and animals is the amazing weather dichotomy. The Olympic Mountains, at the heart of the Peninsula, generate their own weather. As storm clouds sweep off the Pacific Ocean, holding more water than a whole brewpub full of patrons waiting for a single stall, they dump all over the south and west sides of the mountains. Mount Olympus, the highest peak, gets more than 240 inches of precipitation every year. As a result, the clouds don't have much left by the time they pass over the north and east sides of the mountains. Up there, fewer than 30 miles from Olympus, it rains only about 17 inches a year. A day hiker in search of sunshine, then, is more likely to find it on the trails in this so-called "rain shadow": the Dungeness or Gray Wolf Rivers or the peaks and valleys of the eastern Olympics.

Yet as strange as it may seem, some wilderness pedestrians appear to enjoy, or at least tolerate, that wet stuff from the sky, especially in the rain forests where day hiking without moisture just doesn't seem, well, proper.

## Olympic National Park vs. Olympic National Forest

At the core of the Peninsula, and along more than 60 miles of its wild Pacific beaches, is Olympic National Park. It was created in 1938 and provides many of the trails described here. Nearly surrounding the park in a wide, green belt is Olympic National Forest, where you'll find the remaining hikes in this guide. The park is administered by the Department of Interior, while the forest is run by the Department of Agriculture. It is a distinction rightly lost upon many hikers because much of the time you won't know you're crossing the boundary between an Olympic National Forest Wilderness Area and Olympic National Park, except for the occasional sign. What you will notice, however, is how the two agencies arrange for your visit.

In Olympic National Park, parking is free at all trailheads, and only overnight hikers pay fees—but you may be asked to pay an entry fee at major entrances to the park. Fee booths or self-pay stations are located at the Staircase, Heart O' the Hills, Elwha, Sol Duc, and Hoh entrances, and the booths are usually staffed in the summer from 8 a.m. to 5 p.m. In 2022, entry fees were $30 per vehicle and $15 for hikers and cyclists. Depending on your age and where you choose to visit, annual passes range from $55 to $80.

In Olympic National Forest, you must pay a daily or annual fee to park at trailheads, called the Northwest Forest Pass. It is available at all National Forest Ranger Stations, at REI stores throughout greater Seattle, and at a number of retail stores around the Peninsula. Forest passes cost $5 per day and $30 per year.

As a day hiker, you'll need to know several other differences in the rules. In Olympic National Forest, pets on leashes are permitted on all trails, including those within the forest's six Wilderness Areas.

Pets, however, are not permitted on Olympic National Park trails, except on Peabody Creek Trail, Rialto Beach north to Ellen Creek, the beaches between the Hoh and Quinault Reservations, Madison Falls Trail, and Spruce Railroad Trail. Those with permits to carry concealed weapons may do so in both park and forest, but discharging weapons is still against park regulations. Mountain bikes and e-bikes are allowed on many forest trails, while the park permits them only on the Spruce Railroad Trail. The park limits the size of hiking parties to a dozen; the national forest applies that size limit only in forest Wilderness Areas. Several other differences, such as campfire restrictions, aren't likely to affect day hikers.

## Winter Storm Damage

Every winter in the Olympics is severe, causing sometimes catastrophic damage to the trails and trailhead approach roads throughout the region. Flooding rains so bloated the Dosewallips River that it ripped out a 200-yard section of road in 2002; the winter of 2007–2008 demolished trail bridges and backcountry shelters; winds snapped acres of ancient spruce along west side rain forests. Much of the damage from winter is repaired by park and forest trail crews and volunteers, but some—like the Dosewallips and perhaps the Olympic Hot Springs roads—have yet to be fixed. A day hiker should always check with the land managers listed in the "Permits/ Contact" category at the beginning of each hike to make certain the trail is accessible and open for hiking.

## Elwha River

The most dramatic change in the last century of Olympic Peninsula history began in September 2011, with the removal of two dams constructed without permits on the Elwha River. The process took the better part of 4 years and drained two lakes held back by the illegal Elwha and Glines Canyon dams.

During the removal process, access to trailheads and trails west of the Elwha River (Hikes 41–50) were closed. Efforts to reopen the trails and the roads leading to them were hampered by major flood damage to the Olympic Hot Springs Road, which also provided access to several trails on the east side of the river at the Whiskey Bend Trailhead. The road was closed at the Madison Falls trailhead, adding as many as 10 miles to day hikes in the Elwha Valley. A new road is expected to be completed in the fall of 2023, but hikers should always check the status of any approach roads with land managers before leaving home.

In addition to providing miles of spawning waters for salmon and steelhead and creating hundreds of acres of living space for wildlife, removal of the dams also yielded several new opportunities for day hikers. Walks along the beds of the former Mills and Aldwell lakes are outlined here, along with an interesting "urban" walk on the Olympic Discovery Trail.

The Elwha River Valley was the route chosen by the Press Exploring Party of 1889–90 to reach the interior of the mountains. Barely longer than a century ago, while cities had long since sprouted around Puget Sound, the Olympic Mountains had yet to feel the footprints of white men. Though there is archaeological evidence that local tribes visited the mountain core, their permanent villages were located along the more temperate coastlines.

Elwha River trails are generally more dry than trails to the west and south, thanks to the mountains that shield the river from Pacific storms. The water of the river is a startling clear blue because it is fed by snowmelt bereft of glacier flour, and silt collected in the old lakes for a century has begun to clear from the lower river. That material has formed a new delta along the shores of the Strait of Juan de Fuca, and salmon and steelhead are spawning in their new home.

# USING THIS GUIDE

The beginning of each trail description is intended to give you quick information that can help you decide whether the specific day hike is one that interests you. Here's what you'll find:

## Trail Number & Name

Trails are numbered in this guide following a geographical order; see the Overview Map on page vii for general location. Trail names usually reflect those names used by the national park, national forest service, and other land managers. In some cases, portions of very long trails or multiple sections of separate trails have been combined into a single hike and assigned a new name.

## Overall Rating

Assigning an overall rating to a hike is a difficult task, given the fact that one hiker's preferred trail is another's dung-heap. Yet every hike in this guide is worth taking (we're still working on the dung-heap trail guide). Here, the difference between a five-star hike and one with four stars might only be the number and variety of wildflowers along the trail, or the height of the tripping tree-roots arrayed on the path before you. As mentioned earlier, the trails in this book are the best you'll find in the Olympics. Some might not be as good as others, but they are all better than the ones we've excluded.

Another problem is attempting to be objective in rating the trails. Some of us are pushovers for trails above timberline, where the wildflowers wave in gentle summer breezes, where mountains claw clouds, and where cooling snowfields linger through summer. Hikes with these features may be rated higher than you might rate them. If you're a hiker who loves walking along rattling rivers, or padding on rain-forest trails softened by mosses while trying to find the sky through a canopy of 300-foot-tall evergreens, you might add one star to every lowland hike listed here, and subtract one star from every alpland hike.

Finally, many factors must be considered in assigning an overall rating. Besides all that aesthetic stuff like scenery and wildlife and

Really Big Trees, there are objective criteria like trail condition, length and steepness, and obstacles like creek crossings or deadfall. On the other hand, you can forget all that junk and just take our word for it:

★ This hike is worth taking, even with your in-laws.

★★ Expect to discover socially and culturally redeeming values on this hike. Or, at least, very fine scenery.

★★★ You would be willing to get up before sunrise to take this hike, even if you watched an Avengers marathon the night before.

★★★★ Here is the Häagen-Dazs of hikes; if you don't like ice cream, a hike with this rating will give more pleasure than any favorite comfort food.

★★★★★ The aesthetic and physical rewards are so great that hikes given this rating are forbidden by most conservative religions.

## Distance

The distance listed is round-trip, exclusive of any side trips to Really Big Trees or other features mentioned along the way. If these excursions off the main trail are longer than about 0.2 mile, that distance will be mentioned in the description of the hike.

Note: In an effort to prove that trails indeed are getting longer as I grow older, I once pushed a bike wheel equipped with a cyclometer around most of the trails in this guide. I learned to my disappointment that trails aren't getting longer—although there are notable exceptions like Lower Lena Lake—and that I might have equipped myself better by carrying my own oxygen supply instead of a bloody heavy bike wheel.

## Hiking Time

This is an estimate of the time it takes the average hiker to walk the trail, round-trip. Since none of us are average hikers, you may feel free to ignore this entry. For the most part, however, the pace on the trail is calculated at 2 miles per hour. Times are estimated conservatively; even so, this rate might slow on trails with significant elevation gain.

(Some hikers will wonder what sort of trail slug came up with such ridiculously long hiking times—and we're okay with that.)

## Elevation Gain

This is a calculation of the total number of feet you'll have to climb on the trail. Don't assume that all of the elevation will be gained on the way to your destination. Some of these trails actually lose elevation on the way and gain it on the return, or alternately gain and lose elevation along the way. The certainty is that on a round-trip hike, you always gain the same amount of elevation that you lose.

## High Point

This is the highest point above sea level you'll reach on any given hike.

## Difficulty Level

Here's another tough one. Experienced hikers might find a hike rated "Moderately Difficult" to be only "Moderate," while beginning trekkers might rate the same hike "Difficult." As with the hiking times, noted above, the difficulty of individual hikes was rated conservatively.

The terms used here are:

♦     Easy: Few, if any, hills; generally between 1 and 4 miles, round-trip; suitable for families with small children.

♦♦     Moderate: Longer, gently graded hills; generally 4 to 6 miles long, round-trip.

♦♦♦     Moderately Difficult: Steeper grades; elevation changes greater than about 1,000 feet; between 6 and 9 miles long, round-trip.

♦♦♦♦     Difficult: Sustained, steep climbs of at least 1 mile; elevation gain and loss greater than 1,500 feet; usually more than 9 miles long, round-trip. Your deodorant may fail you on these trips.

♦♦♦♦♦     Extreme: Sustained steep climbs; distances greater than 10 miles, round-trip. These trails will provide a rigorous test of your hiking skills and muscles.

## Best Season

Here you'll find our recommendation for the best time of year to take any given hike. Trails that are open throughout the year or that make good three-season hikes will be noted here.

## Permits/Contact

This entry will tell you whether you need a Northwest Forest Pass or other permit and which land manager to contact for more information.

## Maps

The two most popular types of maps, United States Geological Survey (USGS) "quads" and Green Trails, are listed for each hike. Custom Correct Maps are used often on the Peninsula, so those are included here as well. Maps are available at outdoor retailers, park visitor centers, and from other sources. Many hikers now use Internet map servers (such as http://mapserver.maptech.com) to download USGS maps, or print their own, customized maps from apps.

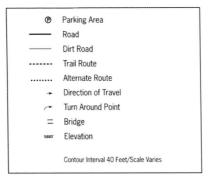

| | |
|---|---|
| ℗ | Parking Area |
| —— | Road |
| —— | Dirt Road |
| ------ | Trail Route |
| ........ | Alternate Route |
| → | Direction of Travel |
| ↱ | Turn Around Point |
| = | Bridge |
| 5880' | Elevation |
| | Contour Interval 40 Feet/Scale Varies |

Each hike in this book includes a trail map of the route, featuring parking and trailhead, alternate routes, direction, elevation profile, and more. Our maps are based most often on USGS; use the legend above.

## Trail Notes

Look here for a quick guide to trail regulations and features: Leashed dogs okay; no dogs; bikes allowed; kid-friendly; good views.

After the at-a-glance overview of each hike, you'll find detailed descriptions of the following:

## The Hike

This section is an attempt to convey the feel of the trail in a sentence or two, including the type of trail and whether there's a one-way hiking option.

## Getting There

You'll either find out how to get to the trailhead or, God forbid, become hopelessly lost. The elevation at the trailhead is also included here.

The main access highway for all of these hikes, save the first two, is the Olympic Loop Highway, or US Highway 101. It circumnavigates the Peninsula, and the order of the trails in this book follows the circle beginning on Hood Canal at the South Fork of the Skokomish River, and moves north, or counter-clockwise as you look at a map.

Keep in mind that at some point, both on the east and west sides of the Peninsula, it actually will be a shorter distance to the trailhead if you follow US 101 South, that is, go clockwise. On the Hood Canal side of the Peninsula, the difference in time isn't significant. Approach any trailheads north of the Dosewallips River from the north, across Hood Canal Bridge on Highway 104. Follow the Quilcene Cutoff Road to US 101 in Quilcene. For trails south of the Dosewallips River, you'll likely reach the trailhead faster by following Highway 106 around the southern end of Hood Canal to US 101 at Potlatch. Motorists headed to the Peninsula from Seattle or Tacoma might instead follow Interstate-5 South to Olympia, then take US 101 North from there.

For hikes on the west side of the Peninsula that are north of the US 101 crossing of the Hoh River, I'd recommend approaching from the north. If you plan to take hikes south of the Hoh River on US 101, the approach from the south, through Aberdeen, might be faster.

## The Trail

Here's where you'll get the blow-by-blow, mile-by-mile description of the trail. It's information your feet will find useful, and we apologize if, every now and then, we take time to recognize a Really Big Tree or an awesome view, since you'll probably recognize these features without much coaching.

## Going Farther

In this section, you can learn about good options to take a longer hike along the same trail. Interesting side trips can be found here too. And if there's a nearby campground that could get you on the trail sooner, or a great place to stay while exploring area trails, it also will be mentioned. Not every hike includes this section.

## Other Hikes

The end of some chapters will include a sentence or two describing other trails in the area that you might want to explore. These outings, in our opinion, aren't worthy of making a list of the best hikes, but as some readers regularly point out, some of these hikes can also be quite enjoyable. Please note that not every chapter will include this section.

# BE CAREFUL

It is all too easy on a warm, sunny day on the trail to forget all of the stuff you ought to be carrying in your pack. Day hikers, especially, are likely to leave that extra layer or Gore-Tex parka in the trunk. Some folks even forget that most essential item—a hiking partner. Never hike alone.

Virtually every time, day hikers who forget one or two of the basic rules for safe wilderness travel return to the trailhead smiling and healthy. No trail cop is going to cite you for negligent hiking if you have only nine of the so-called "Ten Essential Systems," or if you hit the trail without registering or telling someone where you're going.

Perhaps the only weighty argument anyone can make to convince another day hiker to follow the rules for safe travel in the outdoors is this: remember the annual, avoidable tragedies that occur because hikers ignore those rules, and become news headlines instead.

## The Ten Essential Systems

Those clever Mountaineers are always certain to stay abreast of the latest trend. Today we live in a world of "systems"—as in "life support systems" or "total system failure"—so the Seattle-based Mountaineers organization, which came up with the original Ten Essentials, has modified the list to the Ten Essential Systems. This fact was called to my attention by a member of the Mountaineers who serves on the club's Subcommittee of the Committee to Change the Names of Everything Familiar So As to Befuddle and Confuse Old Hikers. These new essential systems include:

- **A navigation system**, which might include a global positioning system (GPS) instead of a map and compass. If you choose a GPS, make certain to carry a spare energy system (battery) along. I'd advise carrying a topographic map system as well. A GPS can tell you where you are and where to go, but it can't tell you that your next step will be off a cliff. I suppose under most circumstances you'd know that.

- **A sun protection system**, which might include sunglasses, sunscreen, and one of those big picnic-table umbrellas.
- **An insulation system**, defined in the old Ten Essentials as "extra clothing." It might be a top and bottom insulating layer and a waterproof and windproof top layer, as well as a hat or cap. Or you might prefer an insulation system that includes a body-sized box made from rigid foam insulation. It would be light enough to tote on day hikes and would also serve as an emergency shelter system.
- **An illumination system**, once known as a flashlight with an extra bulb and batteries. Alternative illumination systems might include a carbide miner's lamp or emergency flares—which could double as your fire system. Headlamps with light-emitting diodes (LEDs) and lithium batteries burn longer than other systems but may also deplete your financial accounting system.
- **A first aid system** was formerly defined as a first aid kit, but you might prefer to drag your personal physician along. I suppose a nurse would do just as well, except in emergencies that might involve surgical procedures. If your first aid system doesn't include wraps for sprains, add an ankle support system and be sure you have some kind of blister treatment system.
- **A fire system**, once described as waterproof matches and a firestarter. If your illumination system consists of a couple of emergency flares, you can probably skip this one.
- **A repair and tools system**. The Ten Essentials said a pocket knife would do, but with today's technology no single Swiss Army knife can open every type of beer container.
- **A nutrition system**, once defined as extra food.
- **A hydration system**, known as "water" in the obsolete parlance.
- **An emergency shelter system,** which should be no problem if you opt for a rigid foam insulation system. One of those lightweight plastic/foil blankets or bags might work better.

In addition to these items, most day hikers never hit the trail without toting a toilet paper system in a plastic bag and perhaps some type of bug repellent on summer hikes. A loud emergency whistle is a lightweight addition. Binoculars are worth their weight simply for watching wildlife, and might help you find your route if you become lost.

Consider, too, a walking stick or a trekking pole of some variety; it can take the stress off your knees on steep downhills, help steady you while crossing streams, and serve a wide variety of other useful purposes, such as a support post for a portable lean-to should you need emergency shelter.

## Water

Dehydration is one of the most common ailments that day hikers face. No one should head out on the trail without at least one liter of clean water per person.

You'll find plenty of opportunities to refill your water bottle on most of the hikes outlined in this book. In cases where creek crossings are scarce or obtaining water might be a problem, it will be mentioned in the trail description.

Treat all water in the wilderness as if it were contaminated. The most worrisome problem might be a little critter called *Giardia lamblia*, which can give you a case of the trots that you'll never forget. The most noticeable symptom of giardiasis is "explosive diarrhea." Need you know more? Probably not.

Thankfully, there is an easy way to assure that the water you take from mountain streams and lakes is safe to drink. When used properly, filter pumps eliminate at least 99.9 percent of giardia and other dangerous organisms from the water. A recent and far more convenient addition to filter pumps, especially for day hikers, are the relatively inexpensive water bottles equipped with their own filters. You simply fill the bottle from the stream (taking extreme care not to contaminate the mouthpiece or drinking cap), drop the filter into place, screw on the top, and you're ready to drink filtered water. Conversely, many veteran hikers still choose to forego all this gadgetry and use the old-fashioned method: iodine water treatments, which come in tablets or crystals. The taste might be objectionable to some, but it's a guaranteed way to kill giardia and other water-borne bugs—something a filter, especially an improperly used or maintained one, is not.

Another quick and easy treatment for wild water is to use a device that uses UV light to purify the H2O. It's portable, light weight, and can be used multiple times. The downside: it operates on some form of energy system (batteries), so make certain you carry spares. Remember too that water taken from a cloudy or muddy source by this method will still retain its appearance, even though all harmful bacteria has been killed.

## Weather

In any mountains, weather can change rapidly and with little warning. On most any alpine hike in the fall, you can get snowed upon, rained upon, sleeted upon, blown around, and finally sunburned—all in the span of a day. Hikers in Washington's mountains have frozen to death in July and drowned in the afternoon while fording flood-filled rivers that were shallow in the morning. Mother Nature is most often a friendly, generous old lady who bakes cookies and bread for you, but when you least expect it, she puts on a goalie's mask and whacks at you with an icicle or lightning bolt. So be prepared, scouts.

Possibly the greatest weather-related hazard an Olympic hiker will face is rain. In alpine country, where you are exposed to rain and wind, hypothermia is a real threat. Waterproof, windproof gear can be life-saving in such situations. On hikes below timberline, a more comfortable alternative to waterproof clothing might be an umbrella. On rainy lowland trails, the only sure way to stay dry in a serious rainfall is to stay at home. If you hike on these days, simply consider dampness to be a hiking partner and stow some dry clothes in the car.

## Flora & Fauna

On October 16, 2010, a mountain goat gored Port Angeles resident Robert Boardman to death while he hiked the Klahhane Ridge Trail (Hike 35). It changed forever the way I—and many other day hikers—viewed goats and other Olympic Peninsula wildlife as relatively benign. The tragedy called attention to earlier reports of aggressive goat behavior in the Olympics, and caused both Olympic National Park and Olympic National Forest officials to issue warnings and educate hikers about mountain goat encounters. In one instance, the Mount Ellinor Trail (Hike 6), was closed for at least a month because of aggressive goat reports. Goats aren't as significant a problem in Olympic National Park as they once were, because officials have all but eliminated them by translocation and shooting. You may find a few in the Olympic National Forest, however, particularly around Mount Ellinor

The animals capable of harming you in the Olympics include black bears, cougars, and perhaps elk and deer. The only time you need to worry about the last two is during the fall rut—and a bull elk is certain to let you know when it doesn't appreciate paparazzi—so you'll get plenty of warning.

Black bears are generally more eager to avoid you than you are of them, and will most likely run off if you find them lumbering along the trail. Cougars are extremely shy and at the same time, very curious. You are more likely to see their tracks than the big cats themselves, although encounters are reportedly increasing in the Olympics and elsewhere.

If you do find yourself face-to-face with a mountain goat, bear, or cougar, heed the following advice from the Washington Department of Fish and Wildlife and Olympic National Park:

**Mountain goat:** Try to stay at least 50 yards away from mountain goats at all times. Calmly retreat down the trail if the goat exhibits threatening behavior (such as bowing its head and pointing its horns at you).

If you've done all you can to keep your distance and the goat continues to move toward you, try to scare it off. Scream, blow a whistle, and make loud noises. Wave a jacket or shirt, or if one is handy, a blanket. As a final resort, throw rocks at the animal. Though I have asked officials many times, I have never had a definitive answer about the effectiveness of bear spray repellent on mountain goats.

**Black bear:** Give the bear plenty of room to get away. Never get between a cub and its mother. Avoid eye contact but speak softly to the bear while backing away from it. Try not to show fear and don't turn your back on a bear. If you can't get away from it, clap your hands or yell in an effort to scare it away. If the bear becomes aggressive, fight back using anything at your disposal. Do NOT play dead.

**Cougar:** Don't take your eyes off the cougar. Make yourself appear big by raising your arms above your head, open your jacket if you're wearing one, and wave a stick above your head. If the cougar approaches, yell and throw rocks, sticks, anything you can get your hands on. In the event of an attack, fight back aggressively.

Less dangerous, but more common hazards to day hikers include stinging and biting pests like yellow jackets, particularly in late summer and early autumn, and black flies, mosquitoes, and deer flies. Liberal doses of insect repellent can take care of the mosquitoes and deer flies, but probably won't keep those pesky yellow jackets away.

Poison oak and ivy grow in the Olympics, mostly in sunny, dry areas. A more common plant pest is stinging nettle, which grows in profusion along many trails but is easily avoided if you recognize it in time.

None of this, of course, should be construed as discouragement. We've been hiking in the Olympics for a lifetime, and have yet to get lost in a snowstorm, be menaced by wild animals, attacked by murder hornets, or swept away in a glacial runoff. So tighten your bootlaces, shoulder that pack, and get out on one of the hikes that follow.

## Etiquette/Ethics

On one recent hike on the Sol Duc Falls Trail, it became clear that many day hikers hadn't a clue about trail manners. I resisted the urge to bodycheck a runner and stepped aside as he ran by without a greeting. It's possible that on that crowded, short trail, many tourists aren't aware of trail courtesies. For any trail in the Olympics and elsewhere, hikers must yield to horses, while bicyclists (on Olympic National Forest trails) must yield to hikers and horses. The most often ignored trail courtesy is that of yielding to the uphill hiker. They're working harder than you and you should step aside.

To protect this wonderful landscape so that users in future generations can enjoy it just as much as you, follow a few simple rules. Stay on established trails, don't cut switchbacks, and stay off sensitive areas. Leave no trace, pack out your trash, and respect other trail users. And because you're having such a great time using Washington's trails, why not volunteer your services on a trail building or repair project?

Happy trails!

# KITSAP PENINSULA

# 1. Green Mountain via Wildcat Trail

| RATING | DISTANCE | HIKING TIME |
|---|---|---|
| ★ ☆ ☆ ☆ ☆ | **9.0 miles round-trip** | **5 hours** |
| **ELEVATION GAIN** | **HIGH POINT** | **DIFFICULTY** |
| **1,200 feet** | **1,640 feet** | ♦ ♦ ◇ ◇ ◇ |

| BEST SEASON |
|---|
| Jan Feb Mar Apr May Jun Jul Aug Sep Oct Nov Dec |

## The Hike

This is the long way to the top of Green Mountain, leading through Department of Natural Resources clearcuts and thick green stands of second- and third-growth Douglas fir. The reward for your effort on this trail is the 360-degree view, best seen before the road to the summit opens during the summer.

## Getting There

From Highway 3, north of Bremerton, take the Newberry Hill Road (Silverdale) exit. Turn left, west, onto Newberry Hill Road and follow it uphill for 3.1 miles to the Seabeck Highway. Turn left onto the Seabeck Highway and follow it 2.0 miles to Holly Road. Circle the roundabout to Holly and follow it 1.8 miles to the Wildcat trailhead, 440 feet above sea level.

**PERMITS/CONTACT**
Discover Pass required/State Department of Natural Resources, (360) 825-1631

**MAPS**
USGS Point Misery; DNR Green Mountain State Forest map

**TRAIL NOTES**
Leashed dogs okay; bikes okay

# The Trail

The Wildcat Trail climbs about 1,200 feet in more than 4 miles to the summit of Green Mountain. You passed Wildcat Lake on the way to the trailhead, and that is as close as you will get on this hike. Don't be disappointed: The view from the summit is worth the climb. If you really want to see the lake, stop at the Wildcat Lake County Park on the way home.

The hike begins with a brief detour around a logged section of the Green Mountain State Forest. Hikers realize that as a "working forest," timber harvests are a possibility pretty much anywhere on the mountain. After crossing logging roads several times, the trail enters a kinder, gentler section of the forest where big wild rhododendron splotch the green with pink around mid-May and winter wrens sing spring songs ten times their size.

The first mile of the trail climbs gently, but at **1.2** miles the path turns to serious uphill. This is the very section where my mountain bike, the Great Emasculator, once traded places and rode me for several embarrassing feet in the mud. At **2.2** miles, the trail crosses a road to the Green Mountain Campground, used primarily by equestrian clubs who are among the volunteers who maintain Green Mountain trails. You may walk through the campground on the upper road to find the continuation of the Wildcat Trail.

Beyond the campground, the path climbs steeply before traversing around another clearcut. Here views open to the east, with the big hammerhead crane of Bremerton's Puget Sound Naval Shipyard and the Seattle skyline's prominent features.

You'll climb into forest again, crossing another old logging road at **3.8** miles. Here you can choose to follow the road as it climbs to and joins the main Green Mountain Road, GM-1, or follow a less well-marked trail over the 1,600-foot summit of the hill just north of Green Mountain.

At **4.0** miles you'll cross the Green Mountain Road, and you can follow the trail 0.2 mile or hike the road to the Green Mountain Vista Parking Area. Find the Vista Trail above the picnic area on the left and follow it the final 0.3 mile to the summit.

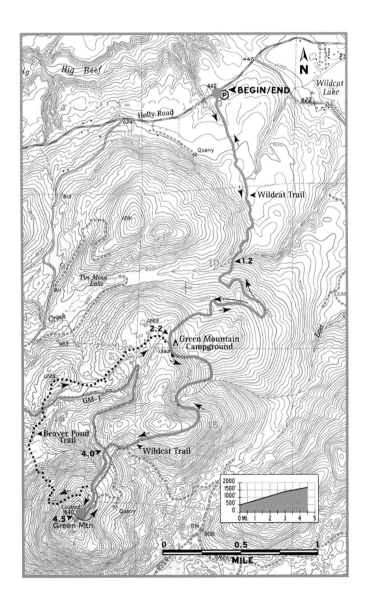

N

Big Beef

447

400

Wildcat
Lake

440'

P ◄BEGIN/END

923

Holly Road

624

600

Quarry

◄Wildcat Trail

813

1291

1200

1.2

900

536

Tin Mine
Lake

811

1000

Creek

983

1269

2.2

Green Mountain
Campground

1345

1225

GM-1

◄Beaver Pond
Trail

4.0►

◄Wildcat Trail

2000'
1500'
1000'
500'
0'
0 Mi.  1  2  3  4  5

Lookout
1540'
4.5►
Green Mtn.

Quarry

BM
808

0          0.5          1
MILE

## Going Farther

For a different route on the descent, you can follow the Vista and Gold Creek Trails down to the junction with the Beaver Pond Trail, then follow the Beaver Pond Trail for 3.1 miles to the Green Mountain Campground. Return to the trailhead via the Wildcat Trail from the campground. ■

# 2. Green Mountain via Gold Creek Trail

| RATING | DISTANCE | HIKING TIME |
|---|---|---|
| ★★ ☆☆☆ | 4.8 miles round-trip | 3 hours |
| **ELEVATION GAIN** | **HIGH POINT** | **DIFFICULTY** |
| 1,000 feet | 1,640 feet | ♦♦ ◇◇◇ |
| **BEST SEASON** | | |
| Jan Feb Mar Apr May Jun Jul Aug Sep Oct Nov Dec | | |

## The Hike

Here's a moderate climb to great views, best when the road to the vista is closed during fall, winter, or spring. You can see all the way (almost) to Lincoln, Nebraska, from the summit of Green Mountain.

## Getting There

From Highway 3, north of Bremerton, take the Newberry Hill Road (Silverdale) exit. Turn left, west, onto Newberry Hill Road and follow it uphill for 3.1 miles to the Seabeck Highway. Turn left onto the Seabeck Highway and follow it 2.0 miles to Holly Road. Circle the roundabout to Holly and follow it 4.1 miles to the Lake Tahuya Road. Turn left on the Lake Tahuya Road and follow it 1.2 miles to a Y junction with the Gold Creek Road. Turn left at the Y onto Gold Creek Road and follow it around Lake Tahuya for 1.8 miles to the Gold Creek trailhead, 640 feet above sea level.

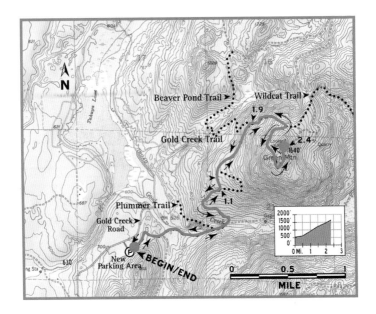

## The Trail

You might think of this trail as a sort of uncrowded Tiger Mountain. On weekends you'll likely share the walk with mountain bikers and perhaps equestrians or dirt-bike riders, although you'll never encounter the masses that wander eastern Puget Sound pathways.

The trail climbs briefly to a traverse on an abandoned road above chattering Gold Creek, a shaded tributary to Tahuya Lake and River. Salal and huck, the brush that provides pickers with the only real gold in these hills, decorates the trailside along with Oregon grape.

At **0.7** mile, you'll cross Gold Creek on a footbridge. Just beyond, the Gold Creek Trail branches sharply to the left and begins climbing through the forest about 100 yards to a junction with the Plummer Trail. Turn right here and continue climbing to a second junction at **1.1** miles. Take the left fork for a steep climb; the right for a slightly longer, more gentle route. Both pathways merge after about 0.5 mile. The grade flattens slightly and at **1.9** miles, joins the Beaver Pond Trail.

Keep right to continue to the Vista Parking Area at **2.2** miles, where you'll find an outhouse and several picnic tables. Turn right and find the Vista Trail at the southwestern end of the parking area. Follow it 0.3 mile to the summit, where you'll find several more picnic tables.

For views toward Seattle, Mount Rainier, Mount Baker, and Puget Sound, climb to the rocky overlook to the east. Until she blew her top, Mount St. Helens was visible from this viewpoint to the southeast. Green Mountain is the second-highest point on the Kitsap Peninsula, offering 360-degree views. Only Gold Mountain, the

The view from the Green Mountain summit includes, from left,
Mount Jupiter, Warrior Peak, and Mount Constance

summit to the southeast above the city of Bremerton's protected watershed, is higher at 1,761 feet.

For a good look at some of the country holding the remaining seventy-two trails in this book, turn around and look across Hood Canal to the Olympic Mountains. From the south to the north, the major summits include Ellinor, Washington, Stone, the Brothers, Jupiter, and Constance. ■

# SKOKOMISH RIVERS

---

# 3. Lower Skokomish River

| RATING | DISTANCE | HIKING TIME |
|---|---|---|
| ★★★☆☆ | 6.5 miles round-trip | 3 hours |
| ELEVATION GAIN | HIGH POINT | DIFFICULTY |
| 350 feet | 850 feet | ♦♦♦♦♦ |

| BEST SEASON |
|---|
| Jan Feb Mar Apr May Jun Jul Aug Sep Oct Nov Dec |

## The Hike

If you're looking for a little walk and a big picnic in a parklike forest by a gently flowing river, this might be just the day hike for you. As you're hiking this trail, silently thank the US Forest Service and Washington Trails Association for the work they've done in improving this pathway over the years.

## Getting There

From the intersection of US Highways 101 and 106 at Potlatch at the south end of Hood Canal, follow US Highway 101 south to the Skokomish Valley Road. Turn west and follow the road for 5.1 miles to Forest Road 23. Turn right and follow FR 23 for 9.5 miles to FR 2353. Turn right and cross the river to a junction with the Brown Creek Campground road. Turn left and follow FR 2353 for 0.2 mile to the Lower Skokomish Trail No. 873 parking area, 500 feet above sea level.

### PERMITS/CONTACT
Parking pass required/Hood Canal Ranger Station, (360) 877-5254

### MAPS
USGS Mount Tebo; Green Trails Mount Tebo

### TRAIL NOTES
Leashed dogs okay; kid-friendly; bikes okay

## The Trail

Don't let the steep climb at the trailhead fool you; this walk is as gentle as a summer breeze. Look at it this way: After the first mile the path through this river valley is as flat and green as a pool table.

You'll climb to a trail junction at **0.4** mile, with the right fork leading to LeBar Horse Camp. Stay left and climb around the ridge separating LeBar Creek from the Skokomish River. Once you crest the ridge above the Skokomish at **0.6** mile, you'll drop in switchbacks down to riverside at **1.0** mile.

Cross a creek and follow the trail as it meanders along the river valley to a campsite at the LeBar claim at **2.0** miles. The trail continues through the forest along the river bottom for about another mile, with excellent picnic spots anywhere along the river off the trail to the left. At **3.0** miles the trail climbs a bench above the river and crosses a bridge over a tributary creek. You'll cross a second creek at **3.25** miles, a good turnaround point.

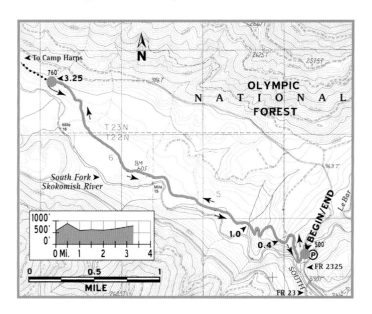

## Going Farther

The Lower Skokomish Trail continues upstream for about another 6 miles, making round-trip day hikes or backpacks of 18 miles possible. The trail eventually joins Forest Road 2361 near Camp Harps and continues upstream another 8.0 miles to Sundown Pass. ■

# 4. Big Creek Loop

| RATING | DISTANCE | HIKING TIME |
|---|---|---|
| ★★☆☆☆ | 4.6 mile loop | 3 hours |
| **ELEVATION GAIN** | **HIGH POINT** | **DIFFICULTY** |
| 1,200 feet | 1,950 feet | ♦♦◇◇◇ |

| BEST SEASON |
|---|
| Jan Feb Mar Apr May Jun Jul Aug Sep Oct Nov Dec |

## The Hike

This loop trail follows old logging roadbed up one side of the Big Creek Canyon and descends the other side, with peekaboo views through mature second-growth forest of Mount Washington and Mount Ellinor above.

## Getting There

From US Highway 101 in Hoodsport, turn west on the Lake Cushman Road and follow it 9.0 miles to the junction with Forest Road 24.

**PERMITS/CONTACT**
Parking pass required/Hood Canal Ranger Station, (360) 877-5254

**MAPS**
USGS the Brothers; Custom Correct Mount Skokomish–Lake Cushman;
Green Trails the Brothers

**TRAIL NOTES**
Leashed dogs okay; kid-friendly

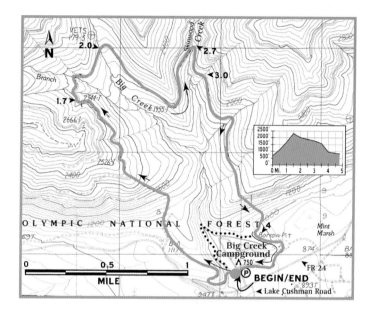

Turn left on FR 24 and immediately right at the Big Creek Campground Road. The Big Creek Loop Trail No. 827 begins at the parking area at the campground entrance, 750 feet above sea level. The Big Creek Campground was rehabilitated in 2014 and makes an excellent base camp for several of the hikes that follow.

## The Trail

This is one of the new Olympic National Forest trails constructed mainly by volunteers over the past few years. It's a splendid example of the extent to which a bunch of dedicated hikers will go to get their Vibrams on a new trail. You can hike this loop in either direction; it's described here starting west, or clockwise, from the trailhead. Begin with a short walk to a bridge across Big Creek, which tumbles from the snowfields of Mount Ellinor and Mount Washington, lurking like gnarly trolls above.

The trail forks just across the bridge. Turn left and follow Big Creek Loop Trail No. 827-1 as it climbs steeply to the ridge crest on the west side of the creek. After about 0.25 mile the trail flattens as it joins an abandoned logging road in a meadow area. You'll get a brief breather before beginning to climb again, never far from the rushing of Big Creek below.

Benches have been placed at strategic locations along the trail for those early-spring hikers who, like me, are preceded up the trail by bellies fed by winter hiking hibernation. One bench is especially welcomed at the 1-mile mark, overlooking the Big Creek Canyon.

The trail forks at **1.7** miles. The path to the right drops to Branch Creek and rejoins the main trail, to the left, in about 0.2 mile. Stay on the main trail to the left and climb to the upper junction and a footlog bridge across Branch Creek at **1.9** miles. Another trail climbs to the left at Branch Creek to join with the lower Mount Ellinor Trail (Hike 6). Keep right here and cross Branch Creek.

Gray jays are more likely company than ants on picnics in the Olympics

At **2.0** miles you'll cross Big Creek on another footlog bridge and traverse around a ridge to climb and then drop to Skinwood Creek, at **2.7** miles. It's pretty much all downhill from here. The trail contours around another ridge to No Name Creek at **3.0** miles, then cascades like the creeks below down to a junction with the Big Creek Campground Loop at **4.0** miles. Turn left for the 0.7-mile-long loop around the campground to the trailhead, or continue right to cross Big Creek and walk downstream to close the loop in about 0.6 mile. ■

# 5. Dry Creek Trail

| RATING | DISTANCE | HIKING TIME |
|---|---|---|
| ★★☆☆☆ | **7.2 miles round-trip** | **4 hours** |

| ELEVATION GAIN | HIGH POINT | DIFFICULTY |
|---|---|---|
| **700 feet** | **1,360 feet** | ◆◆◇◇◇ |

| BEST SEASON |
|---|
| Jan Feb Mar Apr **May Jun Jul Aug Sep Oct** Nov Dec |

## The Hike
Here's a lakeshore walk followed by a tough climb on an abandoned logging road to a picnic by a rushing creek that is often a trickle by late summer. You can make this a one-way hike during summer with two cars and a key exchange.

## Getting There
From US Highway 101 at Hoodsport, turn west on the Lake Cushman Road and follow it 9 miles to Forest Road 24. Turn left on FR 24 and follow it around Lake Cushman to Bear Gulch at the end of the lake. Turn left and cross the causeway on FR 2451. The trailhead is on the left, 100 yards west of the causeway at 660 feet above sea level. During winter, the gate across the Bear Gulch causeway may be closed. In that case, hikers with parking permits can park at the Bear Gulch Day Use Area, just west of the causeway.

# The Trail

Here's a walk you can literally warm up to, even overheat on, if you're not careful. The funny thing is, Dry Creek isn't very dry in the spring.

The first 1.4 miles of this trail is deceptively flat, meandering along the southwestern shore of the lake. You'll pass a number of private homes along the lakeshore on a fire lane. In about 0.7 mile, the road turns into a foot trail and climbs above the lake shore. When the lake is lower in winter, this section reveals the stumps of massive trees that were cut before the Cushman Dam was built. You'll pass under fern-covered cliffs, where in the spring creeks cascade down to the trail and offer cooling showers to hikers.

At about **1.3** miles the trail gets serious and begins to climb steeply along the northern side of the canyon above Dry Creek. In another 0.1 mile, you'll climb steps to a junction with the Dry Creek Campsite trail. Stay right at the junction and continue climbing up the steep trail. Here's where the trail-builders have conspired to whip you into shape for summer hiking: You'll climb about 700 vertical feet in the next mile.

The walk is in shaded second-growth forest, with alders growing along the old roadbed. Springtime is just starting to show itself along the trail, with trillium flashing white in the forest duff. After sweating and straining for about a mile, you'll get a rest as the trail begins to traverse into the upper Dry Creek basin. It crosses several small streams before turning toward chattering Dry Creek.

---

**PERMITS/CONTACT**
Parking pass required/Hood Canal Ranger Station, (360) 877-5254

**MAPS**
USGS Mount Tebo; Custom Correct Mount Skokomish–Lake Cushman;
Green Trails Mount Tebo

**TRAIL NOTES**
Leashed dogs okay; bikes okay

---

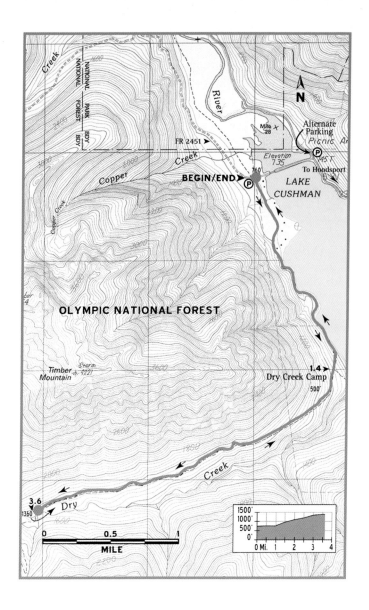

N

Alternate
Parking
Picnic Ar

FR 2451 ▶

River

Mile
28

Elevation
735

P
745 T

Creek

Copper

Creek

BEGIN/END ▶
760
P

To Hoodsport

LAKE
CUSHMAN

Copper Creek

NATIONAL
NATIONAL
PARK
FOREST
BDY
BDY

OLYMPIC NATIONAL FOREST

Timber
Mountain

Timber
4221

1.4 ▶
Dry Creek Camp
500'

Creek

3.6
1360

Dry

Creek

| | 1500' | | | |
|---|---|---|---|---|
| | 1000' | | | |
| | 500' | | | |
| | 0' | | | |
| 0 Mi. | 1 | 2 | 3 | 4 |

0          0.5          1
MILE

At **3.6** miles, you can wade the creek and continue in switchbacks to a 3,600-foot-high pass above LeBar Creek, which would make the hike longer and steeper than many prefer for a day. A better option would be to make the crossing a picnic and turnaround spot, descending the way you came.

Like most of the trailheads in the Olympic Mountains, the Dry Creek trailhead displays the warning about cougar encounters. Read it well. Many years ago, local hikers were not only approached by a cougar, but they were able to snap a great photo of the beast on the trail between them.

## Going Farther

Beyond the creek crossing, the trail climbs over the 3,600-foot-high pass to a trailhead above LeBar Creek, 7.0 miles upstream from Brown Creek Campground off Forest Road 2353-200. This road is closed in spring to give newborn wildlife some peace and quiet and is too long for day hiking.

The trailhead at LeBar Creek makes a one-way hike possible if you've hiking friends with a second car. Your friends park on the LeBar Creek side; you park on the Cushman side.

Both parties hike to the crossing, enjoy a picnic lunch together, and trade car keys. **Don't forget to trade car keys.** Everybody meets in Hoodsport for refreshments after the hike. ■

# 6. Mount Ellinor

| RATING | DISTANCE | HIKING TIME |
|---|---|---|
| ★★★★★ | 4.4 miles round-trip | 3.5–4.5 hours |

| ELEVATION GAIN | HIGH POINT | DIFFICULTY |
|---|---|---|
| 3,244 feet (lower trailhead) 2,244 feet (upper trailhead) | 5,944 feet | ◆◆◆◆◇ |

| BEST SEASON |
|---|
| Jan Feb Mar Apr May **Jun Jul Aug Sep Oct Nov** Dec |

## The Hike

Try this strenuous climb up a real mountain to one of the finest views in all of the Eastern Olympic Mountains.

## Getting There

The Mount Ellinor Trail No. 812 has two trailheads. From US Highway 101 in Hoodsport turn west on the Lake Cushman Road and follow it 9.0 miles to the junction with Forest Road 24. Turn right on FR 24 and drive 1.7 miles to its intersection with FR 2419. Turn left and follow FR 2419 for 4.6 miles to the lower trailhead at 2,700 feet. To reach the upper trailhead, continue on FR 2419 for another 1.6 miles to FR 2419-014, turn left and follow FR 2419-014 for 1.1 miles, where you'll find an outhouse at the trailhead, 3,700 feet above sea level.

**PERMITS/CONTACT**
Parking pass required/Hood Canal Ranger Station, (360) 877-5254

**MAPS**
USGS Mount Washington, Mount Steel; Custom Correct Mount Skokomish–Lake Cushman; Green Trails Mount Steel

**TRAIL NOTES**
Leashed dogs okay

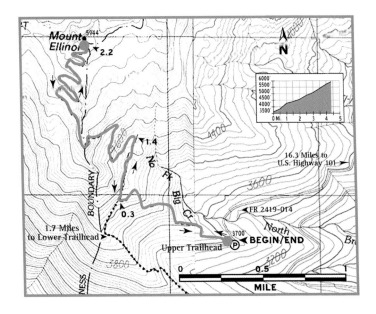

## The Trail

The rough path up Mount Ellinor is another example of the excellent work of Olympic National Forest volunteers and staff. Over the past decade they've turned what used to be an entry-level mountain-climb into a trail that can be followed by those without climbing skills in the late summer all the way to the summit. And what a summit it is: airy and rock-bound, with views all the way to Wall Drug, South Dakota. Or so it seems on a clear day. Besides views of the interior Olympic Mountains to the north and west, you can gaze east to the snow giants of the Cascades: Baker, Rainier, Adams, St. Helens, and on crisp, clear fall days, all the way to Mount Hood.

Hikers climbing up Ellinor in the summer often find hairy company waiting for them near the summit. The area around the mountain is one of the few places left in the Olympics frequented by mountain goats. If you don't see the actual critter, you'll most certainly find goat wool festooning the low bushes around the summit.

Unless getting to the top of the mountain is a secondary goal, I'd recommend starting at the upper trailhead. This will leave you more rubbernecking time on the summit, time to wish you could store a few more digits on that megapixel imaging device. The upper trail begins with a junction in the path about 100 feet past the parking area. Savor this section: it is one of only two flat spots in the trail short of the summit. The left trail contours in about a mile to a junction with the lower Mount Ellinor Trail.

You'll climb to the right up a steep, root-filled way that follows a minor ridge for 0.3 mile to a second trail junction with the lower footpath. Stay right at this junction, although you shouldn't be confused since the path to the left drops almost as steeply as you're climbing. You must continue upward and if there's any doubt, simply hike in the opposite direction of the sweat pouring from your body.

The trail here is in shaded forest, which may help keep the aforementioned sweat from forming a river deep enough to support salmon migration. In the summer white blobs of beargrass blossoms shine like beacons in the darker woods. The trail continues to climb relentlessly for almost a mile, sometimes in switchbacks but often simply and purposely heading straight up the fall line. At **1.3** miles you'll find the second flat spot in the trail. Rejoice and rest here on a meadow bench with a campsite and small creek in the early summer. The climbers' route, used in the spring, begins at the head of the meadow and climbs the steep snow-filled chute directly in front of you.

The summit trail turns left at a junction at **1.4** miles. A way trail leads right to the campsite and climbers' route. Beyond the junction the trail climbs steeply again, first through subalpine forest in switchbacks and then breaking into open alpland along a steep, rocky ridge. Cross a steep meadow where you can look down on the trailhead parking area, waaaay down there, then switchback under the eastern face of the mountain before turning to climb along a ridge to the summit.

There's room for several parties of hikers on the summit, which yields stunning views in every direction. Directly below to the southeast is Lake Cushman; farther east you'll pick out the great bend of Hood Canal and beyond, Puget Sound.

The summits of Mount Pershing, foreground, and Mount Stone, left, can be seen from the top of Mount Ellinor

Ellinor, named for Seattle pioneer Ellinor Fauntleroy, was the summit from which Olympic surveyors Arthur Dodwell and Theodore Rixon viewed the territory they planned to map more than a century ago, and the view of the interior mountains has changed little. The closest peaks are Mount Washington to the east and Mount Pershing and Mount Stone to the north. The glacier-clad mountains beyond include Mount Anderson and Mount Olympus, the Big Kahuna of the Olympic range.

A dramatic event in 2011 added impact to the always-keep-your-pet-leashed rule: Sasha, a Bernese Mountain Dog off her leash for but a second, jumped in pursuit of a mountain goat off the north face cliffs of the peak. Though the dog was feared dead, Olympic Mountain Rescue volunteers responded 2 days later and found Sasha alive on a ledge and reunited her with her human partner.

## Going Farther

The climb of Ellinor from the lower trailhead adds 2.8 miles to the round-trip distance. Many hikers feel this is a small price to pay for the solitude they gain in the old forest, with peekaboo views down to Lake Cushman. The lower route might also be a good alternative for families with children who aren't summit-bound. The lower trail climbs in switchbacks to a forested ridge and then angles toward a junction with a new path that contours to the right to the upper trailhead parking area, at 1.3 miles. It then switchbacks and climbs more steeply to a junction with the upper trail at 1.7 miles. For a real knee-whacker, you can begin your hike from the Big Creek Campground and follow the Big Creek Loop Trail clockwise to a connector with the lower Mount Ellinor Trail. ■

# 7. Mount Rose

| RATING | DISTANCE | HIKING TIME |
|---|---|---|
| ★★☆☆☆ | 6.4 miles round-trip | 3.5 hours |

| ELEVATION GAIN | HIGH POINT | DIFFICULTY |
|---|---|---|
| 3,500 feet | 4,300 feet | ◆◆◆◇ |

| BEST SEASON | | | | | | | | | | | |
|---|---|---|---|---|---|---|---|---|---|---|---|
| Jan | Feb | Mar | Apr | May | Jun | Jul | Aug | Sep | Oct | Nov | Dec |

## The Hike

It's a strenuous, steep climb to the summit of Mount Rose; the payoff is the view down to Lake Cushman and west, toward the peaks and forests of the Skokomish River.

## Getting There

From US Highway 101 in Hoodsport, turn west on the Lake Cushman Road and follow it 9.0 miles to the junction with Forest Road 24.

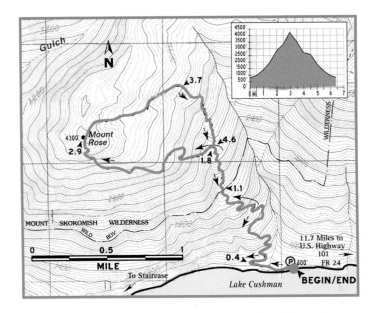

Turn left on FR 24 and drive 2.7 miles to the trailhead, located on an abandoned spur road to the right, where you'll find an outhouse at the trailhead, 800 feet above sea level.

## The Trail

The steepness of this trail, built and maintained largely by Olympic National Forest volunteers, rivals that of the notorious Tunnel Creek Trail from the Dosewallips River (Hike 16). It climbs 3,500 feet in just under 3 miles and provides a thigh-frying, calf-cramping workout for the strongest day hikers. One of the appealing features of this knee-buckler is that it can allow you to suffer pain without boredom: You can punish yourself with separate trails on the way up and down. This is a loop trip, with the summit about half-way around the loop. The ridge walk beyond the rocky zit-summit might be a better spot for lunch, with peekaboo views to the north of Mount Ellinor and Mount Washington.

Marmots keep hikers company on most of the high-country hikes in the Olympics

Begin by climbing in steep switchbacks from the trailhead for 0.4 mile to the boundary of Olympic National Forest past a big moss-covered spine of bedrock dotted with red-barked madronas. This area has been used for rock-climbing practice in the past, with the trail access convenient to the top and bottom of the rock. The path continues to climb through increasingly dense forest, switching back again and again as it passes the boundary of the Mount Skokomish Wilderness at **1.1** miles. After another 0.7 mile of relentless climbing, the trail forks to begin the loop over the summit of Mount Rose.

**PERMITS/CONTACT**
None required/Hood Canal Ranger Station, (360) 877-5254

**MAPS**
USGS Mount Steel; Custom Correct Mount Skokomish–Lake Cushman; Green Trails Mount Steel

**TRAIL NOTES**
Leashed dogs okay

Turn left at this junction to climb to the summit, first in more switchbacks but later along a kinder, gentler traverse past a forested bench where you may find water in early summer. Beyond, the route turns tough again and grows steeper by the step, culminating in a scramble to the northeast to the rocky, narrow summit of the mountain, 2.9 miles from the trailhead. This final section is not recommended for your in-laws from Kansas, unless they are faint of heart and you don't like them very much.

For the loop hike climb over the summit and follow the newest section of trail along the ridge northerly for 0.6 mile as it descends past lumpy rocks where more imaginative hikers might think they're climbing along a stegosaurus's back. Perhaps I'm thinking of a teleosaurus—it's been a few years since I've seen *Jurassic Park*.

Anyway, at **3.7** miles, you'll leave the ridge and drop in bigger chunks of altitude to the junction with the loop trail, at **4.6** miles. Turn left here (unless, God forbid, you forgot your camera on the summit), tighten the shoelaces on your boot toes, and begin the knee-grinding 1.8-mile descent to the trailhead.

## Going Farther

Are you out of your freaking mind? ■

## 8. Silver Snag Hill, Wagonwheel Lake

| RATING | DISTANCE | HIKING TIME |
|---|---|---|
| ★★★★☆ | 6.6 miles round-trip | 4 hours |
| ELEVATION GAIN | HIGH POINT | DIFFICULTY |
| 3,775 feet | 4,600 feet | ◆◆◆◆◇ |

| BEST SEASON |
|---|
| Jan Feb Mar Apr May **Jun Jul Aug Sep Oct Nov** Dec |

### The Hike
This is a steep climb past a tree-shaded lake to a sunny hillside with views of Copper Peak and the Sawtooth Range.

### Getting There
From US Highway 101 in Hoodsport turn west on the Lake Cushman Road and follow it 9.0 miles to Forest Road 24. Turn left on FR 24 and follow it 6.0 miles around Lake Cushman to the Staircase Ranger Station. Be prepared to pay a fee on entering Olympic National Park at Staircase. Turn right just before the ranger station to the trailhead parking lot, 825 feet above sea level.

**PERMITS/CONTACT**
None required/Hood Canal Ranger Station, (360) 877-5254

**MAPS**
USGS Mount Steel; Custom Correct Mount Skokomish–Lake Cushman;
Green Trails Mount Steel

**TRAIL NOTES**
No dogs or bikes

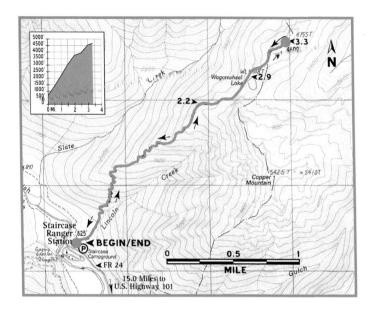

## The Trail

One of the nicest things about this trail is the opportunity to cool off after the tough climb by taking a swim in Wagonwheel Lake before returning to the trailhead. One of the worst things about this trail is that by the time you return to the trailhead, you'll be just as hot and sweaty as you were before you cooled off. No matter. The view from the hillside above Wagonwheel Lake, amid a silver forest of trees burned nine decades ago, might be worth the effort.

The trail to Wagonwheel Lake takes no prisoners. It begins with a straightforward climb up a ridge past a minor's (an underage prospector) exploratory dig. You'll pass through a salal- and Oregon grape–carpeted forest of second-growth timber before beginning a series of switchbacks up the ridge as it steepens to the northeast.

At about **1.0** mile the trail climbs to a viewpoint along the ridge where the hiker can look across the canyon carved by Slate Creek toward Mount Lincoln and across the Skokomish Valley, to the south, to Lightning Peak. You'll climb the ridge in several switch-backs before turning to climb no-whiners-allowed sections of trail, which must have been built by Bunyanesque creatures who wouldn't recognize a switchback if it whacked them alongside the head with a frying pan.

The route continues to climb directly up the ridge to about 2.2 miles. The aforementioned Bunyanesque creatures undoubtedly expired from heart failure here, because the trail becomes a more gentle climbing traverse across an open avalanche slope towards a subalpine forest. In the forest it crosses the Wagonwheel Lake outlet stream at **2.8** miles and climbs another 0.1 mile to the lake.

Anglers and swimmers may find little reason to climb the remaining 0.4 mile and 450 feet up past the lake, but the lake itself is surrounded by forest and the shoreline isn't particularly hospitable for picnic lunches. No established trail climbs the burned-over ridge north-northwest of the lake, but the way is straightforward and perhaps easier than parts of the trail below. Climb the ridge, which tops out at about 4,700 feet, and pick a spot overlooking the Slate Creek saddle and jagged slopes of Mount Lincoln.

You can look back across the lake to Copper Peak and east, to the summit of Mount Ellinor.

## Going Farther

If you'd like a better view and more exercise—although it is difficult to imagine—you can climb open avalanche slopes that sweep down to the lake from Copper Peak to the ridge just west of Copper Peak and follow the ridge to the 5,425-foot summit that towers above Staircase. ■

# 9. Spike Camp

| RATING | DISTANCE | HIKING TIME |
|---|---|---|
| ★★☆☆☆ | 7.2 miles round-trip | 3.5 hours |
| ELEVATION GAIN | HIGH POINT | DIFFICULTY |
| 625 feet | 1,500 feet | ♦♦◇◇◇ |
| BEST SEASON | | |
| Jan Feb Mar Apr May Jun Jul Aug Sep Oct Nov Dec | | |

## The Hike
This is a good walk along an abandoned road to a forested campsite that five decades ago was the trailhead for the Flapjack Lakes Trail.

## Getting There
From US Highway 101 in Hoodsport turn west on the Lake Cushman Road and follow it 9.0 miles to Forest Road 24. Turn left on FR 24 and follow it 6.0 miles around Lake Cushman to the Staircase Ranger Station. Be prepared to pay a fee on entering Olympic National Park at Staircase. Turn right just before the ranger station to the trailhead parking lot at 825 feet above sea level.

## The Trail
The paths up the North Fork of the Skokomish River Valley were among the first in the Olympic Mountains to be blazed by white explorers. This trail follows an old roadbed that was closed in the early 1970s. Begin by climbing around a washed-out section of the abandoned road in forest, then dropping gently in 0.5 mile to a crossing of Slate Creek. You'll be in the midst of an ancient forest where some trees were saplings before Columbus arrived on our shores.

At **1.0** mile the trail branches. The left fork drops to the river where a new suspension bridge crosses to the Four Stream Trail on the opposite bank. Stay right at the junction and continue upstream to Slide Camp, at **1.5** miles. Here the river flows languidly past parklike river bottom land where elk can sometimes be seen in the early spring.

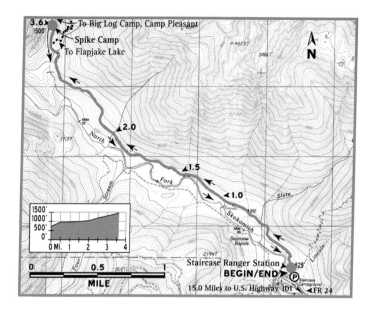

At **1.6** miles the trail crosses the 200-yard-wide 1986 mudslide that gave the camp below its name. And in another 0.1 mile you'll enter a 2-mile stretch of trail that traverses the burned forest of the Beaver Fire. Newborn trees are reclaiming the land from the 1985 fire, believed to have been started by a camper on the opposite side of

**PERMITS/CONTACT**
None required/Hood Canal Ranger Station, (360) 877-5254

**MAPS**
USGS Mount Steel; Custom Correct Mount Skokomish–Lake Cushman;
Green Trails Mount Steel

**TRAIL NOTES**
Kid-friendly

A suspension bridge connects the Spike Camp and Four Stream Trails

the river. It is thought that the mudslide a year later occurred because no vegetation was left to hold the land in check.

At about **2.0** miles the trail begins to climb more steeply past a spring-fed creek. The Mount Lincoln Way Trail junction, at **2.5** miles, begins climbing into the fire debris at this point. Stay left here.

The trail continues to climb, crossing a creek to a campsite at **3.4** miles to a junction with the Flapjack Lake Trail at **3.5** miles. Stay left here and continue another 0.1 mile to Spike Camp, where you'll find an outhouse and another campsite complete with a bear wire, the turnaround point for most day hikers.

## Going Farther

If you'd like a longer hike, two options are possible: You can continue up the North Fork Trail past Spike Camp for another 2.0 miles to Big Log Camp or another 3.0 miles to Camp Pleasant; or you can climb up to Flapjack Lakes, 3.5 miles from the trail junction—making a round-trip hike to the lakes of 14.2 miles and about 3,000 vertical feet. ∎

# 10. Four Stream

| RATING | DISTANCE | HIKING TIME |
|---|---|---|
| ★★☆☆☆ | 4.2 miles round-trip | 2.5 hours |

| ELEVATION GAIN | HIGH POINT | DIFFICULTY |
|---|---|---|
| 140 feet | 960 feet | ◆◇◇◇◇ |

| BEST SEASON |
|---|
| Jan Feb Mar Apr May Jun Jul Aug Sep Oct Nov Dec |

## The Hike

This is a half-day walk for the entire family through an ancient forest scarred by a fire 15 years ago, with peekaboo views of mountains and the North Fork of the Skokomish River beside the trail.

## Getting There

From US Highway 101 in Hoodsport, turn west on the Lake Cushman Road and follow it 9.0 miles to Forest Road 24. Turn left on FR 24 and follow it 6.0 miles around Lake Cushman to the Staircase Ranger Station. Be prepared to pay a fee on entering Olympic National Park at Staircase. Turn right just before the ranger station to the trailhead parking lot, 825 feet above sea level.

## The Trail

This pleasant path follows the North Fork of the Skokomish River upstream along the route taken by the O'Neil Expedition in 1890.

**PERMITS/CONTACT**
None required/Hood Canal Ranger Station, (360) 877-5254

**MAPS**
USGS Mount Steel; Custom Correct Mount Skokomish–Lake Cushman;
Green Trails Mount Steel

**TRAIL NOTES**
Kid-friendly

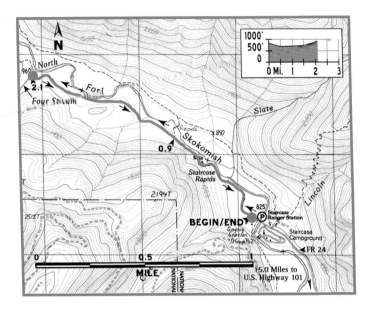

You'll see everything from huge cedar trees to rumbling rapids around Red Reef, 0.4 mile from the trailhead.

The path splits at **0.9** mile, with the right fork dropping to a new suspension bridge that crosses the river and climbs to the Spike Camp Trail. At **1.0** mile a sign marks the eastern boundary of the 1985 Beaver Fire, believed to have been started by a camper. The blaze spread across the river and burned up the side of Mount Lincoln, as you'll see by walking off the trail to the river's edge and looking up.

The trail continues through the burned area on this side for about a quarter-mile before rounding a ridge and entering old-growth forest again. Here the path follows the river closely, and at **1.7** miles it circumvents river flats that would make an excellent picnic stop on the return trip. At **1.9** miles the trail turns uphill, following a curve in the river, and climbs into the wide drainage basin of Four Stream. At **2.1** miles the trail meets Four Stream, which spills into the North Fork and your turnaround point. There's a nice riverside camp on the

The North Fork of the Skokomish River rolls through the forest beside the Four Stream Trail

opposite side of the stream, and an improved trail leads upstream from here. Though the trails from Staircase are all well-marked and easy to follow, hikers still sometimes lose their way. In 2006, for example, a hiker left his car in the Staircase parking area for a short walk. Despite days of searching by park officials and Olympic Mountain Rescue volunteers, he has never been found.

## Going Farther

If you cross the stream, you can climb up the ridge that divides Four and Five Streams on a rough trail that ends at the Olympic National Park boundary, about 1.4 miles and 900 feet up from Four Stream. Another option is to cross the concrete bridge at Staircase and follow the Shady Lane Trail downstream for 1.4 miles to the park boundary, then climb to Forest Road 2451, turn left and follow the road to the Bear Gulch causeway, cross the causeway and turn left up Forest Road 24, returning to Staircase. It's a loop hike of about 3.2 miles. ■

# OTHER HIKES

A restored 2.0-mile loop trail circles little Spider Lake, apparently named for one of the many bugs certain to bug you in midsummer. The lake is located in an island of old forest surrounded by clearcuts near the South Fork Skokomish–Satsop River divide.

The Upper South Fork Skokomish River Trail 873 continues from the end of Forest Road 2361 (closed for wildlife protection October 1–April 30) for 6.8 miles to Sundown Lake and an old connecting trail from Wynoochee Pass. While the first few miles make a good walk, the last are not maintained regularly and are difficult to follow.

A restored trail climbs and drops just as steeply above the head-waters of Church Creek off Forest Road 2361-600 (closed for wild-life protection October 1–April 30) over a pass for 3.3 miles to the Satsop Lakes. Carry bug repellent.

The Copper Creek Trail, off the Bear Gulch Road, Forest Road 2451, is one of a number of trails rebuilt by a bunch of hardy volun-teers who are older than dirt. It is a fiercely steep, 5.0-mile round-trip.

Local hiker-volunteers have made the abandoned Mount Lincoln Way Trail easier to find and follow. It begins about 2.5 miles up the trail to Spike Camp (Hike 9).

# HAMMA HAMMA RIVER

## 11. Lena Lake

| RATING | DISTANCE | HIKING TIME |
|---|---|---|
| ★★★ ☆ ☆ | 6.4 miles round-trip | 3.5 hours |

| ELEVATION GAIN | HIGH POINT | DIFFICULTY |
|---|---|---|
| 1,250 feet | 1,935 feet | ♦ ♦ ◇ ◇ ◇ |

| BEST SEASON |
|---|
| Jan Feb **Mar Apr May Jun Jul Aug Sep Oct Nov** Dec |

## The Hike

This is a moderate climb through old- and second-growth forest to a large subalpine lake with a big picnic rock overlooking the water.

## Getting There

From US Highway 101 at Eldon, 13.0 miles north of Hoodsport, turn west on the Hamma Hamma River Road, Forest Road 25, and drive 8.0 miles to the Lena Lake Trail No. 810, 685 feet above sea level.

## The Trail

Here's a wilderness walk that proves, once and for all, that trails *do* get longer as you get older. When I first walked this path, shortly after the discovery of America, it was 2.0 miles long. It has subsequently grown, first to 2.5 miles in the 1970s and in the past decade to 3.2 miles. The trail begins with a series of long, flat switchbacks climbing the round ridge above Lena Creek. The route here intersects

**PERMITS/CONTACT**
Parking pass required/Hood Canal Ranger Station, (360) 877-5254

**MAPS**
USGS the Brothers, Mount Washington; Custom Correct the Brothers–Mount Anderson; Green Trails the Brothers

**TRAIL NOTES**
Leashed dogs okay; kid-friendly

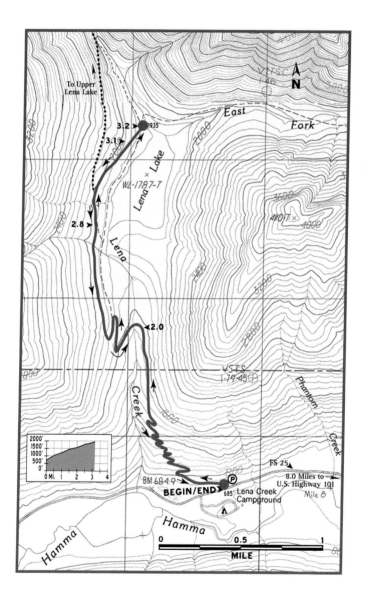

To Upper
Lena Lake

East

Fork

3.2
1935
3.1

Lena × Lake
WL-1787-7

2.8

Lena

2.0

Creek

2000'
1500'
1000'
500'
0'
0 Mi. 1 2 3 4

FS 25

8.0 Miles to
U.S. Highway 101
Mile 8

Phantom

Creek

BM 684.9
BEGIN/END
685'
Lena Creek
Campground

Hamma

Hamma

0          0.5          1
MILE

VTSC
146

4101.7 ×

VFTS
1-79-45

traces of the steeper, old trail at several points and climbs so gently that Olympic National Forest rangers and volunteers must keep busy blocking off all the way trails made by geeks cutting switchbacks.

At **2.0** miles the trail swings above Lena Creek, which can be seen and heard just below the trail, but when you come to the crossing at the site of an old bridge, you'll probably be surprised to find it as dry as desert sand. Huge boulders from massive slides that created the lake upstream covered the creek at this point, which runs underground to a spot just below your crossing point. Across the creek bed the old trail turned right and climbed up to the lake. The trail forged in the '70s turns left and climbs to a bench above the creek, switching back twice, before traversing under cliffs toward the lake.

At **2.8** miles an old trail leads right to the south end of the lake, but you should keep left on the old Upper Lena Lake Trail. The route climbs through forest about 150 feet above the lake before emerging at **3.1** miles onto Chapel Rock, a splendid viewpoint and picnic spot above the lake. From here the trail descends to a junction with the old lake trail, just above the shore at **3.2** miles. The trail continues around the lake to a junction with the Upper Lena Lake Trail, crosses a footlog to nice campsites and becomes the Brothers Trail.

Chapel Rock holds a plaque commemorating Camp Cleland, an old Scout camp of the 1930s. Scouts from that camp and other hikers packed many of the fish to the high alpine lakes around Lena and named many of the area's features, obviously including Scout Lake.

## Going Farther

Masochistic day hikers in search of a deliriously painful workout will find one by climbing another 3.5 miles, one-way, and 2,900 feet *up* to Upper Lena Lake. It's a beautiful alpine lake surrounded by summer snow-hoarding peaks, including Mount Lena to the north and Mount Bretherton to the south. Another trail leads from the north end of Lower Lena through a forest and field of huge boulders called The Valley of the Silent Men for 3.0 miles, one-way, to the most commonly used climbing route up the Brothers, that twin-summited Olympic Mountain peak so recognizable from Seattle. ■

## 12. Lake of the Angels

| RATING | DISTANCE | HIKING TIME |
|---|---|---|
| ★★★★☆ | 7.8 miles round-trip | 5 hours |
| **ELEVATION GAIN** | **HIGH POINT** | **DIFFICULTY** |
| 3,400 feet | 4,900 feet | ◆◆◆◆◆ |
| **BEST SEASON** | | |
| ~~Jan~~ ~~Feb~~ ~~Mar~~ ~~Apr~~ ~~May~~ ~~Jun~~ ~~Jul~~ Aug Sep Oct Nov ~~Dec~~ | | |

### The Hike

Try this tough climb up a no-nonsense pioneer trail to a beautiful gem of an alpine lake set in meadows under snowy Mount Skokomish and rocky—who would know from the name?—Mount Stone.

### Getting There

From US Highway 101 at Eldon, 13.0 miles north of Hoodsport, turn west on the Hamma Hamma River Road, Forest Road 25, and drive 12.0 miles to the Putvin Trail No. 813, located at 1,500 feet above sea level.

### The Trail

This hike takes no prisoners and virtually guarantees a double-ibuprofen drive home if you intend to get out of the car when you get there. I got in trouble for rating this hike as "difficult" in the first edition. It seems most hikers agreed that I underrated climbing the rocky headwall to the lake, where the trail—such as it is—is decidedly

---

**PERMITS/CONTACT**
None required/Hood Canal Ranger Station, (360) 877-5254

**MAPS**
USGS Mount Steel; Custom Correct Mount Skokomish–Lake Cushman;
Green Trails Mount Steel

**TRAIL NOTES**
Leashed dogs okay

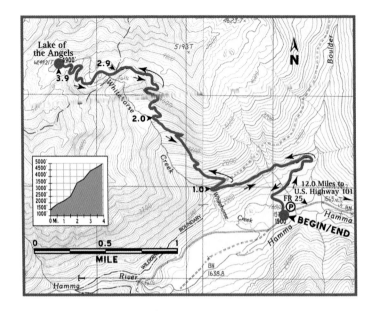

more vertical than horizontal. It climbs and climbs, and then climbs some more. But the lake and alpine meadow at the east end, nestled under the cliffs and snowfields of Mount Skokomish, make the climb seem worthwhile. It is easily one of the most beautiful spots in the southeastern Olympics.

Begin by climbing along an old Forest Service road to the edge of the Mount Skokomish Wilderness and switching back steeply at the location of the old trailhead, just below tumbling Whitehorse Creek. Here, at **1.0** mile, is where the serious climbing begins.

With few switchbacks to ease the climb, you'll follow the rough trail through subalpine forest and steep, open slopes alongside Whitehorse Creek, which drains Lake of the Angels. At **2.0** miles you'll climb closest to the creek and find a way trail leading to what surely is the only flat camp spot in the Western Hemisphere. You'll get a slight breather here as you keep to the right at the junction and cross a basin to the toughest part of the trail up a rocky, steep wall

The Putvin trail to Lake of the Angels begins with a gentle climb

where occasional vegetable belays might be necessary. (A vegetable belay is a technical mountaineering term. Grab hold of anything with solid root structure and pull yourself up, or at the very least, keep from sliding backward.)

At **2.9** miles the trail actually goes downhill long enough that Olympic athletes will be able to catch their breath, past a campsite and several small ponds. This is the Olympic National Park boundary, and hikers who have made their dogs suffer the same climb should not proceed farther.

The trail then crosses Whitehorse Creek and begins a final climb up steep open meadows painted by a kaleidoscope of wildflowers. If you pause to catch your breath, look behind you, out over the Hamma Hamma Valley all the way to Mount Rainier. At **3.8** miles you'll crest the ridge above Whitehorse Creek. The lake is 0.1 mile ahead, in a meadow that cups late-lingering snowfields that will chill that fine chardonnay you toted up here. You did remember the corkscrew, eh? ■

# 13. Mildred Lakes

| RATING | DISTANCE | HIKING TIME |
|---|---|---|
| ★★★ ☆☆ | 7.4 miles round-trip | 5 hours |

| ELEVATION GAIN | HIGH POINT | DIFFICULTY |
|---|---|---|
| 2,500 feet | 3,950 feet | ♦♦♦♦ |

| BEST SEASON |
|---|
| Jan Feb Mar Apr May Jun Jul **Aug Sep Oct Nov** Dec |

## The Hike

The strenuous climb on an angler's trail to picturesque Mildred Lakes is even tougher because you must do it twice, with descents of several hundred feet between climbs, fording two streams. But if you like to fish, this is the hike for you.

## Getting There

From US Highway 101 at Eldon, 13.0 miles north of Hoodsport, turn west on the Hamma Hamma River Road, Forest Road 25, and drive 14.1 miles to the Mildred Lakes Trail No. 822, located at 1,800 feet above sea level.

## The Trail

The path to Mildred Lakes hasn't improved significantly since I first hiked it more than four decades ago. The first time I hiked this trail, I couldn't figure out why every hiker I spoke to who had done it before me whined about it. Sure, walking it involved hopping from one slippery root to another, but the climb up to a rocky ridge crest didn't seem all that tough and I was certain the lakes couldn't be far away. I climbed through the dense forest, perhaps singing lusty trail ditties with my ex-wife, Old Iron Knees (we were married then, of course), and our hiking buddy, Eric Cederwall. At **1.8** miles, after cresting a ridge at 3,200 feet where the root-hopping switched to boulder-hopping, the stupid trail began to descend. Rather steeply, it seemed to me.

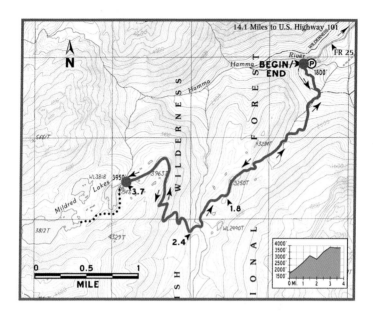

It dropped about 250 feet in the next 0.5 mile, emerging onto forested flats where a large stream blocked our path at **2.4** miles. There was a footlog that looked mighty slippery, so we waded the creek, climbed over a forested hump, then waded a second, smaller creek.

On the other side, we encountered one of those spots in the trail where you begin to question the sanity of trail planners. You take one

**PERMITS/CONTACT**
Parking pass required/Hood Canal Ranger Station, (360) 877-5254

**MAPS**
USGS Mount Steel; Custom Correct Mount Skokomish–Lake Cushman;
Green Trails Mount Steel

**TRAIL NOTES**
Leashed dogs okay

Mildred Lakes nestle in a basin below the Sawtooth Ridge

look at the steep gully and the log that crosses it and wonder: "They want me to cross that? They don't have all their bootlaces tied." Instead, we clambered down the steep hillside and up the other side to regain the trail, such as it was. Continue climbing steeply around rocks in dense forest about 500 feet to a second heathered ridge crest at 3,950 feet and 3.2 miles.

From here, the trail drops 100 feet to the first Mildred Lake, a small pond 3.7 miles from the trailhead. On that first hike, many years before the invention of the wheel, it felt to me more like 370 miles. Hikers gazing across the lakes to the Sawtooth Range above will soon see the reason such a tortuous trail came to be: rainbow trout splash hungrily in all the lakes and share one lake with cutthroat. At more than thirty-six acres, the largest Mildred Lake is one of the biggest subalpine lakes in the Olympics, and it holds some lunker fish.

## Going Farther

Unless you love fishing, you may not want to hike farther than the first lake. The largest lake is 0.7 mile farther along a trail and another 100 feet higher. A third lake, about 0.2 mile southwest of the first lake and slightly larger, holds cutthroat trout as well as rainbows. ∎

# OTHER HIKES

A 2.0-mile trail leads from unusually rough Forest Road 2421 up to usually crowded Elk Lakes, largely because they are also reached by auto on a much smoother Jefferson Creek Road.

The Jefferson Ridge Way Trail climbs through a clearcut to the ridge overlooking the Hamma Hamma River. Drive or hike Forest Road 2421 a mile to the 1.2-mile trail, which ends at the summit of Peak 3850.

# DUCKABUSH
# RIVER

# 14. Jupiter Ridge

| RATING | DISTANCE | HIKING TIME |
|--------|----------|-------------|
| ★★☆☆☆ | 7.2–9.2 miles round-trip | 4 hours |

| ELEVATION GAIN | HIGH POINT | DIFFICULTY |
|----------------|-----------|------------|
| 1,600 feet | 3,300 feet | ♦♦♦♦ |

| BEST SEASON |
|-------------|
| Jan Feb Mar Apr May **Jun Jul Aug Sep Oct** Nov Dec |

## The Hike

This is a strenuous hike up to and along a ridge crest that divides the Duckabush and Dosewallips rivers, with excellent views of the big peaks above the valleys. Strong hikers can continue from the recommended turnaround spot for another 3.6 miles, one-way, to the 5,701-foot summit of Mount Jupiter.

## Getting There

From the Dosewallips River bridge in Brinnon, drive south on US Highway 101 for 2.6 miles to the Mount Jupiter Road. From the south, it is 9.3 miles north from the Hamma Hamma River Road on US Highway 101 to the Mount Jupiter Road. Turn west on the Mount Jupiter Road and drive 3.2 miles to Forest Road 2610-011 and turn left.

### PERMITS/CONTACT
Permit required/Hood Canal Ranger Station, Quilcene, (360) 765-2200; www.RayonierHunting.com

### MAPS
USGS Brinnon, Jupiter; Custom Correct the Brothers–Mount Anderson; Green Trails the Brothers

### TRAIL NOTES
Leashed dogs okay. Both the road and trail traverse portions of private property and the road may be closed several miles below the trailhead. The road is also closed for wildlife protection from October 1 to May 1. Call Hood Canal Ranger Station before taking this hike.

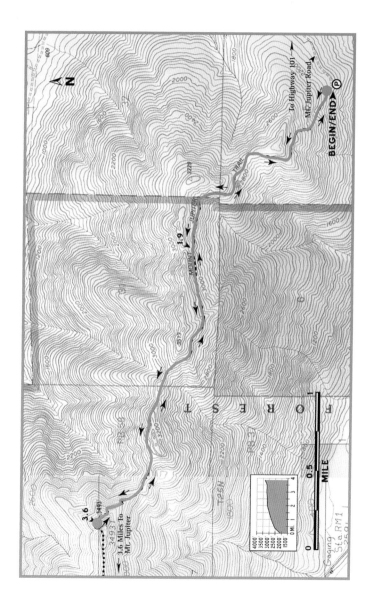

N

To Highway 101

Mt. Jupiter Road

BEGIN/END (P)

TRAIL

1.9

MT JUPITER TRAIL

2229

3.6

3493

3.6 Miles To
Mt. Jupiter

FR-39

F O R E S T

T26N
T25N

FR-37

Gaging
Sta RM1
2550

MILE

0      0.5     1

0 MI    1    2    3    4

1500
2000
2500
3000
3500
4000

Drive 3.0 miles up this rough road to the trailhead, 2,100 feet above sea level. The last 2.0 miles of this road are on private timberland and may be gated. Signs posted at the closed gate in 2021 indicated the road is gated from August 1 through December 31 and gave the website RayonierHunting.com for more information.

## The Trail

The most important thing to remember about this hike—and generally about any hike that follows the crest of alpine ridges—is that there's no water to re-supply your bottle or hydration pack. Carry twice your normal amount, because you'll be doing a lot of climbing, both up and down along the way.

Begin by climbing on switchbacks through south-facing logged-over hillsides that can be hot on summer days, climbing a steep road for 2.0 miles before crossing from private land to Olympic National Forest and the official trailhead. Here you'll find your views spoiled by all those trees and in late May and in early June, a fine pink display of rhododendrons. The trail levels a bit and traverses the forest on the Duckabush side of the ridge. At **1.9** trail miles, emerge on the ridge crest, where you can look north through trees to the Dosewallips valley and to the first views of Mount Jupiter, to the west, and the Brothers, to the south.

Just after cresting the ridge, the trail begins to drop again along the north side, winding down to a saddle before climbing once again. Get used to it: the up-down-up theme features more repetitions than Ravel's Bolero. Perhaps the only relief from this tiresome tedium is the peekaboo views you get of Mount Constance on the north side and the Brothers to the south. The path meanders from one side of the ridge to the other, heading west for about 1.7 miles to a rocky viewpoint just off the trail to the left. Here's your turnaround point, with a fine vista of the Duckabush River and the broad snow bowl that identifies the Brothers to folks watching the sunset in Seattle.

## Going Farther

Hikers in good physical condition, capable of hiking an alpine venue like the Mount Jupiter Trail, can continue another 3.6 miles to the summit of Mount Jupiter, the site of an old lookout. That makes a day hike of between 14.4 to 18.4 miles if the road is gated. Be forewarned: the trail gets steeper, culminating in a rocky switchback climb to the summit. On the plus side, the view from the peak is spectacular. ■

## 15. Big Hump

| RATING<br>★★☆☆☆ | DISTANCE<br>10.4 miles round-trip | HIKING TIME<br>5 hours |
|---|---|---|
| ELEVATION GAIN<br>1,500 feet | HIGH POINT<br>1,700 feet | DIFFICULTY<br>◆ ◆ ◆ ◇ ◇ |

| BEST SEASON |
|---|
| Jan Feb Mar Apr May Jun Jul Aug Sep Oct Nov Dec |

### The Hike

The 1,000-foot climb up and over the Big Hump on the Duckabush River Trail makes an excellent tune-up for long day hikes later in the season. Many local hikers make this a conditioning trek in spring, getting an added workout ducking under and climbing over deadfalls not yet cleared by trail crews.

**PERMITS/CONTACT**
Permit required/Hood Canal Ranger Station, Quilcene,
(360) 765-2200; www.RayonierHunting.com

**MAPS**
USGS Mount Jupiter; Custom Correct the Brothers–Mount Anderson;
Green Trails the Brothers

**TRAIL NOTES**
Leashed dogs okay; wildfire closed trail in 2011—currently open to hikers only

## Getting There

From the Dosewallips River bridge in Brinnon, drive south on US Highway 101 for 2.8 miles to the Duckabush River Road and turn west. From the south, it is 9.0 miles north from the Hamma Hamma River Road on US Highway 101 to the Duckabush River Road. Follow the Duckabush River Road, Forest Road 2510, for 6.0 miles to the trailhead, just right off FR 2510-060, 300 feet above sea level.

## The Trail

Possibly because of the notorious Big Hump—a steep 1,050-foot climb above the Duckabush valley—the hike may not be as popular as others along the Hood Canal side of the Olympic Mountains. But the river is splendidly wild; Duckabush water is exceptionally clear because no glaciers grind silt into the infant stream upriver. Another plus is that Olympic National Forest stretches to within 3 miles of the river mouth. Few farms and residences line the river valley; wilderness reaches upriver from the old Interrorem Ranger Station, less than 4 miles west of Hood Canal.

The trail, No. 803, follows an abandoned road that once climbed through the forest for another mile to the top of Little Hump. That's a 600-vertical-foot warm-up for the Big Hump beyond, and it should get your heart bouncing. Just beyond the 900-foot-high summit of the Little Hump, you'll enter the Brothers Wilderness. Motorized vehicles are prohibited in wilderness areas, but you can take Fido along. The trail drops about 200 feet back down to riverside, about **1.7** miles from the trailhead. Families with younger children might find the flats beside the river a good turnaround spot.

Beyond, the trail begins a 1.5-mile climb to the top of Big Hump, 1,700 feet above sea level. This section of the trail is a series of anywhere between 38 and 58 switchbacks, depending upon how you define a switchback and whether you count the hairpins on the trail back down to the river. The climb up gets interesting near the top when several moss-covered rock outcroppings offer excellent views of the Duckabush valley and St. Peter's Dome across the river. From the top of Big Hump, the trail drops in switchbacks down to the river.

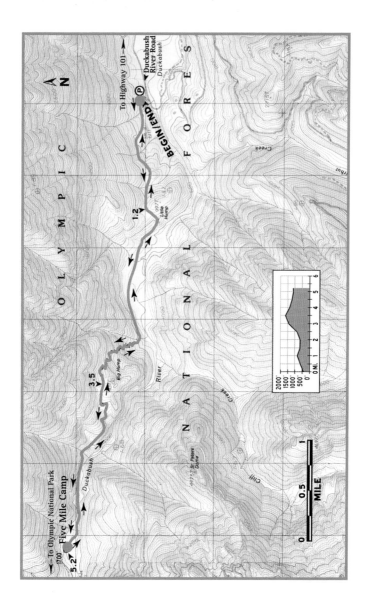

OLYMPIC

N

To Highway 101

Duckabush
River Road
Duckabush

BEGIN/END

FOREST

NATIONAL

Little
Hump

1.2

Big Hump

3.5

River

Creek

St. Peters
Dome

Cliff

To Olympic National Park

Five Mile Camp

Duckabush

5.2

2000
1500
1000
500
0 MI.  1  2  3  4  5  6

0        0.5        1
MILE

You'll cross two sparkling streams and walk about 1.8 miles to Five Mile Camp. The riverside camp is **5.2** miles from the trailhead and makes a good turnaround point.

## Going Farther

Once over the Big Hump, the Duckabush River Trail makes an excellent backpack of 3–5 days. The trail enters Olympic National Park at **6.0** miles, where Fido will have to turn around and you'll have to issue yourself an overnight backcountry use permit. Campsites are located at **10.0** and **15.4** miles along the trail, where pathways lead steeply up over LaCrosse Pass or farther upriver to Marmot, Hart, and LaCrosse Lakes. ■

# OTHER HIKES

Ranger Hole Trail is a 1.6-mile round-trip from the Interrorem Guard Station down to a fishing hole on the Duckabush River. It got its name from the forest rangers who fished there for years.

The Interrorem Nature Trail circles the old guard station in about 0.3 mile and can serve as a beginning or ending loop for the Ranger Hole Trail.

The Murhut Falls Trail leads 1.6 miles up and down along an abandoned logging road to the two-tiered, 120-foot falls.

# DOSEWALLIPS RIVER

# 16. Tunnel Creek, Dosewallips

| RATING | DISTANCE | HIKING TIME |
|---|---|---|
| ★☆☆☆☆ | 6.6 miles round-trip | 5 hours |
| **ELEVATION GAIN** | **HIGH POINT** | **DIFFICULTY** |
| 4,500 feet | 5,050 feet | ◆◆◆◆◆ |

| BEST SEASON |
|---|
| Jan Feb Mar Apr May **Jun Jul Aug Sep** Oct Nov Dec |

## The Hike

Here's an extremely steep, rough trail that offers only three good reasons for its existence: the view of Mount Constance, the rhododendron bloom in mid-June, and the option of hiking one-way.

## Getting There

From Brinnon on US Highway 101 take the Dosewallips River Road 9.0 miles to a wide parking area on the north side of the road, just across from the former Steelhead Campground. Look for the beginning of Tunnel Creek Trail No. 841 as a wide dirt path descending the bank at the west end of the parking area, 500 feet above sea level. This trailhead had no signs on the road when last checked.

## The Trail

Unless you are in excellent physical condition, this steep side of the Tunnel Creek Trail is going to empty a two-gallon can of whoop-ass all over you. Parts of this route rival the notorious Lake Constance

---

**PERMITS/CONTACT**
None required/Hood Canal Ranger Station, Quilcene, (360) 765-2200

**MAPS**
USGS the Brothers, Tyler Peak; Custom Correct Buckhorn Wilderness;
Green Trails the Brothers, Tyler Peak

**TRAIL NOTES**
Leashed dogs okay

---

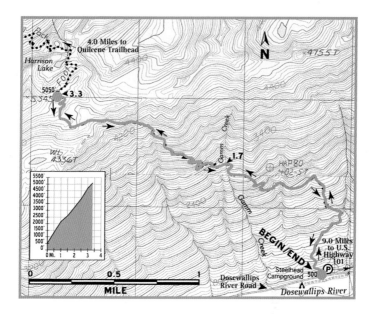

Trail (Hike 17) for steepness. The biggest difference is that Tunnel Creek is more than a mile longer.

Begin by wading through a stinging nettle patch you may encounter blocking your path to the trail, the beginning of which resembles the path left by horses plunging into the river in the Omak Suicide Race. Remember, the Tunnel Creek paths were made by suicidal hikers bound for home, hot tubs, and illegal quantities of ibuprofen. The trail gets only slightly less steep than the beginning, which seems just short of vertical, for the first 1.0 mile. Switchbacks, if indeed they may be called that, involve taking a quarter-turn on the hillside—more to dodge big conifers standing in the way than to provide respite for your lungs.

At **1.1** miles, you'll see that "steep" is indeed a relative term as the trail becomes less steep than it was before becoming more steep than it was before it became less steep. You'll climb again to a spot that could still be washed out at **1.7** miles, just below Gamm Creek.

Cliffs of Mount Constance tower above Lake Constance

Across the creek—the only water on this side of the ridge—you'll find at least 15 feet of trail that could be termed "flat." This is a good spot to pause and attempt to discover if the pounding you hear is your heart or a horny grouse drumming for a mate in the woods.

The trail then climbs again, this time in actual switchbacks for another 1.5 miles through big shady patches of rhododendron that turn the forest pink during their bloom, eventually gaining the crest of the ridge dividing the Dosewallips River from Tunnel Creek.

Continue another 0.1 mile to a rocky perch on the north side of the ridge, where the steep cliffs of the east face of Mount Constance hunker above the trail. The jagged peak is so close you might hear rocks crashing down its cliffs.

## Going Farther

Hikers can park a car at either end of the Tunnel Creek, Quilcene Trail (Hike 20) and—if the party hiking up from the Dosewallips side survives—exchange car keys at the rocky viewpoint. The trail from here down to 5050 Pass may be difficult to follow. The one-way hike would be 7.3 miles. Hikers with titanium knees will be able to withstand the descent to the Dosewallips trailhead with the least pain. ∎

# 17. Lake Constance

| RATING | DISTANCE | HIKING TIME |
|---|---|---|
| ★★★☆☆ | 11.7–13.5 miles round-trip | 6.5 hours |
| ELEVATION GAIN | HIGH POINT | DIFFICULTY |
| 4,060 feet | 4,660 feet | ♦♦♦♦♦ |
| BEST SEASON | | |
| Jan Feb Mar Apr May **Jun Jul Aug Sep** Oct Nov Dec | | |

## The Hike

The steepest trail in Olympic National Park leads to an emerald lake under monstrous cliffs of Mount Constance, setting a scene almost worth the killer climb. With the additional 9.3 round-trip miles of closed road to walk, only the strongest hikers should attempt this hike.

## Getting There

From Brinnon on US Highway 101 take the Dosewallips River Road 9.8 miles to the trailhead and 600 feet above sea level. A washout at a creek 0.9 mile east of the spot where the Dosewallips River closed the road may halt many hikers short of the trailhead. If this is the

**PERMITS/CONTACT**
None required/Hood Canal Ranger Station, Quilcene, (360) 765-2200

**MAPS**
USGS the Brothers, Tyler Peak; Custom Corroot Duckhorn Wilderness;
Green Trails the Brothers, Tyler Peak

**TRAIL NOTES**
No dogs

case, you must add another 1.8 round-trip miles to this hike. Many hikers intent on reaching the lake ride mountain bikes up the Dose Road after bypassing the washout.

## The Trail

One of my four hikes to Lake Constance was most memorable because I had the opportunity to ride back down the trail in a stretcher. I played the victim for the volunteer members of Olympic Mountain Rescue, who used the path for practice sessions.

In fact, to say the trail is regarded by mountaineers as more dangerous than the climb of Mount Constance above is only a slight exaggeration. We can all thank our guardian angels that we probably won't suffer as greatly as my friend Gary Knight's brother Doug, whose boots were stolen years ago by a mountain goat at the lake, leaving the poor fellow with a 2-mile descent in stocking feet the next morning. Even Noah Webster would quibble about using the word "switchback" to describe any of the turns in this trail. Trees along the way make good handles for climbing and good places to arrest sliding plunges on the way down.

Begin by circumnavigating the Dosewallips River Road washout via a new bypass trail that begins 150 feet east of the washout on the north side of the road. It climbs in switchbacks to a flat plateau, then traverses around the washout to descend in switchbacks down to the road. During times of low water, an alternate route is to drop to the river and follow a way trail along river's edge around the washout, then climb back up to the road.

Once there, hike up the road for 3.8 miles, passing the closed Elkhorn Campground on the right at **1.0** mile. The road does not begin to climb in earnest until it passes the closed campground.

This hike was made even more difficult by a fire in 2009 that dropped many trees across the lower part of the path. Follow the trail as it ascends steeply through forest for 1.1 miles before becoming slightly less steep—hikers who call this short section "flat" are suffering delusions brought on by the trail. Just past a huge rock, the trail steepens and follows a traverse across a cliff that mountaineers might call interesting. This is a technical term that means if you slip, you could break something vital to your health and well-being.

The last 0.5 mile of the trail is literally up the (Constance) creek, around a steep cliff overlooking the Dosewallips Valley, and on to the lake. A picnic spot above the lake is 0.2 mile around the lake, with views of lava cliffs that seem to lean over the lake.

## Going Farther

Hikers who won't flop like grounded flounders at the first flat spot they find after the climb begins can continue up the talus slope above the east shore of the lake for better views, or follow the climbers' route up Avalanche Canyon at the north end of the lake. ∎

# 18. Dosewallips Campground

| RATING | DISTANCE | HIKING TIME |
|---|---|---|
| ★★★☆☆ | 10.8–12.6 miles round-trip | 5.5 hours |
| **ELEVATION GAIN** | **HIGH POINT** | **DIFFICULTY** |
| 1,060 feet | 1,540 feet | ◆◆◆◆◇ |

| BEST SEASON |
|---|
| Jan Feb Mar Apr May **Jun Jul Aug Sep Oct Nov** Dec |

## The Hike

It's not likely the Dosewallips Road will be reopened anytime soon, if ever. The lack of vehicle traffic makes this one of the most pleasant walks along a wild river you can find anywhere in the state. Families with young hikers will find the 2.0-mile round-trip walk to the closed Elkhorn Campground a most excellent adventure.

## Getting There

From Brinnon on US Highway 101, follow the Dosewallips River Road 9.8 miles to the trailhead, 600 feet above sea level. A washout at a creek 0.9 mile east of the spot where the Dosewallips River closed the road may halt many hikers short of the trailhead. If this is the case, you must add another 1.8 round-trip miles to this hike.

**PERMITS/CONTACT**
None required/Hood Canal Ranger Station, Quilcene, (360) 765-2200

**MAPS**
USGS the Brothers; Custom Correct the Brothers–Mount Anderson;
Green Trails the Brothers

**TRAIL NOTES**
Leashed dogs okay; kid-friendly

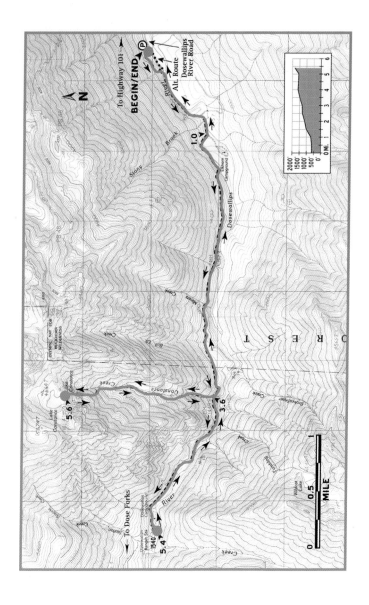

To Highway 101
BEGIN/END
Dosewallips River Road
Alt. Route

River

Stony Brook

1.0

Elkhorn Campground

Dosewallips

Creek

Deception Creek

OLYMPIC NAT'L
PARK WILDERNESS

Lake Constance

5.67

Constance Creek

Constance

3.6

Dosewallips River

To Dose Forks

1540
5.4

Dosewallips Meadph Sta.

Creek

Tunnel Creek

Brinnon Creek

Willock Lake

Station Creek

N

2000'
1500'
1000'
500'
0'
0 Mi. 1   2   3   4   5   6

0      0.5      1
MILE

The Dosewallips River rolls past the chunk it took out of the Dosewallips River Road in 2002

## The Trail

Begin by circumnavigating the Dosewallips River Road washout via a new bypass trail that begins 150 feet east of the washout on the north side of the road. It climbs in switchbacks to a flat plateau, then traverses around the washout to descend in switchbacks down to the road. During times of low water, an alternate route is to drop to the river and follow a way trail along the river's edge around the washout, then climb back up to the road.

Follow the road as it meanders through forest for 1.0 mile to a junction with the short road leading to the left into the closed Elkhorn Campground. If you have young hikers in tow, this is a great spot for a picnic and turnaround, with picnic tables, fire rings, and—unless they've been nailed shut since we last visited—a couple of outhouses.

Keep right at this junction if the Dosewallips Campground is your destination, and begin climbing on the road as it heads toward the old Lake Constance Trailhead and entrance to Olympic National Park, 3.0 miles and 750 vertical feet from the Elkhorn junction.

The climb is on a moderate grade and crosses two major creeks—one on an excellent auto bridge.

The road levels off as you pass the Lake Constance Trailhead, just beyond a gate indicating the Olympic National Park Boundary. It was on this road, years ago, that I was surprised and delighted to find a mountain goat traipsing along. When I approached to take a photo, it ran not uphill, but down towards the Dosewallips River below, crashing through several decades' worth of tin cans discarded by ancient Lake Constance hikers.

Once past the Lake Constance Trail, the road drops steeply to the river, where it ducks under a huge cliff of pillow lava and begins a steep climb alongside the cascading Dosewallips River. The rush and power of the river is palpable here. Beyond, the river is quiet, almost as if gathering strength for the plunge, and the road passes above an old stock loading area before beginning a gradual descent to the campground, 5.4 miles from the washout.

The campground is overgrown with weeds, but you'll find picnic tables and campfire rings along the river for picnicking and a rest before beginning the hike back to the washout. The seasonal ranger station and bunkhouse at the Dosewallips was closed when last visited, but may be open in the summer.

## Going Farther

Strong hikers may wish to continue another 1.4 miles, one-way, to Dose Forks. Here you'll find a wide stock bridge crossing the river, the site of two backcountry shelters burned by Olympic National Park crews in the '70s, and campsites by the river.

The trail forks here, with the left fork leading another 10.2 miles to Anderson Pass and beyond, and the right fork leading 15.2 miles to Hayden Pass and beyond. ■

# OTHER HIKES

Dosewallips State Park, at the mouth of the river, offers up to 5 miles of trails and old fire roads for exploration. The Steam Donkey loop and a wetlands walk on the north side of the river are probably the two most interesting of these trails.

Two abandoned or gated Forest Roads—2810-012 and 2810-10 —begin at a bridge about 5.8 miles up the Dosewallips River Road, offering walks and perhaps mountain bike challenges of up to 6 miles, round-trip.

# QUILCENE RIVER

---

# 19. Mount Walker

| RATING | DISTANCE | HIKING TIME |
|---|---|---|
| ★★★☆☆ | 4.0–6.0 miles round trip | 3–5 hours |

| ELEVATION GAIN | HIGH POINT | DIFFICULTY |
|---|---|---|
| 2,000 feet | 2,800 feet | ◆◆◆◇ |

| BEST SEASON |
|---|
| Jan Feb Mar Apr May Jun Jul Aug Sep Oct Nov Dec |

## The Hike
This is a strenuous climb to a great view of Puget Sound, Hood Canal, and the eastern front of the Olympic Mountains, best done in the winter when the road to two summit viewpoints is closed.

## Getting There
From Quilcene, drive south on US Highway 101 for 5.0 miles to the Mount Walker Road at Walker Pass, turn north on the Mount Walker Road and drive 0.25 mile to the trailhead parking area. The trail begins across the road, 800 feet above sea level.

## The Trail
While the Green Mountain trails (Hikes 1 and 2) might be thought of as Tiger Mountain West, this pathway might be considered an uncrowded, though shorter version, of the Mount Si Trail. It's half as long and climbs half as far, but the view is just as spectacular.

**PERMITS/CONTACT**
None required/Hood Canal Ranger Station, Quilcene, (360) 765-2200

**MAPS**
USGS Mount Walker

**TRAIL NOTES**
Leashed dogs okay

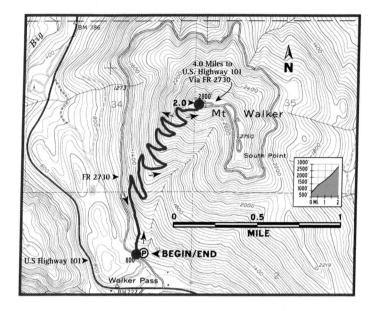

Many day hikers save this trail for the winter, when the road is usually closed, so they can have the option of walking up or down the road. Hiking up the road and down the steeper trail adds 2 miles to the round-trip distance, making it a total of 6 miles. If you choose to wait until warmer, drier months, you can still hike the road, but plan on sharing it with autos and bicyclists in search of serious punishment. One advantage to hiking the road is the round-the-mountain view it affords, starting on the south side of the mountain and climbing clockwise, reaching the summits on the east side of the hill.

The trail climbs relentlessly from the start, gaining about 1,000 feet every mile. The lower section of the trail is through rich forest of Douglas fir, with salal, huck, and rhododendron glowing green beneath the second- and third-growth trees. Switching back up the southern flank of Mount Walker, you'll climb to increasingly wider views through the trees of the eastern front of the Olympic Mountains. The second mile of the route climbs along the eastern side of the forested ridge with views through the trees to the southern viewpoint of Mount Walker.

The trail breaks into the open just below the southern viewpoint of the mountain. Here you'll find a picnic table with views to the west of the Olympics. Hike the road north for about a half-mile to the northern viewpoint for a look across Hood Canal towards Seattle and north to Mount Baker and the North Cascades. Though the trailhead is usually free of snow throughout the winter, you are likely to find as much as a foot or two of snow at the summit during winters of heavy snowfall. ■

# 20. Tunnel Creek, Quilcene

| RATING | DISTANCE | HIKING TIME |
|---|---|---|
| ★ ★ ★ ☆ ☆ | 8.4 miles round-trip | 4.5 hours |
| ELEVATION GAIN | HIGH POINT | DIFFICULTY |
| 2,450 feet | 5,050 feet | ♦ ♦ ♦ ♦ |

| BEST SEASON | | | | | | | | | | | |
|---|---|---|---|---|---|---|---|---|---|---|---|
| Jan | Feb | Mar | Apr | May | Jun | Jul | Aug | Sep | Oct | Nov | Dec |

## The Hike
This is the "easy" though longer climb to a great view of the cliffs of Mount Constance past two tiny alpine lakes. You've the option of a one-way hike but face an extremely steep 3.3-mile descent to the Dosewallips River trailhead.

## Getting There
From Quilcene follow US Highway 101 south 1.4 miles to the Penny Creek Road. Turn right and follow Penny Creek Road to its junction with the Big Quilcene River Road; follow it 3.0 miles to Forest Road 2740 and take FR 2740 to the left. Follow FR 2740 for 7.1 miles to the Tunnel Creek Trail No. 841, located 2,600 feet above sea level.

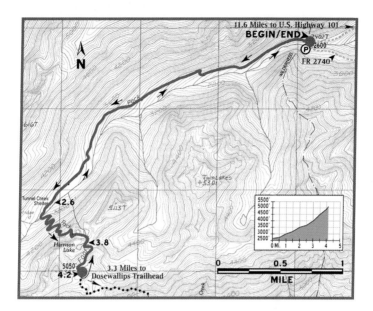

## The Trail

Here's the sane(r) way to get to a ridge crest that divides the Tunnel Creek drainage from the Dosewallips River valley. Begin by climbing along tumbling Tunnel Creek past a creekside campsite across the water at **0.5** mile before turning uphill into woods away from

**PERMITS/CONTACT**
Parking pass required/Hood Canal Ranger Station, Quilcene, (360) 765-2200

**MAPS**
USGS Tyler Peak, the Brothers; Custom Correct Buckhorn Wilderness; Green Trails Tyler Peak

**TRAIL NOTES**
Leashed dogs okay

the stream. The trail plays hide-and-seek with Tunnel Creek for the next 2 miles, dodging into thick forest and then emerging by the water. It climbs steadily until reaching a wide flat stretch at **2.5** miles.

Just above Tunnel Creek Shelter, at **2.6** miles, the trail crosses the creek. You can follow the trail to the horse ford, left, or continue right to a steep climb and cross the creek on a footlog. Above the shelter the trail climbs through deep forest in switchbacks before rounding a steep ridge and emerging at tiny Karnes Lake, at **3.7** miles. The trail climbs again, arriving at larger Harrison Lake after 0.1 mile. Past the lake you'll climb steeply to the ridge at a rocky promontory with a splendid view of the east face of Mount Constance. This viewpoint is 4.2 miles from the trailhead and a good turnaround spot.

## Going Farther

From the viewpoint it is a short climb over 5050 Pass before beginning a knee-punishing, thigh-burning descent to the Dosewallips River, 3.3 miles below (Hike 16). Two-car parties can trade keys at the viewpoint, assuming the hikers climbing up from the Dosewallips haven't dropped from exhaustion along the way. ∎

# 21. Lower Big Quilcene Trail

| RATING | DISTANCE | HIKING TIME |
|:---:|:---:|:---:|
| ★★☆☆☆ | 9.8 miles round-trip | 4.5 hours |

| ELEVATION GAIN | HIGH POINT | DIFFICULTY |
|:---:|:---:|:---:|
| 700 feet | 2,000 feet | ◆◇◇◇◇ |

| BEST SEASON |
|:---:|
| Jan Feb Mar Apr May Jun Jul Aug Sep Oct Nov Dec |

## The Hike

This is a nice, gentle walk above and along the tumbling Quilcene River through second-growth forest and reforested clearcuts, with views of mountains above the Quilcene watershed. There's an optional one-way hike for two-car parties.

## Getting There

From Quilcene follow US Highway 101 south 1.4 miles to the Penny Creek Road. Turn right and follow Penny Creek Road to its junction with the Big Quilcene River Road; follow it 3.0 miles to Forest Road 27. Take FR 27 for 0.3 mile to FR 2700-080 and follow it downhill for 0.4 mile to the trailhead at 1,300 feet above sea level, where a primitive campsite with an outhouse is located.

**PERMITS/CONTACT**
Parking pass required/Hood Canal Ranger Station, Quilcene, (360) 765-2200

**MAPS**
USGS Tyler Peak; Custom Correct Buckhorn Wilderness; Green Trails Tyler Peak

**TRAIL NOTES**
Leashed dogs okay; bikes okay

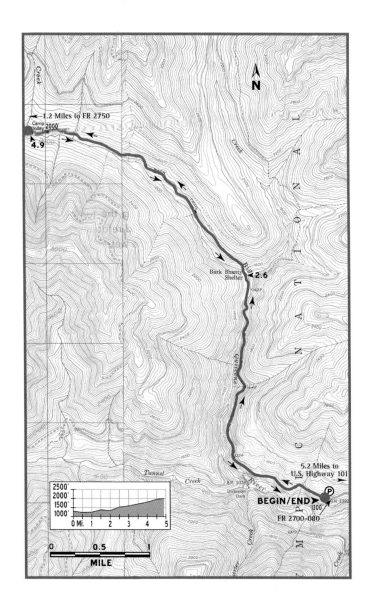

N

1.2 Miles to FR 2750

Camp
Jolley 2000'

4.9

Bark Shanty
Shelter

2.6

5.2 Miles to
U.S. Highway 101

BEGIN/END
FR 2700-080

Tunnel

Creek

BM 1022

Diversion
Dam

1300'

BM 1392

2500'
2000'
1500'
1000'
0 Mi.   1   2   3   4   5

0          0.5          1
MILE

## The Trail

This route follows an abandoned logging road as it first drops gently for about a half-mile through second-growth forest along a grassy, alder-lined bench above the Quilcene River. You'll see a forest road below the path, which ends at the river less than a mile upstream.

The trail, No. 833, stays above the river on the old roadbed for the first couple of miles, crossing a tributary creek at **1.0** mile before traversing the steep hillside. The Quilcene River churns through the forest below, and views through the trees are of the steep slopes of Mount Crag.

The trail drops gently to cross the river at **2.5** miles on a plank bridge, then climbs slightly to a wide bench beside the river called Bark Shanty Shelter. Huge fir trees tower above the river here, 2.6 miles from the trailhead. This was the end of the old road, and the narrower trail now strays through the forest, farther from the river before crossing the Quilcene once again just past the confluence of Townsend Creek and the river, at **3.1** miles. The walls of the Quilcene

The Lower Big Quilcene hike starts on an abandoned logging road

Valley become steeper, and the trail climbs more steeply through old logged areas where sunlight on good days warms the trail.

The path returns to the forest, where rhododendrons bloom in late May and salal provides a green carpet. You'll cross two creeks before crossing Jolley Creek and Camp Jolley, below the main trail, at **4.9** miles.

## Going Farther

Those looking for more exercise can continue past Camp Jolley on the trail for another 1.2 miles to Ten Mile Shelter and Forest Road 2750. Hikers looking for a one-way walk can leave cars at the upper and lower trailheads, or exchange car keys with friends hiking from the opposite direction. ■

# 22. Marmot Pass

| RATING | DISTANCE | HIKING TIME |
|---|---|---|
| ★★★★★ | 10.4 miles round-trip | 5.5 hours |
| ELEVATION GAIN | HIGH POINT | DIFFICULTY |
| 3,500 feet | 6,000 feet | ♦♦♦♦ |
| BEST SEASON | | |
| Jan Feb Mar Apr May **Jun Jul Aug Sep Oct Nov** Dec | | |

## The Hike

Try this strenuous climb to alpine meadows and one of the most scenic views of the Northern Olympic Mountains to be found, made better still by the greater chance for dry weather. Hikers placing two cars at separate trailheads have a one-way option.

## Getting There

From Quilcene follow US Highway 101 south 1.4 miles to the Penny Creek Road. Turn right and follow Penny Creek Road to its junction with the Big Quilcene River Road; follow it 3 miles to Forest Road 27.

Follow FR 27 for 6.1 miles to FR 2750 and follow FR 2750 for 4.5 miles to the Upper Big Quilcene Trail No. 833, at 2,500 feet above sea level.

## The Trail

The hike to Marmot Pass is the champagne walk of the Northeastern Olympics. It starts with a shaded forest walk and ends high above timberline, where you will keep company with the cute little furballs for whom the pass is named. The view will melt your mind.

The trail, located on the fringes of the dry section of the park known as the "rain shadow," begins with a gentle climb through a rhododendron grove that is spectacular in mid-spring, which is a bit too early if you plan to reach Marmot Pass without wading through snow in the high country. After climbing above the river for 1.1 miles, the path switches back away from the river and climbs steeply to another switchback, then traverses through a big forest back to the river. It crosses one major creek before climbing gently towards Shelter Rock, at **2.6** miles. This is the trail's final brush with the Quilcene, which is reduced to a chattering creek.

Beyond Shelter Rock you'll begin climbing steeply, first alongside a little creek that dives through the meadow beside the trail. The path eventually crosses the creek and begins a climbing traverse of the slopes of Buckhorn and Iron Mountains. If you're hiking this section in early summer, expect to cross the snowfields of at least two avalanche paths—the springtime goal of backcountry snowriders. At **4.4** miles the trail switches back twice, where expansive views to the northeast include the Cascade Mountains and Puget Sound basin, then climbs along a creek to Camp Mystery at **4.6** miles.

---

### PERMITS/CONTACT
Parking pass required/Hood Canal Ranger Station, Quilcene, (360) 765-2200

### MAPS
USGS Tyler Peak; Custom Correct Buckhorn Wilderness; Green Trails Tyler Peak

### TRAIL NOTES
Leashed dogs okay

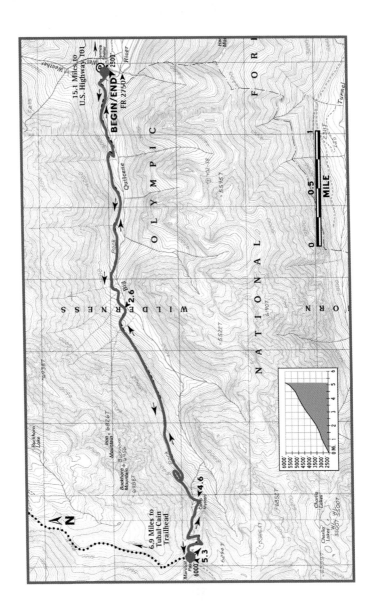

Boulder Ridge hangs above the Marmot Pass Trail below the pass

The camp, an excellent picnic spot, is located in a windbreak of alpine trees. Beyond, the trail follows the creek before climbing into a wide, wildflower-filled bowl just below the pass. Here's another spot sheltered from the frequent winds you may encounter at Marmot Pass, another 0.6 mile up the trail. Continue to the pass for stunning views of the highest peaks of the Northeastern Olympics, including Mount Deception and The Needles.

## Going Farther
A 12.2-mile one-way option for two-car parties can be made by following the Tubal Cain Trail No. 840 (Hike 26) right at the pass and first climbing then descending 7.3 miles to the trailhead. ▪

# 23. Mount Townsend

| RATING | DISTANCE | HIKING TIME |
|---|---|---|
| ★★★★☆ | 8.0 miles round-trip | 4.5 hours |

| ELEVATION GAIN | HIGH POINT | DIFFICULTY |
|---|---|---|
| 2,000 feet | 6,280 feet | ◆◆◆◆◇ |

| BEST SEASON |
|---|
| Jan Feb Mar Apr May **Jun Jul Aug Sep Oct Nov** Dec |

## The Hike
Save this tough climb for a bluebird day of summer, when you can soak up the sunshine and the incredible views of just about everything west of the Mississippi River and south of Fuzzbeak, Alaska.

## Getting There
From Quilcene follow US Highway 101 south 1.4 miles to the Penny Creek Road. Turn right and follow Penny Creek Road to its junction with the Big Quilcene River Road; follow it 3.0 miles to Forest Road 27. Follow FR 27 for 14.8 miles, passing a sign at 14.3 miles directing traffic left to the lower Mount Townsend trailhead. Instead, continue right on FR 27 to FR 27-190 and turn left on FR 27-190, following it 0.7 mile to the upper Mount Townsend Trail No. 839, at 3,400 feet above sea level.

---

**PERMITS/CONTACT**
None required/Hood Canal Ranger Station, Quilcene, (360) 765-2200

**MAPS**
USGS Tyler Peak; Custom Correct Buckhorn Wilderness; Green Trails Tyler Peak

**TRAIL NOTES**
Leashed dogs okay

---

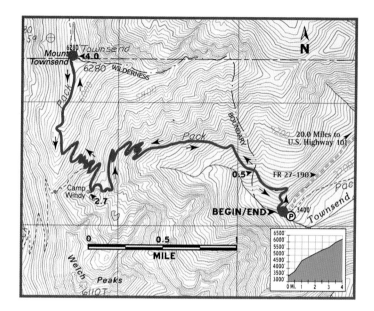

## The Trail

There are twenty-seven switchbacks on the Mount Townsend Trail. One of them is sure to reach up and whack you on the knee. The first half-dozen of these switchbacks help you climb the first **0.4** mile through a nice forest of rhododendrons that usually bloom long before the snow melts from the trail at Camp Windy. Past the switchbacks the trail enters the Buckhorn Wilderness at **0.5** mile.

You'll begin a long climbing traverse through the forest, arriving at a steep subalpine meadow and open avalanche chutes at **1.1** miles. Hikers with sufficient courage can look up, waaaay up, to the barren slopes of Mount Townsend above. Courage. You'll be there as soon as your heart stops its silly jackhammering.

The trail climbs above a waterfall on the major tributary to Townsend Creek, then begins the remaining two-dozen switchbacks to the summit. On crowded summer days you'll be able to hear the moans and incessant whinings of distant trail weenies headed to the summit.

If you are still alive 2.7 miles up the trail, you'll find a pleasant flat spot at Camp Windy, where collapsing of exhaustion may be the prudent option. Look south of the trail for a small tarn and climb a big rock for views to Mount Baker to the north. At the **3.0**-mile mark you'll find the junction with the Silver Lakes Trail (Hike 24). Stay right at the junction and continue upward toward the spot at **4.0** miles where a trail leads to the right to the summit. Most hikers continue another half-mile to a rock overlooking the north side of Mount Townsend.

While you catch your breath, point yourself toward Mount Rainier and rotate counterclockwise to see the Cascades, Glacier Peak, and Mount Baker, the mountains of Vancouver Island with The Needles in front, the Brothers toward the west, and Mount Constance to the south.

A hiker descends from the summit of Mount Townsend, with the peaks of Mount Buckhorn and Constance in the distance

## Going Farther

Hikers wishing to take the short, steep route to Mount Townsend can follow Forest Road 2870 to the Dirty Face Ridge Trailhead, across and just up the road from the Tubal Cain Trailhead, and climb 3.2 miles and 3,300 feet to the summit. If you're planning a key exchange, it's 7.2 miles to the Mount Townsend Trailhead. ∎

## 24. Silver Lakes

| RATING | DISTANCE | HIKING TIME |
|---|---|---|
| ★★★★☆ | 11.0 miles round-trip | 5.5 hours |
| ELEVATION GAIN | HIGH POINT | DIFFICULTY |
| 2,300 feet | 5,700 feet | ♦♦♦♦ |
| BEST SEASON | | |
| Jan Feb Mar Apr May Jun Jul Aug Sep Oct Nov Dec | | |

### The Hike

This tough climb to a lofty alpine lake in flowered meadows is the angler's or swimmer's alternative to hiking the Mount Townsend Trail (Hike 23), which shares the first 3 miles of pathway.

### Getting There

From Quilcene follow US Highway 101 south 1.4 miles to the Penny Creek Road. Turn right and follow Penny Creek Road to its junction with the Big Quilcene River Road; follow it 3.0 miles to Forest Road 27. Follow FR 27 for 14.8 miles, passing a sign at 14.3 miles directing traffic left to the lower Mount Townsend trailhead. Instead, continue right on FR 27 to FR 27-190 and turn left on FR 27-190, following it 0.7 mile to the upper Mount Townsend Trail No. 839, at 3,400 feet above sea level.

Mount Baker is visible as a hiker climbs towards Silver Lake

## The Trail

As with the previous hike, follow the Mount Townsend Trail for 0.5 mile, where it enters the Buckhorn Wilderness. Continue up this trail, which climbs steeply into the high country at **1.1** miles, where you can look up open avalanche chutes to Mount Townsend's summit.

The trail switches back around a waterfall and climbs steadily toward the alpine flats at Camp Windy, 2.7 miles, where you'll find a small tarn and snow lingers to early summer. Climb 0.3 mile to the Silver Lakes Trail junction. Turn left here, traversing and then climbing to a notch in the ridge at **3.5** miles that divides Townsend and Silver Creeks. This is the high point of the hike, at 5,700 feet above sea level.

**PERMITS/CONTACT**
None required/Hood Canal Ranger Station, Quilcene, (360) 765-2200

**MAPS**
USGS Tyler Peak; Custom Correct Buckhorn Wilderness; Green Trails Tyler Peak

**TRAIL NOTES**
Leashed dogs okay

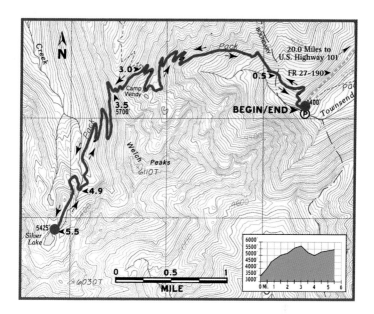

The trail drops gently in several switchbacks from here, descending from the rocky, open alpine slopes into subalpine forest. It crosses Silver Creek 4.9 miles from the trailhead, then climbs 0.6 mile to the largest lake, set in a wide alpine bowl below snowy peaks to the south. Silver Lake and the smaller lake over a saddle 0.2 mile north both contain Eastern Brook trout. ■

# OTHER HIKES

The Falls View Trail is a short-but-steep drop and return climb of 1.5 miles, round-trip, from Falls View Campground to whitewater rapids on the Big Quil.

The Notch Pass Trail, off Forest Road 27-010, is a steep, 2,000-vertical-foot, 2.1-mile climb to a forested defile leading to an abandoned logging road with views of the Quilcene Valley below. Almost a decade of volunteer trail work has made this a popular hike for Kitsap and Olympic Peninsula pedestrians.

The Mount Zion Trail leads 3.6 miles, round-trip, to a 4,270-foot summit off Forest Road 2810, and is used by Kitsap and Olympic Peninsula hikers as a conditioning and rhododendron walk.

# DUNGENESS RIVER

---

Please note, some of these trails may have been affected by recent weather patterns and repairs may be underway. Always call ahead to guarantee trail accessibility.

# 25. Gray Wolf Trail

| RATING | DISTANCE | HIKING TIME |
|---|---|---|
| ★☆☆☆☆ | 7.0 miles round-trip | 3.5 hours |

| ELEVATION GAIN | HIGH POINT | DIFFICULTY |
|---|---|---|
| 280 feet | 1,380 feet | ♦♦♦♦♦ |

| BEST SEASON | | |
|---|---|---|
| Jan Feb **Mar Apr May Jun** Jul Aug Sep Oct Nov Dec | | |

## The Hike

Walk along an abandoned logging road and follow an old trail along the forest bottomland beside one of the clearest streams in the Olympics.

## Getting There

From the Highway 104-101 junction near Discovery Bay, follow US Highway 101 west 16.0 miles to Louella Road, just south of Sequim Bay State Park. Turn left on Louella Road and drive 1.0 mile to Palo Alto Road. Turn left on Palo Alto Road and drive 6.0 miles to a junction with Forest Road 2880.

Turn right onto Forest Road 2880 and descend to a crossing of the Dungeness River, and in 1.7 miles, turn right at a junction with Forest Road 2870. Follow FR 2870 for 1.8 miles to the trailhead on the left, 1,350 feet above sea level.

## The Trail

The big question I kept asking myself as I walked through second-growth forest along the clay banks of an old logging road for 1.1 miles was, "Is it Gray Wolf or Graywolf?" All my maps say it is two words, but there are signs right on this trail that tell me otherwise. Is this a name conspiracy or what? Such questions help pass the time on trails where you really can't see much and the path is about as interesting as the wrinkles on your thumb knuckle. Keep

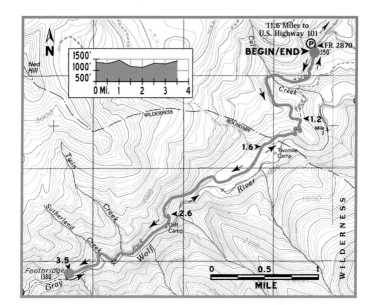

the faith, however, the trail gets more interesting as it plunges steeply down to join the old Gray Wolf Trail at **1.2** miles.

Turn right at this junction, and follow the trail down to a flat bench on the river bottom, **1.6** miles from the trailhead. This is the site of the old Twomile (Or is it Two Mile? Who knows?) Camp. Walk through the flats for 0.4 mile before beginning a climb away from the river to a wooded notch in the hillside and dropping back to the river

**PERMITS/CONTACT**
None required/Hood Canal Ranger Station, Quilcene, (360) 765-2200

**MAPS**
USGS Tyler Peak; Custom Correct Gray Wolf–Dosewallips;
Green Trails Tyler Peak

**TRAIL NOTES**
Leashed dogs okay; kid-friendly

**2.6** miles from the trailhead. This is Cliff Camp, which I am pretty sure is two words.

The trail follows the river a short distance and climbs around a slide area near Twin Creek at **3.2** miles, then begins a series of switchbacks as the trail climbs around Sutherland Creek, at **3.3** miles. You'll drop back to the river at **3.4** miles, where a campsite by the river makes the best picnic spot. The trail ends for day hikers at the site of a bridge that was destroyed several years ago, **4.2** miles from the trailhead. ■

## 26. Tubal Cain Mine

| RATING | DISTANCE | HIKING TIME |
|---|---|---|
| ★★★ ☆☆ | 7.2 miles round-trip | 3.5 hours |
| **ELEVATION GAIN** | **HIGH POINT** | **DIFFICULTY** |
| 1,050 feet | 4,350 feet | ◆◆◆ ◇◇ |

| BEST SEASON | | | | | | | | | | | |
|---|---|---|---|---|---|---|---|---|---|---|---|
| Jan | Feb | Mar | Apr | May | **Jun** | **Jul** | **Aug** | **Sep** | Oct | Nov | Dec |

### The Hike

Take this moderate climb to an alpine creek and site of a historic mine, with a possible side trip to the wreckage of a World War II bomber. There's a one-way option by climbing over Marmot Pass (Hike 22).

### Getting There

From US Highway 101 just south of Sequim Bay State Park, turn left on Louella Road and follow it for 0.9 mile to Palo Alto Road. Turn left on Palo Alto Road and follow it for 4.6 miles, where it becomes Forest Road 28. Turn right on FR 2880, passing the Dungeness Forks Campground and crossing the river to FR 2870. Turn left and follow FR 2870 for 12.5 miles to the Tubal Cain Trail No. 840, on the right, located 3,300 feet above sea level.

## The Trail

One of the best things about this hike is the likelihood of better weather in the Dungeness drainage. Clouds sweeping off the Pacific Ocean have dumped loads of rain on the coastal mountains, and the average amount of rainfall here is about ten times less than it is 30 miles to the west. The trail begins with a brief and gentle descent past the Silver Creek Shelter to cross Silver Creek and climb around a rhododendron-covered hillock. It then begins a gentle grade above Copper Creek. After entering the Buckhorn Wilderness at **0.5** mile, you'll climb through forest and rhododendron thickets for another mile as the trail begins to steepen slightly.

At **3.1** miles you'll strike the junction with the Tull Canyon Trail, which climbs steeply to the left. Stay right here as the main trail takes a climbing traverse for another 0.5 mile to the alpine meadows around Tubal Cain Mine. The mine itself is off the trail, and uphill to the left, and is closed to exploration. Hikers are asked to stay away from the mine shaft and surrounding area, which is private property. The property boundary may be posted with signs; leave any equipment there alone.

## Going Farther

The trail crosses Copper Creek at the mine site and begins to climb in 3.3 miles to a high traverse before dropping to Marmot Pass. Parties planning a key exchange might plan to meet at the pass for a one-way hike option of 12.2 miles, following the Marmot Pass Trail (Hike 22). The Tull Canyon Trail is worth the steep climb, passing a mine entrance at the beginning of the trail and climbing for

**PERMITS/CONTACT**
Parking pass required/Hood Canal Ranger Station, Quilcene, (360) 765-2200

**MAPS**
USGS Tyler Peak; Custom Correct Buckhorn Wilderness; Green Trails Tyler Peak

**TRAIL NOTES**
Leashed dogs okay

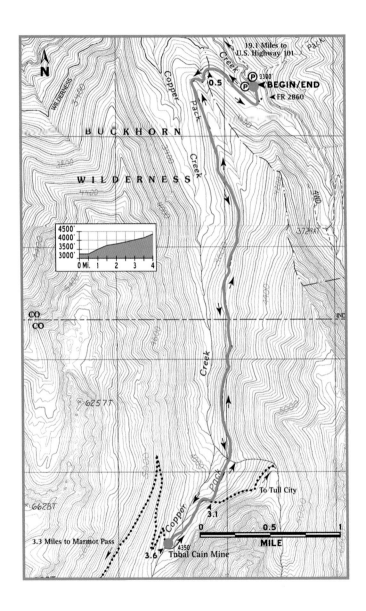

19.1 Miles to
U.S. Highway 101

0.5

BEGIN/END

3300'

FR 2860

Copper

Creek

Pack

B U C K H O R N

Creek

W I L D E R N E S S

4500'
4000'
3500'
3000'
0 Mi. 1 2 3 4

CO
CO

IND

Creek

To Tull City

Pack

3.1

Copper

0     0.5     1
MILE

3.3 Miles to Marmot Pass

3.6  Tubal Cain Mine  4350'

0.25 mile to a junction. Continue climbing to the left to find the wreckage of a B-17 bomber that crashed into the ridge above in January 1952 and tobogganed down the slope to its final resting place.

The remains of Tull City, a mining community built around 1900 and destroyed by heavy winters a decade later, can be found by taking the right fork of the trail and following it for 0.4 mile. ∎

# 27. Camp Handy

| RATING | DISTANCE | HIKING TIME |
|---|---|---|
| ★★★★☆ | 6.6 miles round-trip | 3 hours |

| ELEVATION GAIN | HIGH POINT | DIFFICULTY |
|---|---|---|
| 600 feet | 3,100 feet | ◆◆◇◇◇ |

| BEST SEASON | | | | | | | | | | | |
|---|---|---|---|---|---|---|---|---|---|---|---|
| Jan | Feb | Mar | Apr | May | Jun | Jul | Aug | Sep | Oct | Nov | Dec |

## The Hike

Here's a wildlife-watcher's walk to a sunny subalpine meadow beside a clear creek that makes a great picnic spot for the whole family. A shelter stands ready in the unlikely event that rainfall tries to spoil the fun.

## Getting There

From US Highway 101 just south of Sequim Bay State Park, turn left on Louella Road and follow it for 0.9 mile to Palo Alto Road. Turn left on Palo Alto Road and follow it for 4.6 miles, where it becomes Forest Road 28. Turn right on FR 2880, passing the Dungeness Forks Campground and crossing the river to FR 2870. Turn left and follow FR 2870 for 9.1 miles to the Upper Dungeness Trail 833, 2,500 feet above sea level.

**PERMITS/CONTACT**
None required/Hood Canal Ranger Station, Quilcene, (360) 765-2200

**MAPS**
USGS Tyler Peak; Custom Correct Buckhorn Wilderness; Green Trails Tyler Peak

**TRAIL NOTES**
Leashed dogs okay; kid-friendly

## The Trail

This hike is one of my personal favorites. It starts at an elevation that allows an easy climb to subalpine country yet stays low enough to avoid the chance of extreme weather in the high country. And it is located in the dry rain shadow of the Olympics. Begin by climbing out of the parking lot in a short switchback and contouring along the hillside back to river level. You'll climb gently along the river for 1.0 mile to a junction with the Royal Basin Trail. Turn left here and cross Royal Creek at the Buckhorn Wilderness boundary.

The trail continues to climb gently along the river, passing a mineral lick at **1.5** miles where game trails radiate into the forest. The trail steepens briefly, then drops back to cross the river, 2.4 miles from the trailhead. The path gets slightly steeper across the river as it climbs past a rounded forest ridge. At about **3.0** miles the trail becomes gentle again and contours toward the scenic meadows of Camp Handy, 3.3 miles from the trailhead.

The Dungeness River rumbles through forest below Camp Handy

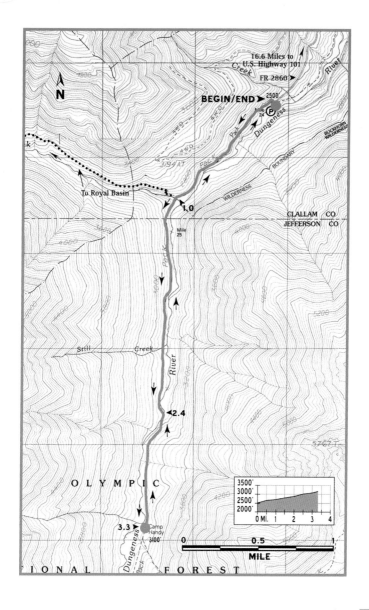

16.6 Miles to
U.S. Highway 101

Creek

FR 2860 ▶

River

BEGIN/END ▶

2500'

Dungeness

BUCKHORN
WILDERNESS

To Royal Basin

WILDERNESS

1.0

CLALLAM CO
JEFFERSON CO

Mile
25

Still    Creek

River

Pack

2.4

O L Y M P I C

3500'
3000'
2500'
2000'

0 Mi.  1    2    3    4

3.3 ▶ Camp
Handy
3100'

Dungeness

0              0.5              1

MILE

I O N A L        F O R E S T

The shelter is located off the trail to the right, overlooking the meadows. Hikers seeking a more solitary setting will find a way trail leading upstream to larger meadows on the creek. I've seen bears in the meadows along the creek above the shelter almost every time I've visited Camp Handy in the late spring. It's a great spot for wildlife-watching; families with small children should also know that it is the site of one of the very rare cougar attacks recorded in the Olympics during the past 20 years.

## Going Farther

You have two options for a longer hike. First, follow the way along Heather Creek for a mile before crossing the creek and meandering another mile up the valley.

A second choice is to follow the trail past Camp Handy, which climbs 3.0 miles to Boulder Camp, where you'll find another shelter, great views, and a trail junction to Home Lake and Buckhorn Pass. ■

# 28. Royal Lake

| RATING | DISTANCE | HIKING TIME |
|---|---|---|
| ★★★★☆ | 14.0 miles round-trip | 7.5 hours |
| **ELEVATION GAIN** | **HIGH POINT** | **DIFFICULTY** |
| 2,600 feet | 5,100 feet | ◆◆◆◆◇ |
| **BEST SEASON** | | |
| Jan Feb Mar Apr May **Jun Jul Aug Sep Oct Nov** Dec | | |

## The Hike

This is a long, scenic climb to a sunny alpine lake surrounded by some of the highest peaks in the Olympics. You'll find a number of great picnic spots by Royal Creek if you're looking for a shorter walk.

## Getting There

From US Highway 101 just south of Sequim Bay State Park, turn left on Louella Road and follow it for 0.9 mile to Palo Alto Road.

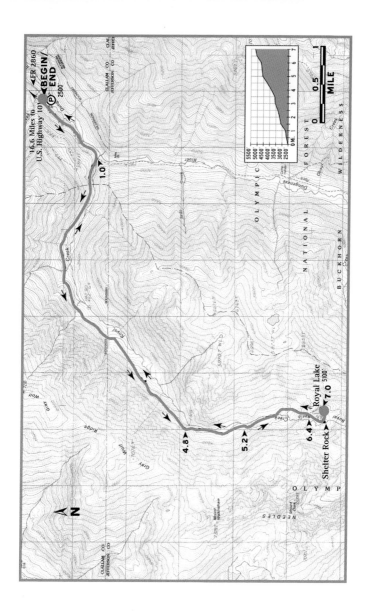

BEGIN/END

FR 2860

16.6 Miles to
U.S. Highway 101

2500

1.0

Creek

Creek

Royal

Wolf

Ridge

4.8

5.2

6.4 Shelter Rock

7.0 Royal Lake
5100'

Royal Creek

Creek

Gray

Ridge

OLYMP

NEEDLES

OLYMPIC

NATIONAL

FOREST

BUCKHORN

WILDERNESS

Dungeness

CLALLAM CO.
JEFFERSON CO.

CLALLAM CO.
JEFFERSON CO.

N

5500
5000
4500
4000
3500
3000
2500

0 MI.   1   2   3   4   5   6   7

0      0.5      1
MILE

Turn left on Palo Alto Road and follow it for 4.6 miles, where it becomes Forest Road 28. Turn right on FR 2880, passing the Dungeness Forks Campground and crossing the river to FR 2870. Turn left and follow FR 2870 for 9.1 miles to the Upper Dungeness Trail 833, 2,500 feet above sea level.

## The Trail

Although your muscles may demand obscene amounts of ibuprofen after this long trek, deal with it. The climb to Royal Basin is one of the best hikes in the Olympics, and if you don't think so, write your congressperson.

The first mile of this trail is a gentle walk along the upper Dungeness River, which you'll share with hikers bound for Camp Handy (Hike 27). You'll part company with them at **1.0** mile, where the trail forks. Keep right for Royal Basin and Lake, climbing around a muddy switchback to barely discernible remains of a trail leading off to the right. This is the old Maynard Burn Way Trail, once used as a shortcut to Royal Basin by a foolish backpacker who forgot the steep climb on the way home and crashed on the trail, whining and blubbering loudly until friends threatened to leave him (me) there.

Anyway, ignore this junction if you see it and keep left on the obvious main trail, which enters Olympic National Park at **1.5** miles. The trail continues to climb gently through a dry forest away from Royal Creek, crossing several small tributaries. You'll climb farther away from the river to a spot where you can look up the valley toward Mount Deception, the 7,788-foot monarch of the Northern Olympics. The trail drops here to a campsite beside the river, 4.8 miles from the trailhead, which makes a good turnaround for hikers looking for a shorter hike.

Hikers bound for the lake can climb over the next avalanche mound as the trail enters the high country and streams tumble down open cliffs from the Gray Wolf Ridge to the right. The trail drops to another picnic area and possible turnaround spot at **5.2** miles. The trail here is not much higher than Royal Creek and is often covered by water, which turns to ice in the winter and caused a foolish backpacker to slip and slide toward the creek, whining and blubbering loudly until friends threatened to leave him (me) there. It was so icy in this spot one February that I actually donned crampons to climb the trail, which steepens considerably.

You'll climb a forested knoll, then contour into the wide lower Royal Basin, 6.4 miles from the trailhead. The trail crosses the creek and climbs up the final pitch to Royal Lake at **7.0** miles. Although the lake is scenic, the meadows below might make a better spot to sprawl out in the sun and soothe your tired body.

## Going Farther

It might be difficult to imagine hiking beyond 7 miles, but the off-trail 0.8-mile climb to upper Royal Basin is definitely worth the effort. Climb up Royal Creek, past Shelter Rock at the head of the basin, passing a swampy meadow on the left; or scramble directly up the rocky headwall to a beautiful rock-bound tarn underneath Mount Deception and The Needles. ■

# 29. Maynard Burn

| RATING | DISTANCE | HIKING TIME |
|---|---|---|
| ★★★★ | 4.5 miles round-trip | 4.5 hours |

| ELEVATION GAIN | HIGH POINT | DIFFICULTY |
|---|---|---|
| 3,137 feet | 6,537 feet | ♦♦♦♦♦ |

| BEST SEASON | | |
|---|---|---|
| Jan Feb Mar Apr May Jun Jul **Aug Sep** Oct Nov Dec | | |

## The Hike

This extremely steep climb along an old fire line leads to the spectacular, sunny high country of Gray Wolf Ridge.

## Getting There

From US Highway 101 just south of Sequim Bay State Park, turn left on Louella Road and follow it for 0.9 mile to Palo Alto Road. Turn left on Palo Alto Road and follow it for 4.6 miles, where it becomes Forest Road 28. Follow FR 28 another 1.1 miles to FR 2880. Turn right on FR 2880 and cross the Dungeness River to FR 2870. Turn left and follow FR 2870 for 7.4 miles to a junction with FR 2870-120, which may not be marked but is the only road climbing to the right. Follow FR 2870-120 for 1.6 miles to a wide parking lot or another 0.1 mile to the dirt blockade over the road and the start of the trail at 3,400 feet above sea level.

## The Trail

You'll want to be in great physical condition to enjoy this climb. The first 1.7 miles is no indication of the pain and suffering you'll experience in the next 1.8 miles. Begin by following the old roadbed, crossing Mueller Creek—the only available water source on this trail—at **0.1** mile. The trail continues to climb gently for 0.8 mile to a switchback and trail junction, where the old lower Maynard Burn Trail plunged down to the Royal Lake Trail, below. Past the switchback the trail continues to climb gently for another 0.7 mile to round a steep ridge.

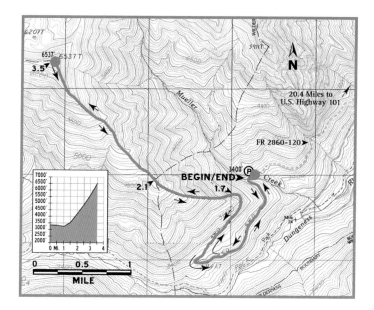

Look up the bank on the left to see the beginning of the old Maynard Burn path, cut and later bulldozed to halt the advance of a forest fire at the turn of the twentieth century.

The trail ascends the ridge directly, with but a few switchbacks to ease the climb. This route is only slightly less steep than the path to Lake Constance but may feel steeper because the country around the Northeastern Olympics is usually sunnier and hotter.

**PERMITS/CONTACT**
Parking pass required/Hood Canal Ranger Station, Quilcene, (360) 765-2200

**MAPS**
USGS Tyler Peak; Custom Correct Gray Wolf–Dosewallips; Green Trails Tyler Peak

**TRAIL NOTES**
Leashed dogs okay

At **2.1** miles you'll find a spot where the old fire line cat-track stops and becomes a single-track trail. Climb left to find the trail if you find no signs at this point, which is located at the boundary of the Buckhorn Wilderness and Olympic National Park.

Although the trail may enter the park from time to time, it is unlikely hikers with leashed dogs would be cited for violating park rules against pets on trails; the path is mostly on the Buckhorn Wilderness side of the ridge. The single-track trail is only slightly less steep than the bulldozed path below.

Continue climbing the ridge, where the forest becomes less sparse and the views more expansive. The path climbs to an end in a steep bowl at the headwaters of Mueller Creek, across from a saddle between Baldy and Tyler Peaks, at **2.8** miles. For the best view continue climbing along the ridge crest another 0.7 mile to an unnamed 6,537-foot summit. The lack of an official path shouldn't matter to anyone who has climbed this far; wildlife and Vibram soles have made the route through scrubby pines on the ridge obvious.

The summit, 3.5 miles from the trailhead, gives hikers a 360-degree view of Vancouver Island, the Strait of Juan de Fuca, the San Juan Islands, Mount Baker, the Cascades, and the Gray Wolf Ridge stretching to the south to The Needles and Mount Deception.

## Going Farther

Strong hikers can scramble south along the crest of the Gray Wolf Ridge over the summit of Baldy, 6,827 feet, for almost 2 miles in Olympic National Park, across the summit of Gray Wolf Peak, 7,218 feet, to Peak 7076, which, curiously enough, is 7,076 feet high. Mountaineering skills are recommended if you intend to venture beyond this point. ∎

# 30. Lower Dungeness Trail

| RATING | DISTANCE | HIKING TIME |
|--------|----------|-------------|
| ★★☆☆☆ | 8.2 miles round-trip | 4.5 hours |
| **ELEVATION GAIN** | **HIGH POINT** | **DIFFICULTY** |
| 800 feet | 2,400 feet | ◆◆◆◇ |
| **BEST SEASON** | | |
| Jan Feb **Mar Apr May Jun Jul Aug Sep Oct Nov** Dec | | |

## The Hike

This is a deviously steep trail; its greatest virtues are the splendid, airy views of the rattling Dungeness River canyon far below, the steep Olympic mountainsides above, and rare wildflowers on usually sunny slopes. You've a one-way option with two cars.

## Getting There

From US Highway 101 just south of Sequim Bay State Park, turn left on Louella Road and follow it for 0.9 mile to Palo Alto Road. Turn left on Palo Alto Road and follow it for 4.6 miles, where it becomes Forest Road 28. Follow FR 28 another 1.1 miles to FR 2880. Turn right on FR 2880, cross the Dungeness River to FR 2870, and turn left. Follow FR 2870 for 2.4 miles to FR 2870-230, and drive 1.6 miles to the Lower Dungeness Trail 833, 1,600 feet above sea level.

**PERMITS/CONTACT**
None required/Hood Canal Ranger Station, Quilcene, (360) 765-2200

**MAPS**
USGS Tyler Peak; Custom Correct Buckhorn Wilderness; Green Trails Tyler Peak

**TRAIL NOTES**
Leashed dogs okay

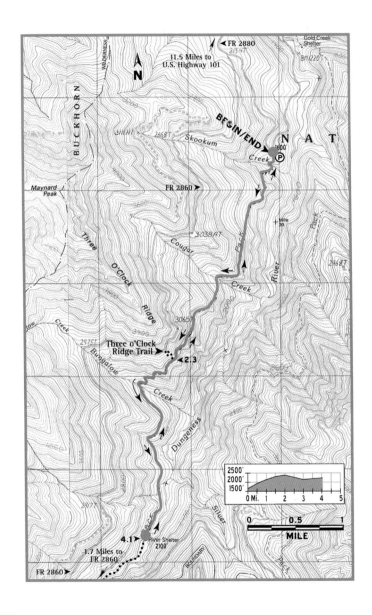

# The Trail

It is a little-known fact that before he was imprisoned in the late eighteenth century, the Marquis de Sade was a trail builder for Olympic National Forest. Disbelievers may feel free to check my research. In any event the following is an unpublished excerpt taken from de Sade's trail log regarding the Lower Dungeness River Trail:

This path, quite simply, shall be the sharpest jewel in my crown of thorns for day hikers. It shall begin, unmarked, at a gate across the road, with no mileages or trail signs to allow the hiker to interpret what eloquent suffering I have planned ahead. And suffering it shall be, for I will lull the hiker with a gentle grade down for the first **0.1** mile before turning through the forest. Just as the path levels out, I shall build a steep grade in the trail, which the hiker will believe is merely a short climb around a slide area.

In fact, however, the trail will continue to climb steeply for 1.7 miles. Ah, were I to live long enough to hear the exquisite sounds of painful panting and sights of serious sweat from wilderness pedestrians who look at a map and believe this to be a gentle river trail!

Then, just as the hiker reaches an airy perch and splendid views of cliffs and mountains, far above the Dungeness River at **1.9** miles and 2,300 feet, I shall add another steep 100-foot hill to a junction with the Three o'Clock Ridge Trail.

This will infuriate the hiker, who will see that Forest Road 2870, which was left at the trailhead 2.3 miles back, is now only 0.5 mile up the Three o'Clock Ridge Trail. Nonetheless, I shall entice the hiker to continue to the left on the Dungeness River Trail with sights of rare spring wildflowers. These shall include the fawn lily, disguised but for its mottled green leaves as an avalanche lily, and Calypso orchids, or lady slipper.

Now, the most cruel trick of all: I shall design the trail so as to drop in switchbacks down, losing almost all the elevation

A footbridge crosses a tributary along one of the only flat sections on the Lower Dungeness Trail

it has gained. Hikers will be so fatigued they will literally flop into Bungalow Creek, at **3.0** miles, writhing in pain.

Finally, I shall build the trail so it drops even farther during the next mile, finally reaching the Dungeness River at an old shelter, 4.1 miles from the trailhead. Although the river has climbed a scant 500 feet in those 4.0 miles, my delightfully miserable hikers have climbed and dropped more than 1,500 feet.

How rewarding it is to know that I can provide such misery to hikers for centuries to come.

As I said in the beginning, disbelievers may feel free to check my research.

## Going Farther

I can't for the life of me imagine anyone wanting to go farther, but just in case your masochism is a match for the trail builder's sadism, you can hike another 1.7 miles from the shelter to the bridge where Forest Road 2870 crosses the Dungeness. This would make a one-way hike of 5.8 miles with cars parked at the upper and lower trailheads and a car-key exchange. If a key exchange is planned, don't assume the downstream hike will be that much easier than the upstream toil. ■

## 31. Dungeness Spit

| RATING | DISTANCE | HIKING TIME |
|---|---|---|
| ★★★★ ☆ | **10.0 miles round-trip** | **5 hours** |

| ELEVATION GAIN | HIGH POINT | DIFFICULTY |
|---|---|---|
| **110 feet** | **120 feet** | ◆ ◇ ◇ ◇ ◇ |

| BEST SEASON |
|---|
| **Jan Feb Mar** Apr May Jun Jul Aug Sep Oct Nov **Dec** |

### The Hike
Walk through the forest for 0.5 mile to drop onto a sandy beach that stretches along the sunny side of the Strait of Juan de Fuca for 5.0 miles.

### Getting There
Drive west on US Highway 101 from Sequim to Kitchen-Dick Road. Turn right and follow it to the ninety-degree corner at Lotzgessell Road and turn left at the entrance to Dungeness National Wildlife Refuge. Follow the road past Dungeness Recreation Area to a parking lot at the trailhead, 120 feet above sea level. The refuge is open daily from 7 a.m. to 30 minutes before sunset. Closing times are posted daily at the trailhead.

### The Trail
I save this walk for the winter, when storms sweep the Strait of Juan de Fuca and the crowds of summer don't exist. Carry rain- and windgear but expect better winter weather here than anyplace on the Olympic Peninsula. After paying a modest fee at the trailhead ($3 per party in 2022), hike the well-graveled, wide path for 0.5 mile to a wooden observation deck overlooking the spit. This portion

**PERMITS/CONTACT**
Trail fee required/Dungeness National Wildlife Refuge, (360) 457-8451

**MAPS**
USGS Dungeness

**TRAIL NOTES**
Dogs not allowed

of the trail is navigable by folks in wheelchairs although many may require assistance if the gravel is soft.

The trail drops steeply here for 0.1 mile to the spit, where it disappears. For the long walk to the New Dungeness Lighthouse, turn right and walk up the spit. The south side of the spit is closed, unless you happen to be a shorebird or other wild creature for whom the inner Dungeness Bay is reserved. That's why they call it a wildlife refuge.

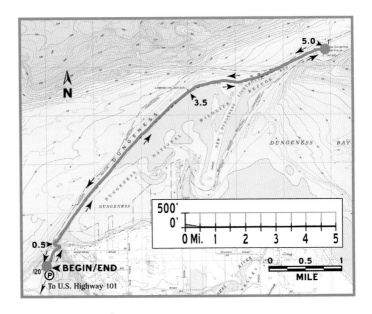

Dungeness Spit stretches for more than 5 miles along the Strait of Juan de Fuca; it is a popular beach in the sunny summer months

Never mind—there's plenty of room to walk along the northern, or Strait, side of the spit. You'll find the easiest going closest to the water, which may also be the wettest walking. Here is one path in this guide where high waterproof boots might be more appropriate than hiking boots. Look seaward for signs of marine mammals, including orcas and seals, and for interesting human-doings: the last time I walked the spit in February, I watched pilots practice landings and takeoffs on one of the navy's supercarriers, and I saw a Trident submarine slipping silently past, like a giant whale.

Hikers can also climb to the high middle ground of the spit, where several observation decks have been built to allow birdwatchers the chance to spot migrating and native waterfowl on the inland bay. Besides wildlife-watching, the view to the northern barrier of the Olympics, dazzling white in the winter, is almost startling. On clear days Mount Baker floats like a big ice cream sundae to the northeast.

Beach hikers often stop to picnic on driftwood perches about 3.5 miles down the spit, choosing not to trek the entire 5.0 miles to the lighthouse. If you do walk all the way, you'll likely find a volunteer lighthouse keeper to welcome you and perhaps provide a spot to warm up before the trek back to the trailhead. ■

# OTHER HIKES

The trail to Ned Hill, the site of an old lookout off Forest Road 2878, is 2.3 miles, round-trip, and used by local hikers as a rhododendron walk and conditioning hike.

The 2.8-mile, one-way trail from Slab Camp to Camp Tony leads downhill, often steeply, to a bridge across the Gray Wolf River. It's used by anglers and backpackers headed up the Gray Wolf.

The little-used path leading from Slab Camp to Deer Park in Olympic National Park climbs, often steeply, for 5.3 miles to the Deer Park auto campground.

# THE HIGH COUNTRY

---

# 32. Roaring Winds, Deer Park

| RATING | DISTANCE | HIKING TIME |
|---|---|---|
| ★★★★☆ | 8.4 miles round-trip | 4.5 hours |
| ELEVATION GAIN | HIGH POINT | DIFFICULTY |
| 1,500 feet | 6,300 feet | ◆◆◆◇◇ |

| BEST SEASON |
|---|
| Jan Feb Mar Apr May Jun Jul Aug Sep Oct Nov Dec |

## The Hike
Hike above the timberline and on some days, above the clouds on this spectacular walk through alpine meadowland to a rocky vista that makes a picnic spot and car-key trade for a one-way option.

## Getting There
From US Highway 101 on the outskirts of Port Angeles, take the Deer Park Loop and follow Deer Park Road south for 17.2 miles to Deer Park. Take the road signed "Deer Park Ranger Station" to the right upon reaching Deer Park. The trailhead, 5,200 feet above sea level, is located below the ranger station. Motorists who have never driven outside of Kansas or Iowa should not attempt the last 8 miles of this steep, winding one-lane road without first gobbling copious amounts of Prozac. Olympic National Park signs warn that Deer Park Road is not suitable for trailers and recreational vehicles, and the road is closed and gated at the park boundary in winter.

## The Trail
The first thing to do on this hike is stock up on water if you aren't carrying any. The only water available on the hike bubbles from a spring just across the road from the trailhead. Another warning: if you hike this trail in August, you will be accompanied by your very own squadron of deer flies, which will buzz you if you keep moving but seldom settle for a bite.

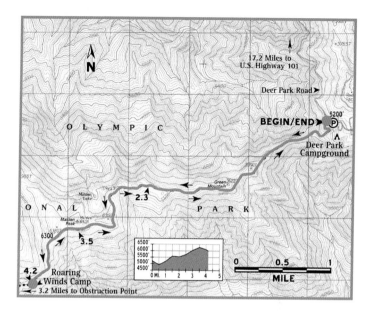

The trail drops almost 400 feet in the first mile, following an old roadbed that was originally planned to connect with the Obstruction Point Road, 7.4 miles distant. The route was never completed, leaving the incredible scenery for lucky wilderness pedestrians. After crossing a wide, flower-filled bench, the trail begins to climb

**PERMITS/CONTACT**
None required/Olympic National Park Wilderness Information Center,
(360) 565-3100; Olympic National Park Visitor Center, (360) 565-3130

**MAPS**
USGS Mount Angeles; Custom Correct Gray Wolf–Dungeness;
Green Trails Mount Angeles

**TRAIL NOTES**
No dogs or bikes

The trail to Roaring Winds from Deer Park follows the ridge to Maiden Peak, center

gradually to a meadow with views to the north of the Strait of Juan de Fuca and south to the cloud-scratching peaks of The Needles. This grassy meadow, 2.3 miles from the trailhead, makes a fine picnic spot for those seeking a shorter hike.

From here the trail begins a steep climb up the slopes underneath 6,434-foot Maiden Peak. The view of the rocky peaks to the east is fantastic, from Mount Walkinshaw to the north and Mount Deception to the south. Beyond Maiden Peak, at **3.5** miles, the trail crosses a flat tundra-like meadow before beginning a steep, rocky descent to Roaring Winds Camp, which often lives up to its name. The camp, at **4.2** miles, makes a good turnaround spot for day hikers.

## Going Farther

Hikers wanting more exercise can continue another 2.8 miles to a flower-strewn meadow overlooking Obstruction Point, with views across Badger Valley to Grand Valley and Grand Pass. Roaring Winds is also the midway point where hikers with cars at Deer Park and Obstruction Point can exchange keys for a one-way hike of

7.4 miles. In 1979, the first of several Great Olympic Mountain Marathons followed the trail from Deer Park to Obstruction Point, then finished after 7.4 miles of road at Hurricane Ridge. The strongest trail runners aimed for under 2 hours for the 16-mile jaunt, gaining and losing nearly a mile in altitude. The race was discontinued several years later, but a number of stalwarts continued the traditional run until 2020.

Deer Park Campground, located just above the trailhead at 5,400 feet above sea level, is easily the most scenic auto campground in the state. Sites are primitive, with vault toilets, but water is available. The steep, narrow approach road keeps most big land yachts in the lowlands. A forest fire more than a decade ago created a silver forest around some of the campsites and opened the incredible view of the Olympic peaks to the south. You couldn't pick a more beautiful spot to stay a weekend to hike to Roaring Winds and Three Forks (Hikes 32 and 33). ∎

# 33. Three Forks

| RATING | DISTANCE | HIKING TIME |
|---|---|---|
| ★★★★☆ | 8.4 miles round-trip | 5.5 hours |
| ELEVATION GAIN | HIGH POINT | DIFFICULTY |
| 3,250 feet | 5,400 feet | ◆◆◆◆◇ |
| BEST SEASON | | |
| Jan Feb Mar Apr May **Jun Jul Aug Sep Oct Nov** Dec | | |

## The Hike

This is a mountain-climb in reverse, beginning in scenic alpine country and dropping steeply to the clear, cold waters of the Grand and Cameron Creeks and the Gray Wolf River. Use it as a bad-weather alternative to the Roaring Winds, Deer Park (Hike 32).

## Getting There

From US Highway 101 on the outskirts of Port Angeles, take Deer Park Loop and follow Deer Park Road south for 17.2 miles to Deer Park. Keep left at the road signed "Deer Park Ranger Station" to a junction at Three Forks trailhead and follow the road past the campground loops to a parking area. The trailhead is located at 5,400 feet above sea level. The last 8 miles up Deer Park Road were not designed for people prone to car sickness. Olympic National Park signs warn that Deer Park Road is not suitable for trailers and recreational vehicles, and the road is closed and gated at the park boundary in winter.

## The Trail

This is not a walk in the park, at least figuratively. Literally, how-ever, that is exactly what it is—a walk in Olympic National Park. If your knees turn to rubber while going down your basement steps, pick a different trail. This trail offers nearly 4 miles and more than 3,000 vertical feet of steps, and all but perhaps two are down. Look at it this way: All but perhaps two steps are up on the return.

What makes this hike so appealing is that you can walk simultane-ously through time and space without taking illegal drugs. While it may be summer in Port Angeles, a mile below, it is still spring at Deer Park. But as you drop in steep switchbacks down to Three Forks,

**PERMITS/CONTACT**
None required/Olympic National Park Wilderness Information Center, (360) 565-3100; Olympic National Park Visitor Center, (360) 565-3130

**MAPS**
USGS Mount Angeles; Custom Correct Gray Wolf–Dungeness; Green Trails Mount Angeles

**TRAIL NOTES**
No dogs or bikes

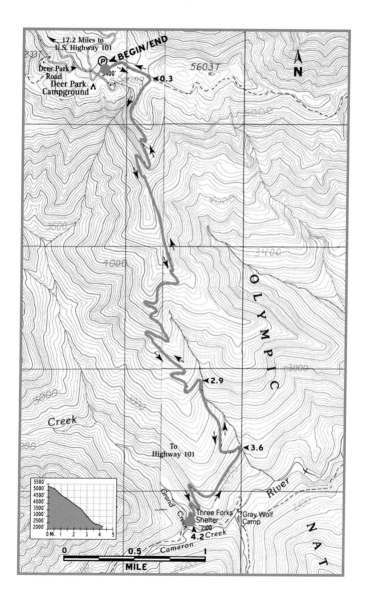

17.2 Miles to
U.S. Highway 101

BEGIN/END

5603

Deer Park
Road

Deer Park
Campground

Spring

0.3

N

OLYMPIC

Creek

2.9

To
Highway 101

3.6

Grand Creek

Three Forks
Shelter
2100
4.2 Creek

River

Gray Wolf
Camp

Cameron

NAT

5500'
5000'
4500'
4000'
3500'
3000'
2500'
2000'

0 Mi.  1  2  3  4  5

0          0.5          1
MILE

you return to summer. By the time you reach Three Forks Shelter at 2,150 feet, the red leaves of vine maple will be telling you it's fall.

Begin the hike by traversing through lupine-filled meadow and scree slopes for 0.3 mile to a junction with the Deer Ridge Trail. Turn right here and begin dropping in some twenty-two switchbacks along a ridge on the fringes of a decade-old forest fire that created a silver forest. Look to the right of the trail, across a steep gully to the Deer Park Campground, to see where the full force of the blaze was felt.

The trail continues to drop steeply down this ridge, traversing from one side to the other, and the spectacular Needles to the south soon play peekaboo with you through the trees. The forest surrounds you as you descend, shading the trail. At **2.9** miles you'll see a dark gully to the left of the trail at a switchback. A trickle of water in fall can be found in the gully during most years; if water is not available here, it will be as you approach the same stream 300 feet and 0.7 mile below. After passing the gully and stream a second time, the trail makes a long descending traverse around a lump in the ridge where the sound of the creeks below rushes to greet you. As if that sound might strengthen your tired legs, the trail steepens as it drops in six switchbacks and 0.6 mile to a junction with the Cameron Creek Trail.

Look to the left of the trail to find Three Forks Shelter in a green meadow above Grand Creek. This is a good picnic area and turnaround spot, with a four-star outhouse up the hill behind the shelter.

## Going Farther

If time and sore muscles permit, explore downriver, or cross the Grand Creek on a footlog to an even higher footlog across Cameron Creek. All three streams are excellent clearwater fishing in the autumn. Possibly the best way to hike the trails of Deer Park might be to plan a weekend car camp at Deer Park Campground—the most beautiful primitive car campground in the state—and hiking to Roaring Winds (Hike 32) one day and Three Forks the next. ■

# 34. Heather Park–Lake Angeles Loop

| RATING | DISTANCE | HIKING TIME |
|---|---|---|
| ★★★★★ | 12.9 mile loop | 7 hours |
| **ELEVATION GAIN** | **HIGH POINT** | **DIFFICULTY** |
| 4,100 feet | 6,046 feet | ◆◆◆◆◇ |

| BEST SEASON | | | | | | | | | | | |
|---|---|---|---|---|---|---|---|---|---|---|---|
| Jan | Feb | Mar | Apr | May | Jun | Jul | Aug | Sep | Oct | Nov | Dec |

## The Hike

Here's a strenuous, beautiful 12.9-mile-loop trip that climbs to high vistas and descends past a clear lake that can put a chill in the heat of the trail for the remaining 3.5 miles.

## Getting There

From US Highway 101 in Port Angeles, turn left on Race Street and follow it past the Olympic National Park Visitor Center to the Hurricane Ridge Road. Turn right and follow Hurricane Ridge Road for 5.7 miles to Heart O' the Hills. Just before reaching the park's fee entrance station, turn right and drive past park staff housing to the

### PERMITS/CONTACT
None required/Olympic National Park Wilderness Information Center, (360) 565-3100; Olympic National Park Visitor Center, (360) 565-3130

### MAPS
USGS Port Angeles, Mount Angeles; Custom Correct Gray Wolf–Dungeness; Green Trails Port Angeles, Mount Angeles

### TRAIL NOTES
No dogs or bikes

Lake Angeles and Heather Park trailheads, located at 1,950 feet above sea level. The Heather Park Trail is located at the far end of the large paved parking area.

## The Trail

The Heather Park–Lake Angeles Loop is one of the premier day hikes on the Olympic Peninsula. It gives you everything the area has to offer except a beach walk: You'll climb from deep forest to airy cliffs and pass a sapphire lake tucked in a snowy cirque.

I'd suggest starting the loop on the Heather Park Trail and proceeding counterclockwise, as you view the loop on a map. This will give you the opportunity to stop at Lake Angeles on the descent, where the effects of a cold swim (for the brave) in the lake won't be lost by having to climb uphill afterward. Start by hiking along a gently graded abandoned logging road for 0.4 mile before the trail turns beside a tributary to Ennis Creek and begins a no-nonsense assault of a forested ridge. You'll climb in switchbacks and, at about 2 miles, begin to get glimpses through the timber of the Strait of Juan de Fuca to the north.

The trail eases slightly as it rounds a timbered bowl above a creek and passes the site of an old shelter—now gone—at Halfway Rock,

The Heather Park–Lake Angeles Loop climbs beside the clouds on Klahhane Ridge

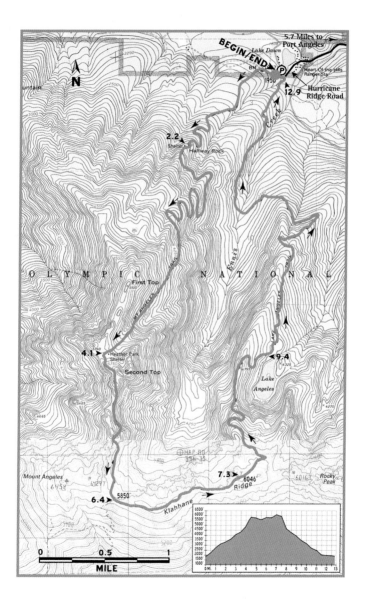

N

BEGIN/END

5.7 Miles to
Port Angeles

Lake Dawn
BM

Heart Of the Hills
Ranger Sta

Hurricane
Ridge Road

12.9

1950

Creek

2.2

Shelter
Halfway Rock

Ennis

O L Y M P I C        N A T I O N A L

First Top

MT ANGELES

Lake Angeles

4.1

Heather Park
Shelter

Second Top

9.4

Lake
Angeles

7.3

6046'
Ridge

Rocky
Peak

Mount Angeles

6.4

5850'

Klahhane

0          0.5          1

MILE

**2.2** miles. After a 0.2-mile traverse to another timbered ridge, the trail switches back and begins steadily climbing, switching back from one side of the ridge to the other.

At **3.1** miles from the trailhead, the path rounds a ridge and begins a steady mile-long uphill traverse to Heather Park, breaking into open alpine slopes filled, not surprisingly, with heather. A tiny stream, the last source of water until just above Lake Angeles, and a big rock mark the entrance to Heather Park.

The trail climbs under the site of another old shelter—this one once must have had an elaborate fireplace—and traverses steep cliffs to pass Second Top, the low peak on the right. The path crosses a wide, flat saddle under the barren summit, Heather Pass.

From here the trail drops slightly underneath red rock cliffs and then begins climbing again, just underneath the bare rock to traverse a steep hillside with mind-melting views to the west and northwest. You'll continue to climb for about a mile to a notch in the ridge at **5.2** miles, then drop in steep, short switchbacks to the east into a bowl underneath the east face of 6,454-foot Mount Angeles.

The trail traverses this bowl, often spotted with snow until late summer, then climbs steeply to a junction with the Switchback Trail (Hike 35), 6.4 miles from the trailhead on Klahhane Ridge. This saddle, 5,850 feet above sea level, offers awesome views of mountains in every direction, including the snowy peaks of northern Vancouver Island and on clear days the glaciers of British Columbia's Coast Range beyond. Although the Klahhane saddle is about halfway on your hike, it isn't the high point, and you might want to get your climbing done before a lunch stop. Turn left and follow the Klahhane Ridge Trail as it alternately climbs and drops—but mostly climbs—to the high point of the hike 0.9 mile beyond the junction and 150 feet higher.

It's almost all downhill from this point, as the trail follows a draw between rock towers toward a descending ridge on your left. You may find a small stream dribbling through this wide gully to replenish your water supply. The trail switches back several times in a steep bowl above Lake Angeles, then traverses down just under the sharp, steep west face of a ridge. As the ridge becomes less steep to the east, you'll cross and switchback down to Lake Angeles, 9.4 miles from the trailhead. The lake, with its islet, is clear and deep, with perhaps warmer water at the northern end away from the snow-hoarding bowl at the southern end. The trail down from the lake drops first in a direct, mile-long shot down a ridge above Lake Creek, then switches back around the headwaters of a creek that eventually bubbles past Heart O' the Hills Campground, 600 feet and 1.8 miles below. You'll follow the ridge above the creek for about 0.3 mile, then switch back to cross it, 11.4 miles from the trailhead. Finally, the trail rounds the ridge above Ennis Creek, drops to the creek and crosses it, climbs briefly to the opposite ridge, then follows the creek down to the trailhead at **12.9** miles.

## Going Farther

If you're looking for an early start, you might plan on car-camping a short half-mile from the trailhead at Heart O' the Hills Campground, just past the Olympic National Park fee entrance booth. The primitive campground, open year-round, provides running cold water and flush toilets but no hookups or sewage dump station. ∎

# 35. Klahhane Ridge

| RATING | DISTANCE | HIKING TIME |
|--------|----------|-------------|
| ★★★★☆ | 4.6 miles round-trip | 2.5 hours |
| **ELEVATION GAIN** | **HIGH POINT** | **DIFFICULTY** |
| 1,846 feet | 6,046 feet | ◆ ◆ ◆ ◆ ◇ |
| **BEST SEASON** | | |
| Jan Feb Mar Apr May **Jun Jul Aug Sep Oct Nov** Dec | | |

## The Hike

This steep climb provides all the scenery and views found on the Heather Park–Lake Angeles Loop (Hike 34), but saves some time, knees, and distance, as it shortens the hike by more than 8 miles.

## Getting There

From US Highway 101 in Port Angeles, turn left on Race Street and follow it past the Olympic National Park Visitor Center to the Hurricane Ridge Road. Turn right and follow Hurricane Ridge Road for 5.7 miles to Heart O' the Hills, where you'll pay a fee to enter the park. Continue up the Hurricane Ridge Road 9.3 miles to the Switchback Trail, located at the base of a hairpin turn underneath Mount Angeles, at 4,400 feet above sea level. Plan to arrive early at the Heart O' the Hills entrance station, or wait until midafternoon for this hike, as wait times often exceed 30 minutes on summer days.

## The Trail

A creek at the trailhead provides the only water on this hike, but remember to filter it before drinking—this stream was blamed for infecting at least one hiker with giardiasis a decade ago. There is little about this trail that is nice, save the expanding, splendid view of the mountains that you'll get as you climb. Perhaps the only flat spot in the first 1.3 miles is at a trail junction at **0.5** mile.

You'll climb through a sparse forest of alpine evergreens that provide some shade on a hot day. The trail wastes little space on the horizontal and gobbles big gulps of vertical, crossing into a wide avalanche path at about **0.3** mile. Continue up to a junction with a trail leading to Hurricane Ridge at **0.5** mile, where you can look down to the parking area and perhaps ask yourself why you are panting loudly enough to be heard in Forks, 70 miles away. Climb to the right at this

---

**PERMITS/CONTACT**
None required/Olympic National Park Wilderness Information Center,
(360) 565-3100; Olympic National Park Visitor Center, (360) 565-3130

**MAPS**
USGS Port Angeles, Mount Angeles; Custom Correct Hurricane Ridge;
Green Trails Port Angeles, Mount Angeles

**TRAIL NOTES**
No dogs or bikes

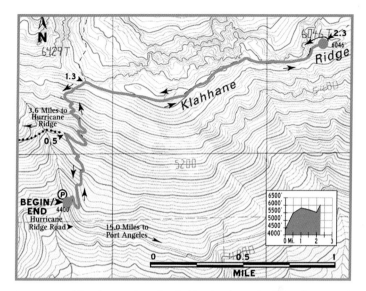

junction and begin a series of switchbacks through alpine forest and next to rocky giant steps tumbling off Mount Angeles above.

The trail emerges on open slopes at about **1.1** miles and climbs to a 5,850-foot saddle on Klahhane Ridge, 1.3 miles from the trailhead. Here it joins the Heather Park–Lake Angeles loop, and you'll turn right. The remaining mile of this hike is up and down along the open, rocky Klahhane Ridge to a 6,046-foot peak that makes a good turnaround and lunch spot, 2.3 miles from the trailhead. The trail begins to drop from this point, losing the incredible view you'll get of surrounding mountains, Vancouver Island, and the Strait of Juan de Fuca.

The upper reaches of Switchback Trail and Klahhane Ridge were once the range of the largest mountain goat herd in the Olympics, which gathered there largely because salt licks were placed in the area by Olympic National Park biologists and student volunteers during goat population studies in the 1970s. The magnificent animals were later trapped and relocated to other Northwest wilderness areas, and goats are all but nonexistent within the park boundary.

The Switchback Trail climbs Klahhane Ridge to the flat saddle, center

About a decade ago, a number of mountain goats migrated from the fringes of the park back to Klahhane Ridge. They became increasingly aggressive, despite hassling by park rangers, until one of them gored and killed Port Angeles resident Robert Boardman on October 16, 2010. The animal was later killed by rangers.

## Going Farther

You can get a longer, one-way hike by leaving one car at the Switchback Trail parking area and a second at Hurricane Ridge. Plan to meet at Klahhane saddle and trade car keys. The party climbing the Switchback Trail would have a 4.9-mile hike back to Hurricane Ridge, while the hikers coming from Hurricane Ridge could follow the Switchback Trail 1.3 miles down to the parking area. ■

# 36. Mount Angeles Saddle

| RATING | DISTANCE | HIKING TIME |
|---|---|---|
| ★★★★☆ | 4.4 miles round-trip | 2.5 hours |

| ELEVATION GAIN | HIGH POINT | DIFFICULTY |
|---|---|---|
| 1,300 feet | 5,471 feet | ◆◆◆◇◇ |

| BEST SEASON |
|---|
| Jan Feb Mar Apr May **Jun Jul Aug Sep** Oct Nov Dec |

## The Hike
Walk a gentle trail along the crest of an alpine ridge to a flat picnic spot beneath Mount Angeles. Be sure to glance at the trail every so often, lest you miss a step while ogling the panorama.

## Getting There
From US Highway 101 in Port Angeles turn left on Race Street and follow it past the Olympic National Park Visitor Center to the Hurricane Ridge Road. Turn right and follow Hurricane Ridge Road for 5.7 miles to Heart O' the Hills, where you'll pay a fee to enter the park. Continue up the Hurricane Ridge Road 11.8 miles to the Hurricane Ridge Visitor Center parking area. The trailhead is located across the road from the lodge, 5,250 feet above sea level. Plan to arrive early at the Heart O' the Hills entrance station, or wait until midafternoon for this hike.

### PERMITS/CONTACT
None required/Olympic National Park Wilderness Information Center, (360) 565-3100; Olympic National Park Visitor Center, (360) 565-3130

### MAPS
USGS Hurricane Hill, Mount Angeles; Custom Correct Hurricane Ridge; Green Trails Mount Olympus, Mount Angeles

### TRAIL NOTES
No dogs or bikes

## The Trail

If there's a single niggle about this path, it is the fact that you don't get the stunning view of the interior Olympic Mountains unless you turn around or wait until the return trip. Alpine wildflowers and views of the Strait of Juan de Fuca may be consolation enough

There's no water available on this hike, so if you haven't brought any, fill up at the Hurricane Ridge Visitor Center. Like several pathways around Hurricane Ridge, this one starts as a paved nature

Wildflowers such as the Columbia Tiger Lily and purple lupine grow profusely along the Switchback Trail

trail and climbs a 5,471-foot hill called Sunrise Point, east and across the parking area from the visitor center. This hill is the site of a snow-sports area in the winter, with a rope tow climbing to the summit.

The pavement continues about halfway to the summit, where the trail drops to the northeast along the crest of the ridge underneath a second 5,400-foot hill. You'll traverse along splendid alpland to a flat saddle where Columbia blacktail deer occasionally harass tourists, then climb around a 5,539-foot peak at **1.3** miles. From here the trail drops steeply in switchbacks—this slope may hold snow until mid-summer—to another saddle where the trail passes through an alpine forest. Finally, you'll skirt the east side of a 5,350-foot hill before emerging onto a flat saddle at the base of the south face of 6,454-foot Mount Angeles. A climber's trail heads uphill to the left from this saddle to a meadow just above the trail, a good picnic perch and turnaround spot, 2.2 miles from the trailhead.

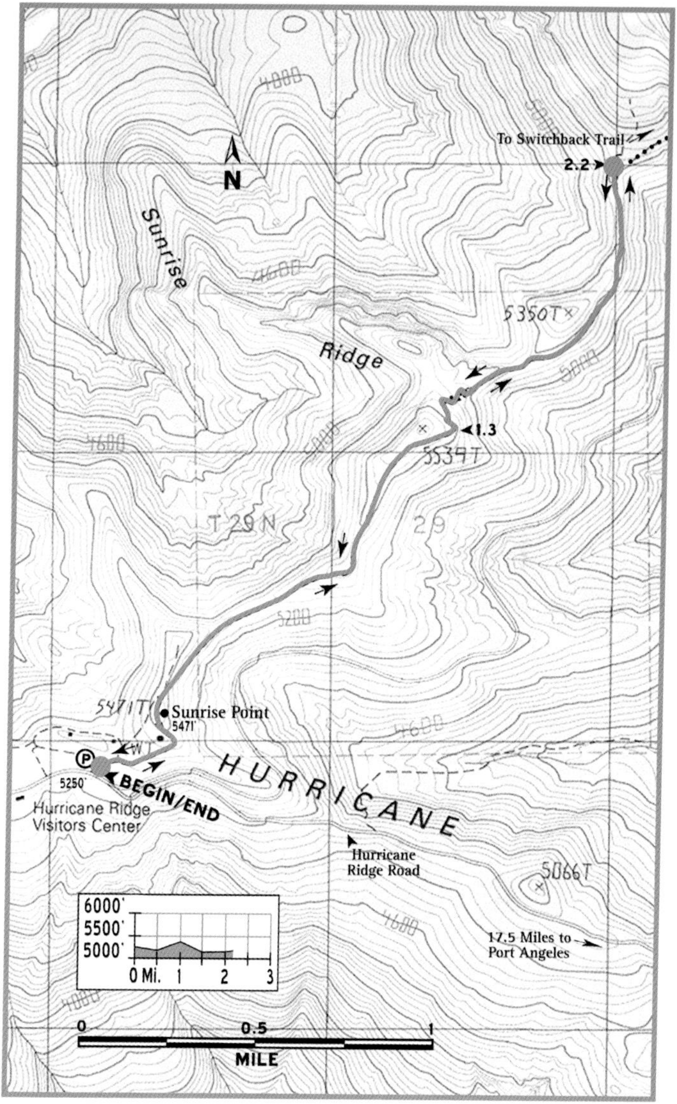

To Switchback Trail

2.2

5350T

1.3

5537T

T 29 N

29

5200

Sunrise Ridge

5471T
Sunrise Point
5471'

P
5250'
BEGIN/END
Hurricane Ridge
Visitors Center

HURRICANE

Hurricane
Ridge Road

5066T

17.5 Miles to
Port Angeles

6000'
5500'
5000'

0 Mi.   1    2    3

0              0.5              1
MILE

## Going Farther

For the one-way option mentioned in the Klahhane Ridge (Hike 35), continue on the main trail to the right for another 1.4 miles to a junction with the Switchback Trail, then climb steeply left 0.8 mile to Klahhane Ridge. ■

# 37. Hurricane Hill

| RATING | DISTANCE | HIKING TIME |
|---|---|---|
| ★ ★ ★ ★ ★ | 6.0 miles round-trip | 3 hours |
| ELEVATION GAIN | HIGH POINT | DIFFICULTY |
| 1,700 feet | 5,757 feet | ◆ ◆ ◆ ◇ ◇ |

| BEST SEASON | | | | | | | | | | | |
|---|---|---|---|---|---|---|---|---|---|---|---|
| Jan | Feb | Mar | Apr | May | Jun | Jul | Aug | Sep | Oct | Nov | Dec |

## The Hike

Climb along a repaved nature walk 1.6 miles to the site where an aircraft spotter's cabin once stood, then follow a trail along a rocky open ridge to a mountain view overlooking the Elwha River valley far below. The paved path to the summit of Hurricane Hill is accessible to folks who do their hiking aboard wheelchairs, although steep sections may require assistance.

## Getting There

From US Highway 101 in Port Angeles, turn left on Race Street and follow it past the Olympic National Park Visitor Center to the Hurricane Ridge Road. Turn right and follow Hurricane Ridge Road for 5.7 miles to Heart O' the Hills, where you'll pay a fee to enter the park. Continue up the Hurricane Ridge Road 11.8 miles to the Hurricane Ridge Visitor Center. Plan to arrive early at the Heart O' the Hills entrance station, or wait until midafternoon for this hike. Follow the road through the parking area 2.5 miles down a steep, curving road past a picnic area—your last chance to stock up on water—and up to a parking loop at the trailhead, 5,075 feet above sea level. In summer, all trailhead parking spots are often taken, but hikers can drive less than a mile down to the picnic area and follow a trail back to Hurricane Hill Trail.

## The Trail

The hike to Hurricane Hill is on paved nature trail the entire distance and offers stunning views of Mount Olympus, the highest peak of the Olympics at 7,965 feet, and Mount Carrie, the 6,995-footer that is so close across the Elwha River valley you might hear its glacier grumble. The path first drops to a little knoll where you can look north across the Strait of Juan de Fuca to Vancouver Island, then it climbs underneath a 5,250-foot peak to a saddle and junction with the Little River Trail. Stay left here and begin a long sidehill climb across steep, open slopes with awesome views to the interior Olympics. You'll round a forested ridge and emerge on a saddle below Hurricane Hill, the grassy-sloped mountain above. The trail begins climbing in switchbacks here to a trail junction at **1.4** miles. Follow the trail to the right through a wide meadow to the rocky summit of Hurricane Hill, 5,757 feet above sea level.

The view from here is enough to whup your eyeballs flat. Mountains everywhere. Forests and river valleys below. Saltwater and foreign nations to the north. Mount Baker out there to the northeast, floating in the haze. An aircraft spotter's cabin was once lashed to the summit rock by cables whose anchors may still be visible. Herb Crisler—the

### PERMITS/CONTACT
None required/Olympic National Park Wilderness Information Center, (360) 565-3100; Olympic National Park Visitor Center, (360) 565-3130

### MAPS
USGS Mount Angeles, Hurricane Hill; Custom Correct Hurricane Ridge; Green Trails Mount Angeles, Mount Olympus

### TRAIL NOTES
No dogs or bikes

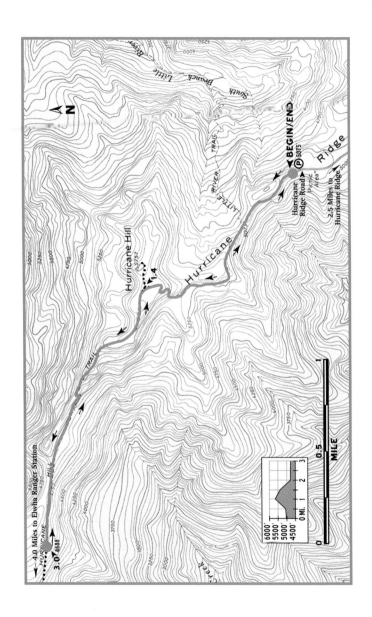

N

Little Branch

South

River

Ridge

BEGIN/END
P 5075
Hurricane Ridge Road
Picnic Area
2.5 Miles to
Hurricane Ridge

LITTLE RIVER TRAIL

Hurricane Hill

5757
1.4

HURRICANE

5075

HURRICANE HILL TRAIL

4.0 Miles to Elwha Ranger Station

3.0 4688

Creek

6000'
5500'
5000'
4500'
0 Mi.  1   2   3

0        0.5        1
MILE

Hikers along the Hurricane Hill Trail

Disney cinematographer who filmed *The Olympic Elk*—spent a winter here with his wife, Lois.

After taking in the view, walk back to the trail junction and turn left, following the trail as it crosses a green, flat meadow to gain the crest of an increasingly narrow, rocky ridge. You'll walk the crest, switching back once to pass on the south under steep rocky peaks, 2.4 miles from the trailhead. Continue past a flat saddle to a point where the trail begins to angle down the grassy knoll in front of you, 3.0 miles from the trailhead.

This is the turnaround point for most hikers, because the trail switches back steeply down the meadow to enter the forest, dropping 4,400 feet and 3.0 miles to the Elwha Ranger Station.

## Going Farther

With the closure of the Olympic Hot Springs Road at Madison Falls, the hike down to the Elwha Ranger Station and out the closed road would make a one-way hike of about 10 miles. However, it may be difficult to find a pedestrian willing to climb up to Hurricane Ridge to retrieve the second car without offering a significant cash bribe. ■

# 38. PJ Lake

| RATING | DISTANCE | HIKING TIME |
|---|---|---|
| ★ ☆ ☆ ☆ ☆ | 1.8 miles round-trip | 1.5 hours |

| ELEVATION GAIN | HIGH POINT | DIFFICULTY |
|---|---|---|
| 1,700 feet | 5,000 feet | ♦ ♦ ♦ ◇ ◇ |

| BEST SEASON |
|---|
| Jan Feb Mar Apr May **Jun Jul Aug Sep** Oct Nov Dec |

## The Hike

Here's a short, steep trail down, then up, to a quiet little lake underneath Hurricane Ridge, perhaps worth the trip if you enjoy angling for little bitty Eastern Brook trout or swimming in cold, clear water.

## Getting There

From US Highway 101 in Port Angeles, turn left on Race Street and follow it to the Hurricane Ridge Road just past the Olympic National Park Visitor Center. Turn right on the Hurricane Ridge Road and drive 17.5 miles to Hurricane Ridge. On entering the parking area, turn left on the single-lane, gravel Obstruction Point Road and follow it as it winds steeply along an alpine ridge for 4.0 miles to the Waterhole Picnic Area. The trailhead, at 5,000 feet above sea level, is located on the north side of the road. Drivers who feel insecure on roads less than interstate widths will freak out on the Obstruction Point Road.

**PERMITS/CONTACT**
None required/Olympic National Park Wilderness Information Center,
(360) 565-3100; Olympic National Park Visitor Center, (360) 565-3130

**MAPS**
USGS Mount Angeles; Custom Correct Hurricane Ridge;
Green Trails Mount Angeles

**TRAIL NOTES**
No dogs or bikes

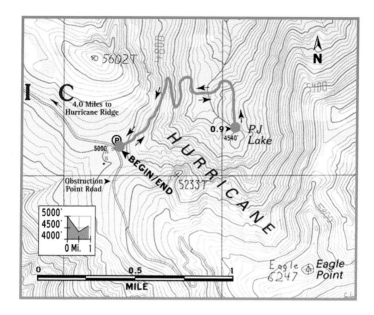

Motorists returning to Hurricane Ridge in the fall will also find visibility hampered by a setting sun shining directly in their eyes.

Plan to arrive early at the Heart O' the Hills entrance station, or wait until midafternoon for this hike, as wait times often exceed 30 minutes on summer days.

## The Trail

I once got a poison-pen letter from a hiker who suggested I should be quartered and fried in extra-virgin olive oil for describing the hike to PJ Lake as downhill. For the record, only 1,000 feet of the total 1,700-feet elevation gain is downhill. The other 700 feet is uphill. So here's the sad truth: After a 0.1-mile traverse, you begin dropping on a trail so steep that if you fall off, you will land in the top of a 100-foot-tall evergreen. You continue downhill for the next 0.4 mile, dropping 500 feet.

PJ Lake

You cross three creeks in flowery subalpine meadows, the last below a photo-op waterfall at **0.6** mile. Then you climb for the last 0.3 mile, up 375 feet to the lake. That means that on the way back, you drop 375 feet, then climb 500. Big deal. It's *mostly* downhill.

The lake contains Eastern Brook trout. Just remember, in the unlikely event you catch and keep a big one, you'll have to carry it up that hill—even if it's mostly downhill to the lake. ■

## 39. Moose Lake

| RATING | DISTANCE | HIKING TIME |
|:---:|:---:|:---:|
| ★ ★ ★ ★ ★ | 8.2 miles round-trip | 5 hours |
| ELEVATION GAIN | HIGH POINT | DIFFICULTY |
| 1,500 feet | 6,450 feet | ♦ ♦ ♦ ◊ ◊ |

| BEST SEASON |
|:---:|
| Jan Feb Mar Apr May **Jun Jul Aug Sep Oct Nov** Dec |

### The Hike
This hike is mostly down to a mile-high lake, worth the accompanying crowds because it is one of the most scenic treks in Olympic National Park.

## Getting There

From US Highway 101 in Port Angeles, turn left on Race Street and follow it to the Hurricane Ridge Road just past the Olympic National Park Visitor Center. Turn right on the Hurricane Ridge Road and drive 17.5 miles to Hurricane Ridge. On entering the parking area, turn left on the single-lane, gravel Obstruction Point Road and follow it as it winds steeply along an alpine ridge for 8.0 miles to the Obstruction Point trailhead, located 6,150 feet above sea level. This road was not built for your timid aunt from Iowa and can be dusty in midsummer. Motorists returning to Hurricane Ridge in the fall will also find visibility hampered by a setting sun shining directly in their eyes.

Plan to arrive early at the Heart O' the Hills entrance station, or wait until midafternoon for this hike, as wait times often exceed 30 minutes on summer days.

## The Trail

Wildflowers, exceptional views, wildlife, the chance to catch a trout, a rugged workout—the hike to Moose Lake has it all. The price for all this splendor is that you must share it with other hikers. Moose Lake and the Obstruction Point area is one of the more popular destinations in the park. Things get even more elbow-to-elbow with backpackers in the evening, making day hiking an excellent option.

Day hikers will want to leave plenty of time for the return climb from Moose Lake because the way is steep and long. Another nag: If there's

**PERMITS/CONTACT**
None required/Olympic National Park Wilderness Information Center, (360) 565-3100; Olympic National Park Visitor Center, (360) 565-3130

**MAPS**
USGS Mount Angeles; Custom Correct Gray Wolf–Dosewallips; Green Trails Mount Angeles

**TRAIL NOTES**
No dogs or bikes

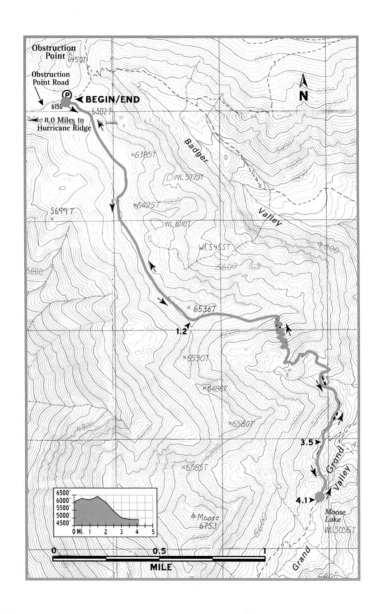

Obstruction
Point ×6507'

Obstruction
Point Road

◄BEGIN/END

6150'          ×6302'

◄8.0 Miles to
Hurricane Ridge

Badger

×6385'

WL 5779'

×6425'

Valley

5699'
×

WL 6110'

WL 5455'

5600

5000

×6536'

1.2

×6530'

×6486'

×6580'

3.5►

Grand

×6385'

Valley

4.1►

Moose
Lake
WL 5055'

▲Moose
6753'

6500'
6000'
5500'
5000'
4500'

0 Mi.  1  2  3  4  5

Grand

0                    0.5                    1
MILE

The trail above Moose Lake climbs towards Grand Pass

any hike where extra clothing might come in handy in an evening chill or sudden alpine storm, this is it. It has snowed at Obstruction Point every month of the year, and the trail has the notorious distinction of being the site where, one summer in the 1960s, two people froze to death less than a mile from their car.

The trail heads south from the parking lot, which at 6,150 feet would appear to be the top of the world. Actually, after dropping onto a marmot-filled meadow that is flat as a pancake griddle, you'll climb almost 200 feet in the next 0.5 mile to another flat plateau filled with phlox and other alpine flowers. Walk another quarter-mile and begin to drop in steep switchbacks where a mountain tarn can be seen to the southeast. You'll drop down to a rocky swale and climb again to a ridge stretching south above Badger Valley. The trail follows the ridge, climbing up and down several times before beginning a long uphill traverse to the high point in the hike, a 6,450-foot peak at **1.2** miles.

The trail rounds the peak and begins to descend immediately into Grand Valley, first with a long downhill traverse, then in steep switchbacks to meadows where creeks gurgle and tarns reflect alpine wildflowers. The trail continues to drop steeply, finally switching back

Lake Lillian is an off-trail destination for those seeking solitude on the Moose Lake hike

in a meadow and crossing a creek above Grand Lake, at **3.0** miles. After crossing the creek, the trail meanders through alpine forest to a meadow overlooking Grand Lake and the trail junction leading to the lake, at **3.5** miles. Keep right here and continue past a waterfall another 0.6 mile to Moose Lake. You'll find a great flower-filled meadow for picnicking at the south end of the lake.

## Going Farther

Hikers can make a loop trip by dropping down to Grand Lake, then following the Grand Valley Trail either directly to Obstruction Point or following the main trail to a junction with the Obstruction Point Trail 2.0 miles west of the trailhead. I wouldn't recommend this alternative for any but the strongest hikers, because it loses another 400 feet below Grand Lake before beginning to climb steeply to Obstruction Point in 4.8 miles. Instead, hikers seeking solitude might find it at little Gladys Lake, another 0.5 mile up the trail from Moose Lake. More exercise and fantastic views await strong hikers who climb past Gladys Lake to Grand Pass, another 1.4 miles and 1,100 feet farther uphill. ■

## 40. Roaring Winds, Obstruction Point

| RATING | DISTANCE | HIKING TIME |
|---|---|---|
| ★★★★★ | 6.4 miles round-trip | 3.5 hours |
| ELEVATION GAIN | HIGH POINT | DIFFICULTY |
| 1,400 feet | 6,700 feet | ◆◆ ◇◇◇ |
| BEST SEASON | | |
| Jan Feb Mar Apr May **Jun Jul Aug Sep** Oct Nov Dec | | |

## The Hike
Here is the highest trail in the park, passing through alpine country of immense beauty and yielding awesome views. If you have time to day hike only one high trail in the Olympics, make it this one. Carry water.

## Getting There
From US Highway 101 in Port Angeles, turn left on Race Street and follow it to the Hurricane Ridge Road just past the Olympic National Park Visitor Center. Turn right on the Hurricane Ridge Road and drive 17.5 miles to Hurricane Ridge. Plan to arrive early at the Heart O' the Hills entrance station, or wait until midafternoon for this hike, as wait times often exceed 30 minutes on summer days.

**PERMITS/CONTACT**
None required/Olympic National Park Wilderness Information Center, (360) 565-3100; Olympic National Park Visitor Center, (360) 565-3130

**MAPS**
USGS Mount Angeles; Custom Correct Gray Wolf–Dosewallips; Green Trails Mount Angeles

**TRAIL NOTES**
No dogs or bikes

A hiker checks the view from Obstruction Point

Stop for water here if you're not carrying any; none is available on this hike. On entering the parking area, turn left on the single-lane, gravel Obstruction Point Road and follow it as it winds steeply along an alpine ridge for 8.0 miles to the Obstruction Point trailhead, located 6,150 feet above sea level. You'll also find what is surely the highest outhouse in Olympic National Park. Flatlanders are likely to feel more comfortable on a roller coaster named Death Monster than they will driving the Obstruction Point Road. Motorists returning to Hurricane Ridge in the fall may find it difficult to see the road, as the setting sun shines directly in their eyes.

## The Trail

In good weather no other hike in the Olympics is better than this one. In weather that is less than great, it can get mighty cold, wet, and windy on this hike. And any month, as my good friend Dan Weaver, the Big Scribe, might tell you: "It could snow, Mister."

The trail begins by following the remnants of an abandoned road at the east end of the parking area, which can get crowded in the

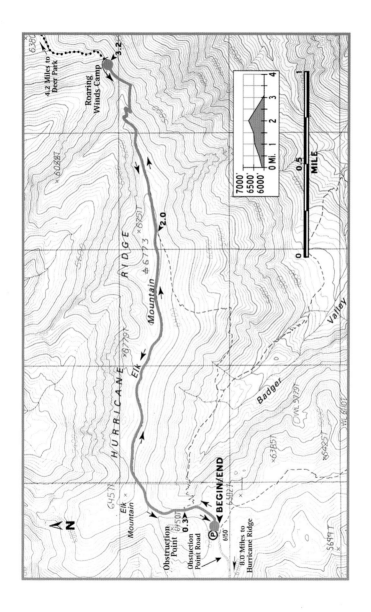

summer. However, most of these hikers are bound for Grand or Moose Lakes (Hike 39). The trail descends gently and rounds a steep rocky ridge falling from 6,450-foot Obstruction Point, above. Just beyond, in a steep gully, you'll likely encounter a short, steep, icy snowfield that usually lingers across the trail until mid-August. Although you might find a hand line and well-trod ledge in the snow, if you aren't comfortable walking in snow, hike the Moose Lake Trail instead

Just beyond the snowfield, the trail joins with the steep switchback trail into Badger Valley, at **0.3** mile. Stay left here and climb steeply across a rock and scree slope where you'll slip back a half step for every one you take forward. This section is only about 0.4 mile long and emerges into a meadow and flat bench overlooking Grand Valley to the south. The hike continues across pool-table flats toward the high point in the hike underneath a rocky 6,773-foot peak to the left. From here the trail drops slightly to a junction with the main Badger Valley Trail at **2.0** miles.

Keep left at this junction and continue east to the crest of the ridge, where the trail switches back down the steep mountainside, rounds a ridge, and settles along a flat saddle at Roaring Winds Camp, 3.2 miles from the trailhead. This is the turnaround point and picnic spot for most day hikers.

## Going Farther

It's 7.4 miles, one-way, from Obstruction Point to Deer Park. Parties with cars at both trailheads can trade keys at Roaring Winds. Read the description of the hike from Deer Park to Roaring Winds (Hike 32). ∎

# OTHER HIKES

The Little River Trail climbs 8.1 miles from the Little River Road to a junction with the Hurricane Hill Trail.

# ELWHA RIVER

---

The closure of Olympic Hot Springs Road at Madison Falls adds between 4.0 and 15.8 round-trip miles to all but two hikes in this section. The road was expected to be rerouted and opened in October 2023. It has been opened to bicycles and e-bikes since it was washed out in 2017.

# 41. Olympic Discovery Trail

| RATING | DISTANCE | HIKING TIME |
|---|---|---|
| ★★☆☆☆ | 4.6 miles round-trip | 2.5 hours |

| ELEVATION GAIN | HIGH POINT | DIFFICULTY |
|---|---|---|
| 190 feet | 240 feet | ◆◇◇◇◇ |

| BEST SEASON | | |
|---|---|---|
| Jan Feb Mar | | Sep Oct Nov Dec |

## The Hike

Get a look at the free-flowing lower Elwha River from a unique pedestrian bridge that hangs underneath the Elwha River Road bridge.

## Getting There

From the western junction of Highway 101 and Lauridsen Boulevard in Port Angeles, follow Highway 101 west for 4.4 miles to Laird Road and turn right. Follow Laird Road for 1.0 mile to a right turn at Dry Creek School to West Edgewood Drive, then follow West Edgewood for a half-mile to Lower Elwha Road. Turn left on the Lower Elwha Road and drive 0.75 miles to an intersection with Kacee Way, crossing the Olympic Discovery Trail just before the intersection. Turn left on Kacee Way and look for a wide parking area on the left. This trailhead, donated by the Lower Elwha Klallam Tribe, is 240 feet above sea level.

Alternative parking access for about 10 cars is off the Elwha River Road, about 200 feet west of the bridge.

**PERMITS/CONTACT**
None required/www.olympicdiscoverytrail.com

**MAPS**
Printable PDF maps available at www.olympicdiscoverytrail.com

**TRAIL NOTES**
Leashed dogs okay; bikes okay; paved asphalt trail

## The Trail

The Olympic Discovery Trail follows the abandoned route to the Spruce Railroad, which hauled spruce for World War I aircraft out of the Olympics to Port Angeles mills. Thanks to the volunteer efforts and planning work of the Peninsula Trails Coalition, this urban trail

The pedestrian deck of the Lower Elwha Bridge is suspended below the auto deck

stretches in sections from Port Townsend to Lake Crescent and beyond. It could eventually reach La Push, mostly on railroad grade free of auto traffic, but for now the most interesting section for pedestrians is the 2.3 miles leading down to the Elwha River crossing.

The hike begins with a level 0.8 mile to the west, paralleling the road and passing several homes before turning to the south and entering a forest of evergreen and maple. The descent is gentle, although it is easy to imagine the old steam logging shays huffing and puffing up this hill with a cargo of giant spruce.

The Elwha River can soon be heard to the west, rushing its final 3.0 miles to the Strait of Juan de Fuca. Almost as quickly, the river wash is drowned by the whine of pumps and clang of machinery at the Elwha Water Treatment Plant and Klallam Tribal Hatchery below the trail. You'll continue downhill, alternately traversing forest and logged sections, before reaching a ramp leading uphill to the bridge and pedestrian walkway that hangs underneath it.

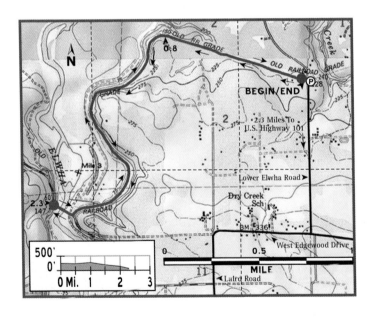

The old railroad bridge was located just downstream from the new bridge, which was completed in 2009. Turnaround for this hike is at the west end of the pedestrian span, with good views upstream and down.

## Going Farther
A number of developed Olympic Discovery Trailheads can be found east of the Lower Elwha Road near the Port Angeles airport and in the city itself. For a longer walk, start at the William Fairchild Airport to a round-trip hike of 8.0 miles. ■

# 42. Mills Lakebed

| RATING | DISTANCE | HIKING TIME |
|---|---|---|
| ★★ ☆ ☆ ☆ | 5.0 miles round-trip | 3 hours |
| **ELEVATION GAIN** | **HIGH POINT** | **DIFFICULTY** |
| 540 feet | 1,150 feet | ◆ ◆ ◆ ◇ ◇ |
| **BEST SEASON** | | |
| Jan Feb Mar Apr May Jun Jul Aug Sep Oct Nov Dec | | |

The Olympic Hot Springs Road was expected to be rerouted and opened by October 2023. If not, add approximately 6.1 miles each way by foot or bike from the Madison Falls parking area.

## The Hike
Here's an excellent chance to walk on land that hasn't seen boot-prints for a century: hike along the bottom of the former Lake Mills and see the Elwha River cut through 100 years of accumulated silt.

## Getting There
Follow US Highway 101 west 8.7 miles past Port Angeles to the Elwha River. If you wish to bypass the downtown section of Port Angeles, turn left on Race Street and follow it to Lauridsen Boulevard. Turn right on Lauridsen and follow it to its junction with US Highway 101 on the west end of town. Just before crossing the Elwha River, turn

left and follow Olympic Hot Springs Road 4.0 miles to Whiskey Bend Road, stopping to pay a fee at the entrance to Olympic National Park. Turn left on Whiskey Bend Road, just past the Elwha Ranger Station. Follow this single-lane, winding gravel road for 4.8 miles to the old Lake Mills Trailhead, on the right, 1,100 feet above sea level. Parking here is limited and the big Elwha River Trailhead parking area is only 200 yards beyond.

## The Trail

The trail dropping steeply to the former Lake Mills once welcomed tired Elwha River hikers as a short walk to swim in the chilly, clear water of the lake. Today, that same trail leads to history. Land exposed by the draining of the lake hasn't seen sunlight since the early 1900s, and exploring the sand, gravel, and mud of the lake bottom makes for a good walk.

Begin by dropping in steep switchbacks through forest for 0.5 mile and 540 vertical feet to the end of the developed trail on the former lakeshore. This section isn't the only descending or climbing you'll do, although it is by far the longest; you'll be walking along the former lake bottom from now on, scaling unstable hillocks of gravel and sand or crossing creek tributaries of the Elwha River.

The river changes course as it snakes through the lake bottom, carving channels in the sediment that the river carried downstream and dumped in the lake for 100 years. Logs and stumps decorate the land, resembling a post-apocalyptic landscape. Signs at the end

**PERMITS/CONTACT**
None required/Olympic National Park Wilderness Information Center,
(360) 565-3100; Olympic National Park Visitor Center, (360) 565-3130

**MAPS**
USGS Hurricane Hill; Custom Correct Elwha Valley

**TRAIL NOTES**
No dogs or bikes, trail not developed

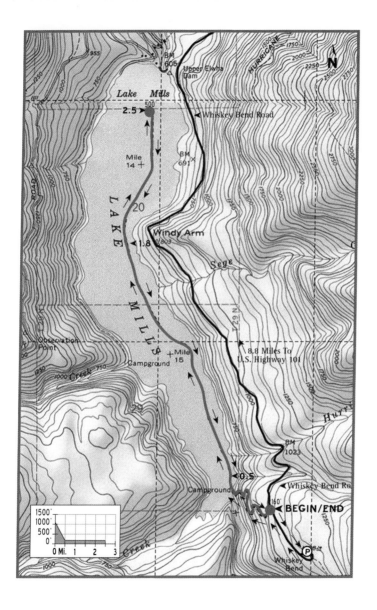

of the trail caution hikers about unstable banks near the river and prudent hikers will stay well away from the river banks.

Once you've negotiated the initially steep bank to the lake bottom, you can turn northeast and walk down the lake bottom for about 2.0 miles before the river canyon becomes too steep as it approaches Glines Canyon.

The river courses along the western shore, and hiking is fairly straightforward and flat along the eastern side. Crossing Wolf, Hurricane, and Sege creeks at about **0.8** and **1.5** miles is not difficult. You'll round Windy Arm, the forested hillside on your right, at **1.8** miles.

If the new river permits, you should be able to hike another 0.7 mile before turning around. Don't try to cross the river at any point. An alternate route back would be to climb the very steep forested hillside to the east and regain the Whiskey Bend Road for a 2.5-mile hike back to the trailhead. ■

The Elwha River carves a new channel through the silt that was the bottom of Lake Mills

# 43. Wolf Creek

| RATING | DISTANCE | HIKING TIME |
|--------|----------|-------------|
| ★★ ☆ ☆ ☆ | **9.0 miles round-trip** | **4.5 hours** |
| **ELEVATION GAIN** | **HIGH POINT** | **DIFFICULTY** |
| **3,900 feet** | **4,000 feet** | ◆ ◆ ◆ ◇ ◇ |

| BEST SEASON |
|-------------|
| Jan Feb Mar Apr May **Jun Jul Aug Sep** Oct Nov Dec |

The Olympic Hot Springs Road was expected to be rerouted and opened by October 2023. If not, add approximately 6.5 miles each way by foot or bike from the Madison Falls parking area.

## The Hike

This is a moderate climb up an abandoned road to the high country underneath Hurricane Ridge, with the possibility of a one-way option from the ridge.

## Getting There

Follow US Highway 101 west 8.7 miles past Port Angeles to the Elwha River. If you wish to bypass the downtown section of Port Angeles, turn left on Race Street and follow it to Lauridsen Boulevard. Turn right on Lauridsen and follow it to its junction with US Highway 101 at the west end of town. Just before crossing the Elwha River, turn left and follow the Olympic Hot Springs Road about 4 miles to

**PERMITS/CONTACT**
None required/Olympic National Park Wilderness Information Center, (360) 565-3100; Olympic National Park Visitor Center, (360) 565-3130

**MAPS**
USGS Hurricane Hill; Custom Correct Elwha Valley; Green Trails Mount Olympus

**TRAIL NOTES**
No dogs or bikes

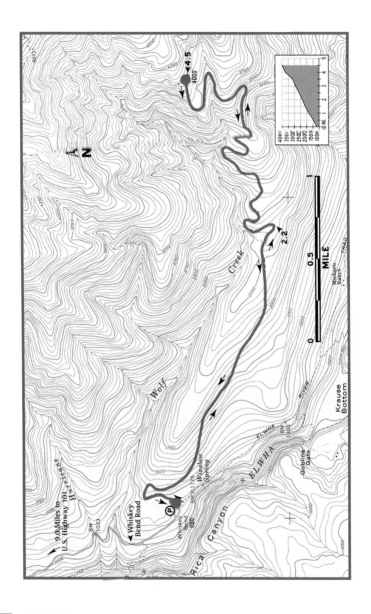

4.5

4000

5

4

3

2

1

0 MI.

400m
350m
300m
250m
200m
150m
100m

2.2

MILE

0     0.5     1

Wolf     Creek

N

Mickush
Ranch

TRAIL

Winslow
Spring

Whiskey Bend Road

Whiskey
Bend
1000

BM 1,175

P

9.0 Miles to
U.S. Highway 101 Hurricane

BM
1023

ELWHA

ELWHA     RIVER

Goblins
Gate

Krause
Bottom

Rica     Canyon

The upper end of Wolf Creek Trail overlooks Sue Peak and Mount Olympus

Whiskey Bend Road, stopping to pay a fee at the entrance to Olympic National Park. Turn left on Whiskey Bend Road just past the Elwha Ranger Station. Follow this single-lane, winding gravel road 5.0 miles to the trailhead, 1,100 feet above sea level.

## The Trail

Until a half-century ago this trail served as the road access to Hurricane Ridge, so the climb is generally not as strenuous as most trails. Climb past the stock facility uphill from the parking area, round a corner, and begin a long traverse along the hillside that ends in the first of several switchbacks at **2.2** miles.

The trail climbs a bit steeper to the next switchback, where you can hear Wolf Creek chattering below the trail. Thirsty hikers should not attempt to climb down to the creek; it is slippery and dangerous and in the 1970s, a hiker was killed in a fall here, apparently trying to reach water. The trail switches back again and climbs the ridge more directly in an alley between the trees, the sound of Wolf Creek below. Continue climbing another six switchbacks, finally crossing Wolf Creek, the first opportunity for water, at **4.0** miles.

The trail rounds a ridge above the creek and in another 0.5 mile, reaches an open slope at 4,000 feet, providing views of the Elwha River valley below and the mountains above. This is a good picnic spot and turnaround point for day hikers.

## Going Farther

Assuming you can convince another party to hike up from Whiskey Bend, you can hike down the Wolf Creek Trail from the Hurricane Hill Road, 1.5 miles past the Hurricane Ridge Visitor Center, for a trek of 8.0 miles. Parking is limited at the upper trailhead, and you may have to park at a picnic area 1.3 miles from the visitor center. ■

# 44. Elwha Loop

| RATING | DISTANCE | HIKING TIME |
|--------|----------|-------------|
| ★★★★☆ | 6.6 mile loop | 3.5 hours |
| ELEVATION GAIN | HIGH POINT | DIFFICULTY |
| 250 feet | 1,150 feet | ◆ ◇ ◇ ◇ ◇ |
| BEST SEASON | | |
| Jan Feb Mar Apr May Jun Jul Aug Sep Oct Nov Dec | | |

The Olympic Hot Springs Road was expected to be rerouted and opened by October 2023. If not, add approximately 6.5 miles each way by foot or bike from the Madison Falls parking area.

## The Hike

This walk is a pleasant day hike along one of the mightiest rivers in the Olympics, where you may see Roosevelt elk, the animals for which the river was named. You'll pass a couple of historic buildings and walk country first seen by white people little more than a hundred years ago.

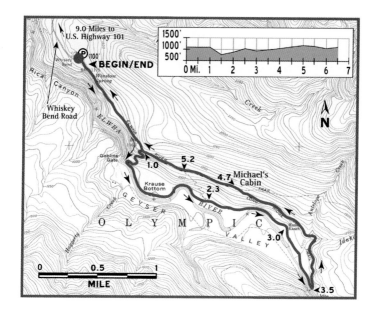

## Getting There

Follow US Highway 101 west 8.7 miles past Port Angeles to the Elwha River. If you wish to bypass the downtown section of Port Angeles, turn left on Race Street and follow it to Lauridsen Boulevard. Turn right on Lauridsen and follow it to its junction with US Highway 101 at the west end of town. Just before crossing the Elwha River, turn left and follow the Olympic Hot Springs Road about 4 miles to Whiskey Bend Road, stopping to pay a fee at the entrance to Olympic National Park. Turn left on Whiskey Bend Road just past the Elwha Ranger Station. Follow this single-lane, winding gravel road 5.0 miles to the trailhead, 1,100 feet above sea level.

## The Trail

This hike follows the route blazed by the first white explorers up the Elwha River valley, the Press Expedition, in 1899–90. Begin by traversing for a mile above the river, which can be heard below. At **0.5** mile

**PERMITS/CONTACT**
None required/Olympic National Park Wilderness Information Center,
(360) 565-3100; Olympic National Park Visitor Center, (360) 565-3130

**MAPS**
USGS Hurricane Hill; Custom Correct Elwha Valley; Green Trails Mount Olympus

**TRAIL NOTES**
Kid-friendly

you'll see a sign directing you to an overlook, and a short, steep trail leading down. Unless you're hiking early in the morning, I'd suggest you save this short side trip for the way home in the evening, for a better chance of seeing elk on the river flats below the overlook.

Continue left for another half-mile to a junction with the Rica Canyon Trail at the edge of an old forest fire scar. Turn right here and plunge steeply down to green flats in the forest above the river. A trail junction here offers a very short, steep side trip to the right to Goblins Gate, where the Elwha River narrows and smashes against cliffs in a steep, rocky canyon. After a gawk and chance to catch your breath, follow the trail to the left toward Krause Bottom, a flat, wide stretch of river flats where, at **2.3** miles from the trailhead, you'll strike another trail descending from the main Elwha Trail above. Keep

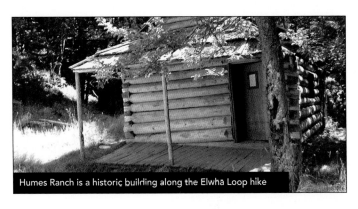

Humes Ranch is a historic building along the Elwha Loop hike

right here and continue along the flats to a wide, grassy field marking the pastureland of the Humes Ranch.

The old building is located at the south end of the field, where Grant and Will Humes homesteaded and Herb Crisler, the last mountain man of the Olympics, later lived. The trail drops to a wide campsite and then winds through woods to a good lunch spot above the river. It climbs around a washout and joins the Dodger Point Trail at **3.5** miles from the trailhead.

If you wish, take a short side trip to the right, down the Dodger Point Trail, to the suspension bridge across the Elwha River. Then return to the trail junction and follow it as it climbs gently for a little more than a mile to a junction with the Lillian River Trail, at **4.7** miles.

This is the site of another historic building, Michael's Cabin. Keep left at the junction and follow the trail as it climbs again through the old burned area to a junction with the Krause Bottom Trail at **5.2** miles. Stay right here and climb more steeply in 0.4 mile to the Rica Canyon Trail junction to close the loop. The trailhead is 1 mile to the right. ■

# 45. Lillian River

| RATING | DISTANCE | HIKING TIME |
|---|---|---|
| ★ ★ ★ | **9.6 miles round-trip** | **5 hours** |
| ELEVATION GAIN | HIGH POINT | DIFFICULTY |
| **500 feet** | **1,600 feet** | ◆ ◆ |
| BEST SEASON | | |
| Jan Feb **Mar Apr May Jun** Jul Aug Sep Oct Nov Dec | | |

The Olympic Hot Springs Road was expected to be rerouted and opened by October 2023. If not, add approximately 7.5 miles each way by foot or bike from the Madison Falls parking area.

## The Hike

Trek along the Elwha River Trail for about 5 miles to a big pony bridge across one of the river's main tributaries, the Lillian, for a good rainy-day hike.

## Getting There

Follow US Highway 101 west 8.7 miles past Port Angeles to the Elwha River. If you wish to bypass the downtown section of Port Angeles, turn left on Race Street and follow it to Lauridsen Boulevard. Turn right on Lauridsen and follow it to its junction with US Highway 101 at the west end of town. Just before crossing the Elwha River, turn left and follow the Olympic Hot Springs Road 4.0 miles to Whiskey Bend Road, stopping to pay a fee at the entrance to Olympic National Park. Turn left on Whiskey Bend Road just past the Elwha Ranger Station. Follow this single-lane, winding gravel road 5.0 miles to the trailhead, 1,100 feet above sea level.

## The Trail

Begin by following the Elwha River Trail (Hike 44) for 1.9 miles, passing a short, steep trail leading to an overlook on the right at **0.5** mile and a steep trail leading down to the right to Rica Canyon, 1.0 mile from the trailhead. In another 0.4 mile, you'll come to a third junction with the Krause Bottom Trail, leading right. Keep left and follow the main Elwha River Trail to Michael's Cabin. This is a good spot for families with smaller children to stop, especially in soggy weather. The cabin, a historic building last occupied by "Cougar Mike" Michaels, was built by "Doc" Ludden in 1906. (There is a little-known rule on the Elwha River that states all settlers must have nicknames. Feel free to check my research on this point.)

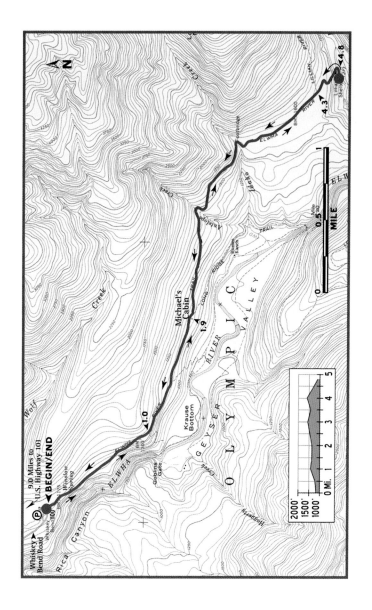

The Lillian River rushes to join the Elwha River below Lillian River Camp

Climb left at the junction at Michael's Cabin with the Dodger Point Trail. The Elwha Trail angles along a sidehill and gets steeper as it climbs around canyons to cross Antelope Creek and, later, Idaho Creek. Look downhill from the steep banks approaching Idaho Creek to see several rare (even rarer since Taxol was discovered) Pacific yew trees. After climbing out of the Idaho Creek canyon, the trail flattens and cuts across a bench where big trees are blackened by an old forest fire. At **4.3** miles it strikes a junction with the Lillian River Trail.

Keep right here and begin a steep half-mile descent to the Lillian River, switching back several times before passing several campsites and an outhouse on the flats by the bridge, at **4.8** miles. The bridge is a good picnic and turnaround spot. ■

## 46. Aldwell Lakebed

| RATING | DISTANCE | HIKING TIME |
|---|---|---|
| ★★☆☆☆ | 3.0 miles round-trip | 2 hours |

| ELEVATION GAIN | HIGH POINT | DIFFICULTY |
|---|---|---|
| Negligible | 187 feet | ◆◇◇◇◇ |

| BEST SEASON |
|---|
| Jan Feb Mar Apr May Jun Jul Aug Sep Oct Nov Dec |

## The Hike

This walk along the bottom of the former Lake Aldwell takes you into the remnants of land near the mouth of the Elwha River that existed more than a century ago. You'll see huge stumps of trees logged before the Elwha River Dam was built, and perhaps find artifacts left by pioneer settlers or Native Americans.

## Getting There

Follow US Highway 101 west 8.7 miles past Port Angeles to the Elwha River. If you wish to bypass the downtown section of Port Angeles, turn left on Race Street and follow it to Lauridsen Boulevard. Turn right on Lauridsen and follow it to its junction with US Highway 101 on the west end of town. Cross the Elwha River Bridge and immediately turn right on Lake Aldwell Road. Follow the road about 0.7 mile to its end at the old Lake Aldwell boat launch, 200 feet above sea level.

### PERMITS/CONTACT
None required/Olympic National Park Wilderness Information Center, (360) 565-3100; Olympic National Park Visitor Center, (360) 565-3130

### MAPS
USGS Hurricane Hill; Custom Correct Elwha Valley

### TRAIL NOTES
No developed trail

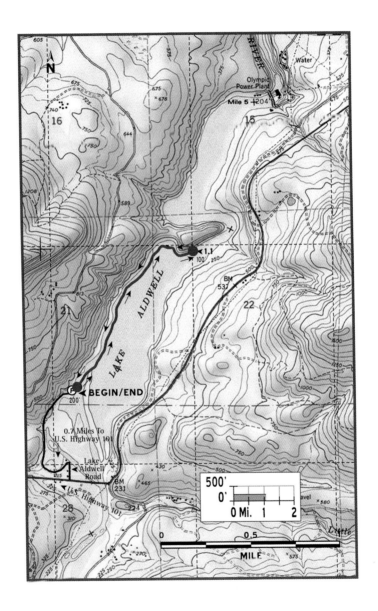

N

16

605
675
725
740
750
678
644
750
1208
589
613
750
500
200

RIVER

Water

Olympic
Power Plant

Mile 5 204

15

1,1
100   250

BM
53?

22

1000

750

1000

LAKE ALDWELL

21

BEGIN/END

0.7 Miles To
U.S. Highway 101

Lake
Aldwell
Road
BM
231
224

28
310

U.S. Highway 101

275

430
465

750

500

1000

270

575

Little

Gravel   580

500'
0'

0 Mi.   1   2

0                    0.5

MILE

## The Trail

One of the things that makes this short hike interesting is the way the land and river are restoring themselves and being restored by Olympic National Park and Tribal workers and volunteers. While the river carves channels in the century-old sediment deposits, man and Mother Nature are dropping hundreds of thousands of native plant seedlings onto the new land.

No trail leads north along the lake bottom, but finding your way is not difficult. Park rangers ask that you watch out for new vegetation sprouting from the ground, and be wary of soft or muddy areas along the way.

Portions of the lakebed were once riverfront areas frequented by settlers and Native Americans who fished for the legendary chinook salmon of the Elwha. Hikers are cautioned about removing any artifacts they might find, and may remember the simpleton who, in 2012, found a wagon wheel on the lake bottom and attempted to sell it on eBay. He was subsequently fined $225.

You should be able to walk about 1.5 miles north along the former lakebed before the walls of the canyon get steep or the river prohibits farther travel. Olympic National Park rangers may be offering guided weekend walks along the former lake bottom. For information, contact the Olympic National Park Visitor Center, (360) 565-3130. ∎

An ancient snag stands sentinel on the Aldwell Lakebed

# 47. Happy Lake

| RATING | DISTANCE | HIKING TIME |
|---|---|---|
| ★★★☆☆ | 9.8 miles round-trip | 5.5 hours |

| ELEVATION GAIN | HIGH POINT | DIFFICULTY |
|---|---|---|
| 3,120 feet | 4,875 feet | ♦♦♦♦ |

| BEST SEASON |
|---|
| Jan Feb Mar Apr May **Jun Jul Aug Sep Oct Nov** Dec |

The Olympic Hot Springs Road was expected to be rerouted and opened by October 2023. If not, add approximately 6 miles each way by foot or bike from the Madison Falls parking area.

## The Hike
It's a tough climb to Happy Lake, located just below a scenic alpine ridge with expansive views in all directions.

## Getting There
Follow US Highway 101 west 8.7 miles past Port Angeles to the Elwha River. If you wish to bypass the downtown section of Port Angeles, turn left on Race Street and follow it to Lauridsen Boulevard. Turn right on Lauridsen and follow it to its junction with US Highway 101 at the west end of town. Just before crossing the Elwha River, turn left and follow the Olympic Hot Springs Road 8.6 miles to the trailhead, just above the former Lake Mills overlook, stopping to pay a fee at the entrance to Olympic National Park. The trailhead is 1,750 feet above sea level. The Olympic Hot Springs Road may be closed at the Glines Canyon Overlook, which is about a quarter-mile east of the trailhead. Check with the Olympic National Park Visitor Center for current road status.

## The Trail
Back in the days when I could catch something other than my ear by casting a fly, Happy Lake was one of my favorite destinations. The shoreline was so open and grassy that my backcast seldom snagged

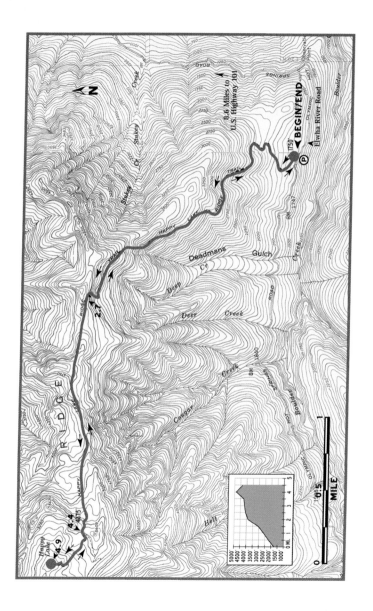

Map labels:
- N
- ROAD
- SPRINGS
- OLYMPIC
- Overhead
- **BEGIN/END**
- 8.6 Miles to U.S. Highway 101
- Elwha River Road
- P
- Boulder
- Creek
- Shakey Cr
- Shakey
- HAPPY
- TRAIL
- BM 1747
- Deadmans
- Gulch
- Creek
- Cr
- Deep
- Deer
- Creek
- RIDGE
- TRAIL
- 2.7
- ROAD
- BM 1840
- Cougar
- Creek
- Boulder
- Creek
- OLYMPIC
- HAPPY
- 4375
- 5.4
- Hell
- Happy Lake
- 4.9

Scale inset:
5000
4500
4000
3500
3000
2500
2000
1500
1000
0 Mi. 1 2 3 4 5

0   0.5   1
MILE

**PERMITS/CONTACT**
None required/Olympic National Park Wilderness Information Center,
(360) 565-3100; Olympic National Park Visitor Center, (360) 565-3130

**MAPS**
USGS Mount Carrie; Custom Correct Lake Crescent–Happy Lake Ridge;
Green Trails Mount Olympus, Lake Crescent

**TRAIL NOTES**
No dogs or bikes

on anything and the Eastern Brook trout in the lake would snap up bare hooks, they were so hungry. Today, of course, I am much too sophisticated to cast a fly to such a lowly char. Besides, as I say, I would only catch my ear.

This hike starts with a climb right out of the gate, and it doesn't let up much for about 3 miles. The grade is steep to moderately steep but consistently *up* more than anything else. If you've not stocked up on water, you'll find a small stream just off the trail at **0.2** mile. The trail climbs on a traverse across the hillside before switching back through an arid draw to a ridge, switching back a couple of times before dropping back into the draw and climbing the ridge on the other side.

The gain in elevation is apparent as Olympic peaks to the southwest begin to peek through the trees at you. Stop panting and peek back. At **2.5** miles you'll cross another stream and contour a sidehill so steep that falling off the trail would not be conducive to a successful hike. In fact, a narrow defile here is called Deadman's Gulch. The trail climbs just underneath the crest of the ridge and makes a final switchback to gain the top at **2.7** miles. You'll hike along the ridge as the trail meanders up and down, offering views through the short alpine forest up the Elwha Valley and across to Mount Carrie and Mount Olympus, beyond.

At a broad saddle, at **3.7** miles, the trail drops under the north side of the ridge where you can look back to see Mount Baker in the distance above the Strait of Juan de Fuca. You'll climb a grassy swale

The trail to Happy Lake passes though a silver forest half hidden in mist

to a junction with the Happy Lake Trail at **4.4** miles. Turn right and descend 0.5 mile to the lake, which is shallow and ringed by wide grassy shores. Unless a cooling dip in the lake or catching some of those little Brookies is on the agenda, I'd suggest climbing back to the ridge, with its better views, for a lunch spot. ■

# 48. Olympic Hot Springs

| RATING | DISTANCE | HIKING TIME |
|---|---|---|
| ★★★★ ☆ | 4.8 miles round-trip | 2.5 hours |

| ELEVATION GAIN | HIGH POINT | DIFFICULTY |
|---|---|---|
| 400 feet | 2,200 feet | ◆ ◆ ◆ ◆ ◆ |

| BEST SEASON |
|---|
| Jan Feb Mar Apr May Jun Jul Aug Sep Oct Nov Dec |

The Olympic Hot Springs Road was expected to be rerouted and opened by October 2023. If not, add approximately 7.8 miles each way by foot or bike from the Madison Falls parking area.

## The Hike
Here's an easy walk along an abandoned road to primitive hot springs along the banks of the tumbling Boulder Creek.

## Getting There
Follow US Highway 101 west 8.7 miles past Port Angeles to the Elwha River. If you wish to bypass the downtown section of Port Angeles, turn left on Race Street and follow it to Lauridsen Boulevard. Turn right on Lauridsen and follow it to its junction with US Highway 101 at the west end of town. Just before crossing the Elwha River, turn left and follow the Olympic Hot Springs Road 9.9 miles to the trailhead. You'll stop

**PERMITS/CONTACT**
None required/Olympic National Park Wilderness Information Center, (360) 565-3100; Olympic National Park Visitor Center, (360) 565-3130

**MAPS**
USGS Mount Carrie; Custom Correct Lake Crescent–Happy Lake Ridge; Green Trails Mount Olympus

**TRAIL NOTES**
Kid-friendly

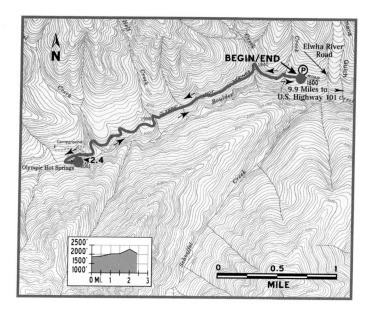

to pay a fee at the entrance to Olympic National Park. The trailhead is
1,800 feet above sea level. The Olympic Hot Springs Road may be
closed at the Glines Canyon Overlook, which is about a quarter-mile
east of the trailhead. Check with the Olympic National Park Visitor
Center for current road status.

## The Trail

This is a good walk in the spring, when things aren't usually so
crowded around the pools, which are constructed of plastic tarps
and logs by the bathers. The hot springs also make a refreshing stop
returning from longer hikes like Boulder Lake (Hike 49) or Boulder
Falls (Hike 50). Depending on the severity of the winter, you can
sometimes ski or snowshoe to the hot springs but often must add
another 4.0 miles round-trip to the walk because the road is closed at
the former Lake Mills overlook.

Bathers soak in one of the Olympic Hot Springs pools

The trail begins at a gate across the abandoned road, where you'll find an outhouse and trail register, and climbs over a hill to descend to the first of three stream crossings. Pavement has been removed from the old road, but some bathers ride mountain bikes to the springs. The road alternately climbs and drops as it traverses around the creek crossings, finally dropping and climbing steeply across Crystal Creek, just below the hot springs at **2.2** miles. You'll enter an abandoned parking lot, where a trail leads uphill to the right to the old Boulder Creek Campground and Appleton Pass and Boulder Lake trailheads.

Keep left here, heading to the east end of the parking lot and the trail leading to the hot springs. The trail follows Boulder Creek upstream for 0.1 mile, then crosses the creek on a footbridge, where years ago a cougar and cub sprawled in the sun and blocked bathers from the pools.. Turn left across the bridge and look for the hot pools on way trails leading uphill to the right. One or two pools once dotted a terrace off the trail to the left, but these may now be gone. The largest pool is located about 0.1 mile along the main trail, on a side trail uphill to the right.

Although nude bathing is discouraged, many of the hot springs visitors let it all hang out. You have been warned. ■

## 49. Boulder Lake

| RATING | DISTANCE | HIKING TIME |
|---|---|---|
| ★★★★☆ | 11.6 miles round-trip | 6 hours |

| ELEVATION GAIN | HIGH POINT | DIFFICULTY |
|---|---|---|
| 2,532 feet | 4,332 feet | ◆◆◆◇ |

| BEST SEASON |
|---|
| Jan Feb Mar Apr May **Jun Jul Aug Sep Oct Nov** Dec |

The Olympic Hot Springs Road was expected to be rerouted and opened by October 2023. If not, add approximately 7.8 miles each way by foot or bike from the Madison Falls parking area.

### The Hike

This is a steep climb to a sunny green alpine lake where a wildflower-filled meadow makes a splendid picnic spot underneath Boulder Peak.

### Getting There

Follow US Highway 101 west 8.7 miles past Port Angeles to the Elwha River. If you wish to bypass the downtown section of Port Angeles, turn left on Race Street and follow it to Lauridsen Boulevard. Turn right on Lauridsen and follow it to its junction with US Highway 101 at the west end of town. Just before crossing the Elwha River, turn left and follow the Olympic Hot Springs Road 9.9 miles to the trailhead. You'll stop

**PERMITS/CONTACT**
None required/Olympic National Park Wilderness Information Center, (360) 565-3100; Olympic National Park Visitor Center, (360) 565-3130

**MAPS**
USGS Mount Carrie; Custom Correct Lake Crescent–Happy Lake Ridge; Green Trails Mount Olympus

**TRAIL NOTES**
No dogs or bikes

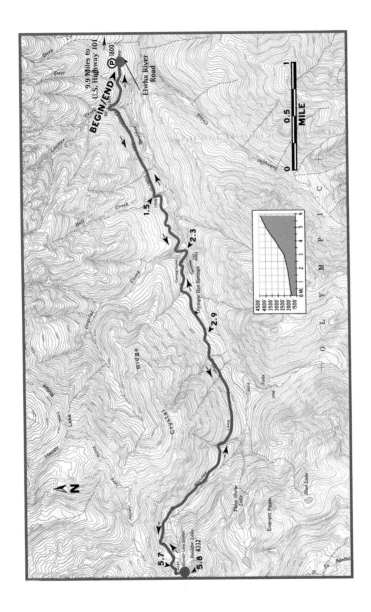

N

9.9 Miles to
U.S. Highway 101

Elwha River
Road

BEGIN/END

P 1800

1.5

2.3

Geyser Valley

Olympic Hot Springs

2.9

5.7

5.8 4332
Boulder Lake

MILE

0       0.5       1

4500
4000
3500
3000
2500
2000
1500
0 MI. 1  2  3  4  5  6

O   L   Y   M   P   I   C

Boulder Lake

to pay a fee at the entrance to Olympic National Park. The trailhead is 1,800 feet above sea level. The Olympic Hot Springs Road may be closed at the Glines Canyon Overlook, which is about a quarter-mile east of the trailhead. Check with the Olympic National Park Visitor Center for current road status.

## The Trail

This path follows the abandoned Olympic Hot Springs Road 2.4 miles to the hot springs (Hike 48). Follow the trail to the right at the abandoned parking lot at the hot springs and take the left branch of the old campground road to find the trailhead at the west end of the campground.

The trail meanders through a forest of huge evergreens for 0.6 mile to a junction with the Appleton Pass Trail. Bear right here and climb more steeply around the first of three creeks that rattle down steep gullies to Boulder Creek, below. The trail is steepest as it ascends the last of these gullies, 3.7 miles from the trailhead. Hikers pausing here can look back to glimpse the cliffs and snows of Mount Appleton to the south.

You'll begin a steady uphill traverse from here above the creek that drains Boulder Lake, rounding a dry gully and finally crossing to a rocky point where you can look down the valley carved by the outlet stream. Finally, the trail parallels the outlet stream and follows an alpine meadow to a junction with the Boulder Ridge Trail, 5.7 miles from the trailhead. Turn left here and climb over a knoll to Boulder Lake. A meadow at the south end of the lake, where the maintained trail ends, is a good picnic spot.

## Going Farther

Strong, experienced hikers looking for a great view can scramble up 5,600-foot Boulder Peak, just west of the lake. The easiest route is to climb up the Boulder Ridge Trail for two switchbacks, then angle off-trail towards the peak's long northeast ridge, climbing along the ridge to the summit. Though it may take you less time, allow at least 1.5 hours for the 1,300-foot climb and return to the lake. ■

# 50. Boulder Falls

| RATING<br>★ ★ ☆ ☆ ☆ | DISTANCE<br>8.4 miles round-trip | HIKING TIME<br>4 hours |
|---|---|---|
| ELEVATION GAIN<br>900 feet | HIGH POINT<br>2,700 feet | DIFFICULTY<br>◆ ◆ ◇ ◇ ◇ |
| BEST SEASON<br>Jan Feb Mar Apr May **Jun Jul Aug Sep** Oct Nov Dec | | |

The Olympic Hot Springs Road was expected to be rerouted and opened by October 2023. If not, add approximately 7.8 miles each way by foot or bike from the Madison Falls parking area.

## The Hike

Climb along tumbling Boulder Creek to a forested spot where it cascades in a big watery staircase over three falls.

## Getting There

Follow US Highway 101 west 8.7 miles past Port Angeles to the Elwha River. If you wish to bypass the downtown section of Port Angeles, turn

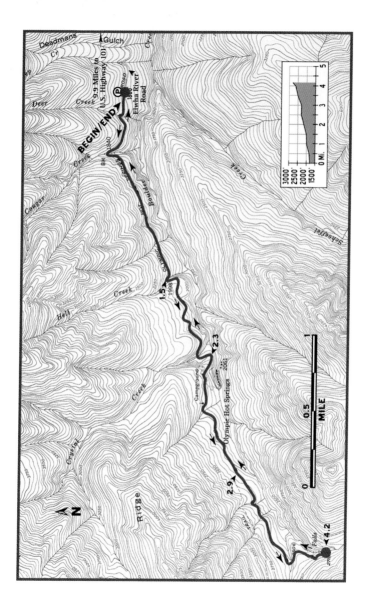

left on Race Street and follow it to Lauridsen Boulevard. Turn right on Lauridsen and follow it to its junction with US Highway 101 at the west end of town. Just before crossing the Elwha River, turn left and follow the Olympic Hot Springs Road 9.9 miles to the trailhead. You'll stop to pay a fee at the entrance to Olympic National Park. The trailhead is 1,800 feet above sea level. The Olympic Hot Springs Road may be closed at the Glines Canyon Overlook, which is about a quarter-mile east of the trailhead. Check with the Olympic National Park Visitor Center for current road status.

## The Trail

This trek makes a good rainy-weather walk, since you are under the expansive canopy of a virgin forest and views are blocked by all those pesky trees that were here quite some time before the Revolutionary War. The hike begins with a 2.4-mile trek up the abandoned road leading to Olympic Hot Springs, a road that you will swear has grown longer on your return.

At the abandoned hot springs parking area, climb right along a trail that leads through the Boulder Creek Campground. Walk through the campground on the old road to the left to find the trailhead at the west end. The trail wanders through a swampy area around the trunks of massive trees and climbs gently to higher ground, where you'll encounter a junction with the Boulder Lake Trail (Hike 49) 0.6 mile from the hot springs. Keep left here and follow the trail along a forested bench to cross two creeks before beginning an angling descent to a main branch of Boulder Creek.

Picnic at Appleton Pass, on the trail above the Boulder Falls hike

Cross the creek and climb over a ridge to the side trail leading to the lower falls, 4.0 miles from the trailhead. The cascade is about 25 feet high and easier to view than the upper falls, and might make the best picnic spot. To reach the upper falls, continue climbing right in switchbacks another 0.2 mile to the side trail leading left to an overlook. The upper of the three cascades is highest but difficult to see.

## Going Farther

Appleton Pass is one of the most scenic alpine areas of the park, but it is a 16-mile round-trip hike from the Olympic Hot Springs trailhead. If you feel like following the trail past the falls, you'll climb another 1.5 miles before reaching beautiful alpine meadows below Appleton Pass. For those who thrive on the high country, the 12.0-mile round-trip might be worth it. ■

# LAKE CRESCENT

## 51. Spruce Railroad Trail

| RATING | DISTANCE | HIKING TIME |
|---|---|---|
| ★★★☆☆ | 8.2 miles round-trip | 4 hours |

| ELEVATION GAIN | HIGH POINT | DIFFICULTY |
|---|---|---|
| 60 feet | 680 feet | ◆◇◇◇◇ |

| BEST SEASON |
|---|
| Jan Feb Mar Apr May Jun Jul Aug Sep Oct Nov Dec |

### The Hike

This 12-foot-wide accessible foot and bike trail is an excellent historical walk along an abandoned railroad grade, through two tunnels, and along the banks of one of the deepest, cleanest lakes in the state.

### Getting There

Follow US Highway 101 west from Port Angeles 27.6 miles to Fairholme at the west end of Lake Crescent. Turn right on the Fairholme/North Shore Road and follow the North Shore Road past Fairholme Campground for 5.0 miles to the trailhead at the end of the road, 680 feet above sea level. For a one-way option, leave a car parked at the east trailhead, located 3.2 miles off US Highway 101 on the East Beach Road, across the Lyre River from the Log Cabin Resort. The US Highway 101–East Beach Road junction is 17.0 miles west of Port Angeles on US Highway 101.

**PERMITS/CONTACT**
None required/Olympic National Park Wilderness Information Center, (360) 565-3100; Olympic National Park Visitor Center, (360) 565-3130

**MAPS**
USGS Lake Crescent; Custom Correct Lake Crescent–Happy Lake Ridge

**TRAIL NOTES**
Kid-friendly; bikes okay

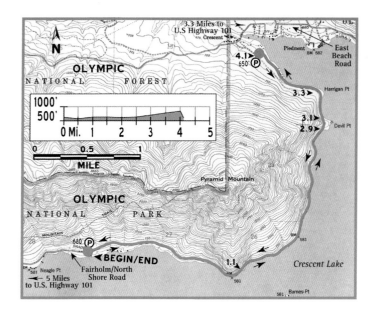

## The Trail

Hikers, equestrians, bicyclists, those who ply pathways aboard a wheelchair, and even leashed dogs should not miss the Spruce Railroad Trail on their visit to the Olympic Peninsula. It is the crown jewel of the longer Olympic Discovery Trail and its $1.2 million renovation was completed in 2020. Besides following the Crescent lakeshore, the trail passes through two tunnels that had been closed for more than five decades.

I prefer to do this hike from west to east because the west trailhead gives a more wild feel to the trail; the east trailhead is next door to several private residences. Because of its low elevation, snow seldom sticks long around Lake Crescent.

For most of the way you'll be hiking the old railbed of the Spruce Railroad, named for the wood it was supposed to haul to the mills to build the frames for World War I aircraft. The trail begins above Lake Crescent, whose jeweled waters seem to vary with the seasons from silver-gray in the winter to emerald, sapphire, and turquoise in the summer. You'll follow the old railbed as it drops gently about 40 feet to the water's edge, passing the only sections of rail remaining from tracks long gone. Once at a level just above the lake, the trail meanders along following the shoreline of the lake, occasionally leaving sight of the shore to traverse cuts made to even the rail grade. At **1.1** miles, as the trail rounds a point, follow the new route left to the first of two railroad tunnels.

Bicyclists cross the footbridge on the Spruce Railroad Trail

Continue around the point and hike above the lake where the cliffs of Pyramid Mountain above dive into the water. You'll walk along ledges cut from the rock and pass several rock retaining walls built along the water side to carry the railbed.

The McFee Tunnel is located at Devil Point, 2.9 miles from the trailhead. You can now walk through the tunnel, which was rebuilt with a 12-foot-wide hard-surface path and new entrances on either side. It opened in the summer of 2018, and bypasses a branch in the trail at **3.0** miles that leads to the Devil's Punchbowl.

The Punchbowl trail climbs in a steep, short pitch past the bridge before reaching the 12-foot-wide section of the route, 3.1 miles from the trailhead. Enjoy the walk through the 450-foot-long McFee Tunnel under Harrigan Point and the final 0.6 mile on the widened and improved trail to the eastern trailhead and your turnaround point. ■

## 52. Pyramid Mountain

| RATING | DISTANCE | HIKING TIME |
|---|---|---|
| ★★★☆☆ | 7.0 miles round-trip | 3.5 hours |

| ELEVATION GAIN | HIGH POINT | DIFFICULTY |
|---|---|---|
| 2,400 feet | 3,100 feet | ◆◆◆◇◇ |

| BEST SEASON |
|---|
| Jan Feb Mar Apr May **Jun Jul Aug Sep** Oct Nov Dec |

### The Hike

Climb this peak above Lake Crescent to the site of an old aircraft spotter's cabin for big views to the north and the interior Olympics.

### Getting There

Follow US Highway 101 west from Port Angeles 27.6 miles to Fairholme at the west end of Lake Crescent. Turn right on the Fairholme/North Shore Road and follow the North Shore Road past Fairholme Campground for 3.1 miles to the trailhead, located at 700 feet above sea level across the road from the North Shore picnic area.

### The Trail

The trail to the summit of Pyramid Mountain is a great early-summer workout for hikers looking for a spectacular view of some of the hikes they might like to try later in the summer. The trail here is generally

---

**PERMITS/CONTACT**
None required/Olympic National Park Wilderness Information Center,
(360) 565-3100; Olympic National Park Visitor Center, (360) 565-3130

**MAPS**
USGS Lake Crescent; Custom Correct Lake Crescent–Happy Lake Ridge;
Green Trails Lake Crescent

**TRAIL NOTES**
No dogs or hikes

---

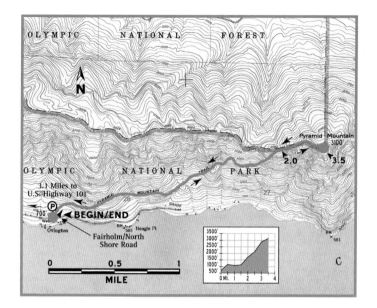

free of snow early in the season—if indeed the winter is severe enough to accumulate snow on the south-facing hillside. Begin climbing steadily from the trailhead through the forest, where you'll get peekaboo views of Lake Crescent below and the Aurora Ridge across the lake. You'll cross a couple of streams 1.5 miles from the trailhead that provide a water source early in the season.

At **1.8** miles, the trail traverses a very steep, exposed landslide where Kitsap and Olympic Peninsula trail volunteers attempted to widen the tread in the summer of 2007. Slides continue to wipe out the trail at this point and crossing this steep sidehill could be dangerous; don't proceed if there's any concern or if the park has closed the trail. Beyond, the trail climbs to a saddle in the ridge west of Pyramid Mountain and begins to follow the ridge along its crest toward the mountain. The view of the Strait of Juan de Fuca is provided courtesy of a clearcut on the north slope of the ridge. The trail climbs under the ridge to the north, then switches back and gains the ridge, following the crest over several lower rocky summits to the old spotter's cabin. You'll scramble around for the best views, across the Strait to the north and inland, across Lake Crescent to Mount Storm King and the snowy north slopes of Happy Lake Ridge. ■

# 53. Storm King

| RATING | DISTANCE | HIKING TIME |
|---|---|---|
| ★★☆☆☆ | 3.8 miles round-trip | 2.5 hours |
| ELEVATION GAIN | HIGH POINT | DIFFICULTY |
| 2.000 feet | 2,650 feet | ◆◆◆◇ |

| BEST SEASON | | | | | | | | | | | |
|---|---|---|---|---|---|---|---|---|---|---|---|
| Jan | Feb | Mar | Apr | May | Jun | Jul | Aug | Sep | Oct | Nov | Dec |

## The Hike
Join crowds of hikers for a tough but short climb to a viewpoint above Lake Crescent.

## Getting There
Follow US Highway 101 west from Port Angeles for 19.7 miles to the Storm King Ranger Station. The trail leaves the parking lot via a highway underpass, 650 feet above sea level.

**PERMITS/CONTACT**
None required/Olympic National Park Wilderness Information Center, (360) 565-3100; Olympic National Park Visitor Center, (360) 565-3130

**MAPS**
USGS Lake Crescent; Custom Correct Lake Crescent–Happy Lake Ridge; Green Trails Lake Crescent

**TRAIL NOTES**
No dogs or bikes

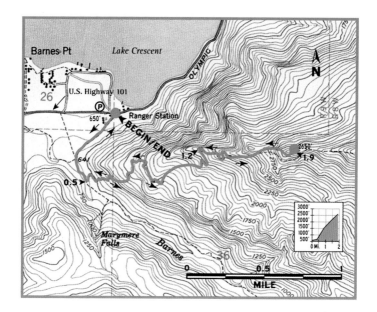

## The Trail

Walk under the highway on a paved path that leads to a junction with the Barnes Creek Trail and Marymere Falls Nature Trail at **0.5** mile, where your real climb begins. The trail scales a ridge in steep switchbacks where you can look through trees to the lake below. You'll continue to climb steeply in switchbacks up the mountain to the first of two overlooks at **1.2** miles. If you've brought children along, this might be the best turnaround spot.

Beyond, the trail climbs another steep 0.7 mile to the second overlook. The trail continues as a rough way path up the mountain from here, but the view doesn't get much better and the route gets a whole lot worse. In 2017, a hiker was killed in a fall from this very steep trail.

## Going Farther

Hikers seeking more exercise might enjoy the nature trail to Mary-mere Falls, 0.3 mile from the Storm King junction and another quarter-mile to the falls. You can also hike the Barnes Creek Trail to the point where the trail climbs above the creek, 3.5 miles from the trailhead, making a round-trip hike of 7.0 miles. The trail up Barnes Creek that connected to the old Aurora Ridge Trail has been improved, largely by Kitsap and Olympic Peninsula volunteers, and makes a good streamside hike of about 6 miles, round-trip. It begins at a junction with the Marymere Falls Trail. ∎

# SOL DUC RIVER

# 54. North Fork Sol Duc

| RATING | DISTANCE | HIKING TIME |
|---|---|---|
| ★★★★☆ | 6.0 miles round-trip | 3 hours |

| ELEVATION GAIN | HIGH POINT | DIFFICULTY |
|---|---|---|
| 400 feet | 1,750 feet | ◆◇◇◇◇ |

| BEST SEASON |
|---|
| Jan Feb **Mar Apr May Jun** Jul Aug Sep Oct Nov Dec |

## The Hike

Hikers seeking a quiet river walk with the chance of spotting wildlife will find it on this hike up the North Fork of the Sol Duc River.

## Getting There

Drive 30 miles west on US Highway 101 from Port Angeles to the Sol Duc Hot Springs Road. Turn left and drive 8.2 miles up the Sol Duc Road, stopping to pay a fee at the Olympic National Park entrance booth. The trailhead, about 5.0 miles up the road from the booth, is located across the road from the parking area, at 1,450 feet above sea level.

## The Trail

I don't think you can beat this trail for solitude on a short river hike. It's downright romantic and relatively few pedestrians take this walk,

---

**PERMITS/CONTACT**
None required/Olympic National Park Wilderness Information Center, (360) 565-3100; Olympic National Park Visitor Center, (360) 565-3130

**MAPS**
USGS Mount Muller, Lake Crescent; Custom Correct Lake Crescent–Happy Lake Ridge; Green Trails Lake Crescent

**TRAIL NOTES**
Kid-friendly

The North Fork of the Sol Duc River below the North Fork Trail

perhaps because it doesn't really go anywhere, or possibly because the final miles are rough and difficult to follow and involve fording the stream twice.

The hike starts with a half-mile climb through the forest over a low ridge. The trail crosses the ridge and in the same gentle grade, descends to the river's edge at **1.0** mile.

A high footlog that used to cross the river at this point is now missing, and you'll have to ford the river, which is lowest in the fall. The best crossing is just downstream from the trail. Once across, the trail turns upriver through a series of grassy lowland meadows that resemble a rain forest. Elk and deer browse here in the spring—a big reason to hike this path at this time of year.

The trail meanders through these meadows for about a half-mile, then settles along the river on black bedrock ledges where the North Fork slips and tumbles by only a few feet away. You'll scramble along more slowly here and might have a tough time getting the kids to go farther at all, simply because the trail here is unique.

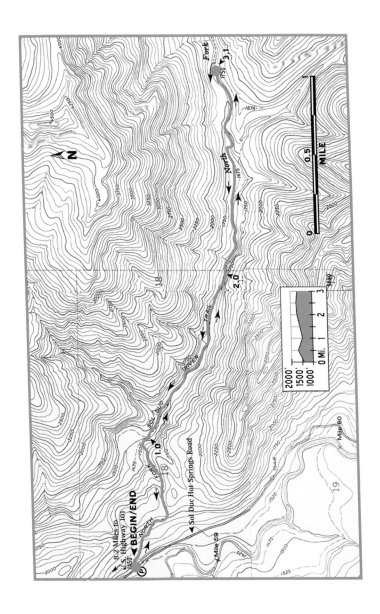

The remaining mile of this hike wanders along the river bottomland, climbing gently from green meadow to deep forest and back to meadow again. You'll find a wide riverside campsite at **3.0** miles and a smaller one another 0.1 mile farther up the trail. Either makes a good picnic spot and turnaround point.

## Going Farther

Wilderness pedestrians seeking more exercise can follow the North Fork Trail another 3.6 miles to a spot where the park trail maintenance ends at the first of two river fords. The trail beyond the 3.0-mile turnaround spot climbs away from the river, however, and doesn't return until it strikes the first ford. The old trail continues 3.0 miles past the ford to the North Fork Shelter, and a faint way trail can be followed by experienced backcountry travelers another mile. The late Robert L. Wood once used the North Fork Trail to access the backcountry between Boulder Lake and Appleton Pass—a rugged ridge marked by alpine tarns and flower-filled basins. ■

# 55. Mink Lake Meadows

| RATING | DISTANCE | HIKING TIME |
|---|---|---|
| ★★★☆☆ | 7.4 miles round-trip | 4 hours |

| ELEVATION GAIN | HIGH POINT | DIFFICULTY |
|---|---|---|
| 1,460 feet | 3,100 feet | ◆◆◆◇◇ |

| BEST SEASON |
|---|
| Jan Feb **Mar Apr May Jun Jul Aug Sep Oct Nov** Dec |

## The Hike

It's a moderate climb on rough trail past shallow Mink Lake to a picnic spot in a flower-strewn meadow, with great views rewarding hikers who are willing to try the strenuous climb an extra mile.

## Getting There

Drive 30.0 miles west on US Highway 101 from Port Angeles to the Sol Duc Hot Springs Road. Turn left and drive 12.3 miles on the Sol Duc Hot Springs Road to Sol Duc Hot Springs Resort. Cross the bridge to the resort and turn right to the Mink Lake trailhead at the northwest end of the paved parking lot at 1,640 feet above sea level.

## The Trail

The Mink Lake Trail has taken Sol Duc Hot Springs visitors up to the shallow, shady subalpine lake for years—and in places the horrid

**PERMITS/CONTACT**
None required/Olympic National Park Wilderness Information Center, (360) 565-3100; Olympic National Park Visitor Center, (360) 565-3130

**MAPS**
USGS Bogachiel Peak; Custom Correct Seven Lakes Basin–Hoh; Green Trails Mount Tom

**TRAIL NOTES**
Kid-friendly

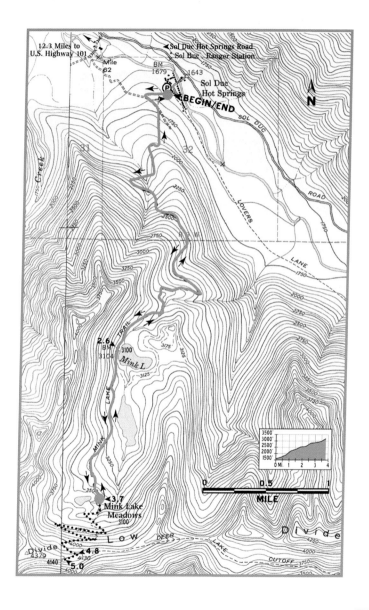

An angler tries his luck at Mink Lake

condition of the trail shows its age. A smoother tread on this trail would upgrade its rating to moderate. But you should find the struggle over slippery rocks, exposed roots, and through knee-deep channels cut by thousands of feet worth the effort simply for the solitude you'll likely find on the trail above Mink Lake.

If you're taking young children along, Mink Lake—2.6 miles up the trail—might be the best destination. The lake offers everything to keep a youngster fascinated for a whole day: small, easily caught Eastern Brook trout, hopping toads and wriggly salamanders, a creek for splashing, and early in the summer, snow banks that stretch to the water's edge.

The trail begins with a couple of switchbacks through thick, young forest above Sol Duc Hot Springs, where sounds of visitors splashing in the pools soon give way to the quiet of the forest. At **0.2** mile the trail flattens and turns to follow an abandoned roadbed for a short distance before beginning its climb again, switching back across a moss-covered rock smoothed by generations of hikers' boots.

It climbs around and follows a minor ridge, where it enters virgin forest, carpeted by fragrant vanilla leaf dotted by Canadian dogwood.

After another switchback at **0.9** mile, you'll begin a mile-long climbing traverse through the forest on benches and sidehill where the rush and tumble of the Sol Duc River can be heard below. Parts of the trail here are as smooth as the day they were first trod, but you won't enjoy these sections for great distances. At **1.8** miles you'll climb to a view down to the rushing, noisy creek that drains Mink Lake. Here the trail turns away from the creek to climb along just under a forested ridge.

The trail switches back and climbs above a basin back to a sidehill above the creek to a trail junction at **2.6** miles. Mink Lake, with its grassy banks and dilapidated shelter, is just off the trail to the left. The main trail continues to climb to the right past the lake, flattening to cross a beautiful moss-banked creek that murmurs its way to Mink Lake, before climbing above a marshy tarn at **3.1** miles. You'll cross a second creek at **3.4** miles and begin a steeper climb toward a noisy waterfall that can be heard through the subalpine forest ahead.

At **3.7** miles, the trail enters a flat subalpine meadow ringed with Alaska cedar. Marsh marigold line the plank bridge across the creek with the waterfall just below, and a faint way trail leads to the right into the meadow. Here's your picnic spot, with peekaboo views to the Mink Lake valley below and forested ridges of Little Divide to the east. The meadow stretches to the west where, just under a forested ridge, you'll find a clear, shady tarn.

## Going Farther

From the meadow the trail begins a steeper climb up the ridge to the southwest, switching back several times before reaching a junction with the Little Divide Loop (Hike 56) at **4.8** miles. This section of the trail is often snow-covered until mid-July. Turn right at the junction and walk another 0.2 mile, crossing the ridge to a steep meadow where you'll find views through the trees of Mount Olympus to the south, across the Bogachiel River valley, below. ∎

# 56. Little Divide Loop

| RATING | DISTANCE | HIKING TIME |
|---|---|---|
| ★★★★☆ | 13.6 mile loop | 7 hours |

| ELEVATION GAIN | HIGH POINT | DIFFICULTY |
|---|---|---|
| 2,500 feet | 4,140 feet | ◆◆◆◆◇ |

| BEST SEASON |
|---|
| Jan Feb Mar Apr May Jun Jul Aug Sep Oct Nov Dec |

## The Hike

Climb up past one subalpine lake to a lonely alpine ridge overlooking the Bogachiel River and Mount Olympus, then return past another lake where you'll meet the crowds.

## Getting There

Drive 30.0 miles west on US Highway 101 from Port Angeles to the Sol Duc Hot Springs Road. Turn left and, after passing the park's fee entrance station, drive 12.3 miles on the Sol Duc Hot Springs Road to Sol Duc Hot Springs Resort. Cross the bridge to the resort and turn right to the Mink Lake trailhead at the northwest end of the paved parking lot at 1,640 feet above sea level.

**PERMITS/CONTACT**
None required/Olympic National Park Wilderness Information Center,
(360) 565-3100; Olympic National Park Visitor Center, (360) 565-3130

**MAPS**
USGS Bogachiel Peak; Custom Correct Seven Lakes Basin–Hoh;
Green Trails Mount Tom

**TRAIL NOTES**
No dogs or bikes

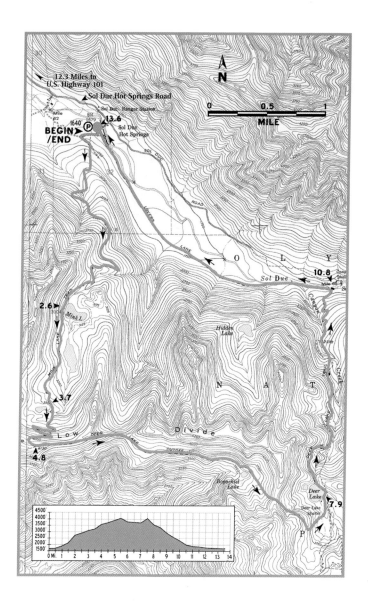

12.3 Miles to
U.S. Highway 101

Sol Duc Hot Springs Road

Sol Duc Ranger Station

13.6

1640'
BEGIN
/END

Sol Duc
Hot Springs

N

0          0.5          1
MILE

SOL DUC

ROAD

LOVERS

O   L   Y

Sol Duc

LANE

10.8

2.6

Mink L.

Hidden
Lake

N     A     T

3.7

Low          Divide

CUTOFF

4.8

Bogachiel
Lake

Deer
Lake

7.9

Deer Lake
Shelter

P

4500'
4000'
3500'
3000'
2500'
2000'
1500'

0 Mi.  1  2  3  4  5  6  7  8  9  10  11  12  13  14

Olympic mountain view from the Little Divide Trail

## The Trail

Don't confuse this Low Divide with the other Low Divide, which is located at the pass between the North Fork of the Quinault River and the Elwha River. But there you have it: Look on any USGS map to see that there are two official Low Divides—one here and one there. Go figure. Perhaps that is why virtually anyone but a terminal anal retentive calls this "Little Divide."

Of course, this Low Divide is higher than the Low Divide on the Quinault, but you can't call this Low Divide "High Divide" because there is only one High Divide, and it is not here. The official, proper name for Little Divide, therefore, should probably be Higher Low Divide. None of this musing is going to get you up the trail, though. So take a deep breath and start with the 2.6-mile climb to Mink Lake and continue past the lake to a sunny meadow and bubbling creek at **3.7** miles.

From here the trail begins a series of steep switchbacks up to a junction with the Little Divide Trail, **4.8** miles from the trailhead. The north side of the ridge below the junction often holds snow until mid-July. Turn left at this junction and walk the broad forested ridge, where the trail alternately climbs and drops along the ridge. The trail passes two ridgetop tarns at **5.7** miles, alternately climbs and drops in short, steep spurts, and finally descends below the crest of the ridge to the southwest. You'll round a rocky promontory overlooking little Bogachiel Lake.

The trail enters the forest again and begins a gradual climb around the Bogachiel Lake basin, switching back at a notch at the northeast end of the valley, **7.5** miles from the trailhead. It's mostly downhill from here. From the notch the trail makes a descending traverse above Deer Lake, crossing the meadows above the lake and joining the Deer Lake Trail, **7.9** miles from the trailhead. It is at this trail junction where, in 1992, German exchange student Stefan Bissert was last seen alive. His body has never been found.

Follow the trail left around the lake and cross the bridge at its outlet. From here the trail climbs briefly, then begins its 2.9-mile descent to the Sol Duc River. Just before reaching Sol Duc Falls, you'll find a junction with the Lover's Lane Trail. Turn left here and follow this trail 2.8 miles back to the trailhead at Sol Duc Hot Springs.

## Going Farther

Although it's doubtful you'll want to hike farther, you might want to set up your car camp in the big Sol Duc Campground, just south of the hot springs, and combine this hike with the High Divide Loop or one of the shorter alternatives. That way, you'll not only get an early start but a soothing soak in the hot pools between treks. ■

# 57. Potholes Meadows

| RATING | DISTANCE | HIKING TIME |
|---|---|---|
| ★★★☆☆ | 10.6 miles round-trip | 5.5 hours |

| ELEVATION GAIN | HIGH POINT | DIFFICULTY |
|---|---|---|
| 1,500 feet | 3,450 feet | ◆◆◆◇ |

| BEST SEASON |
|---|
| Jan Feb Mar Apr May Jun Jul Aug **Sep Oct Nov Dec** |

## The Hike

You'll climb past a subalpine lake surrounded by wide, flower-filled meadows to a splendid alpine plateau overlooking Deer Lake, filled with clear mountain tarns.

## Getting There

Drive 30.0 miles west on US Highway 101 from Port Angeles to the Sol Duc Hot Springs Road. Turn left and, after passing the park's fee entrance station, drive 14.0 miles on the Sol Duc Hot Springs Road to the trailhead at the end of the road, located 1,950 feet above sea level.

## The Trail

I didn't know I was taking this hike the first time I took it. I was trying to find Hidden Lake, which turned out to be well-named. "Just

---

**PERMITS/CONTACT**

None required/Olympic National Park Wilderness Information Center, (360) 565-3100; Olympic National Park Visitor Center, (360) 565-3130

**MAPS**

USGS Bogachiel Peak, Mount Carrie; Custom Correct Seven Lakes Basin–Hoh; Green Trails Mount Tom

**TRAIL NOTES**

No dogs or bikes

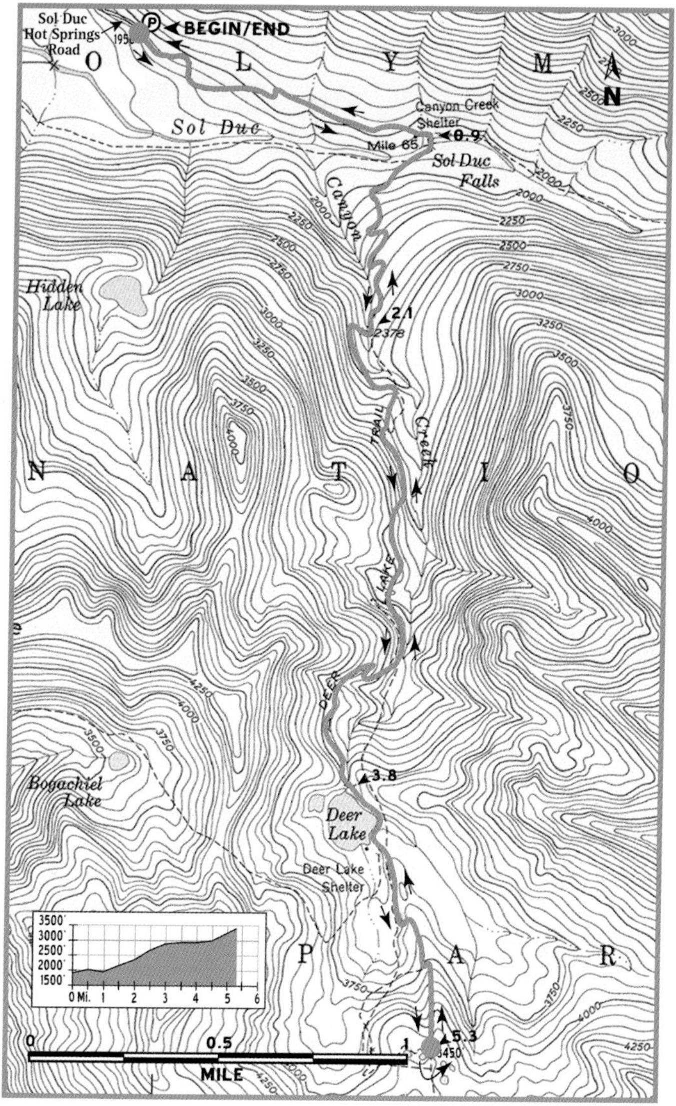

Sol Duc Hot Springs Road
1950
BEGIN/END
O L Y M P
N
Canyon Creek Shelter
0.9
Sol Duc
Mile 65
Sol Duc Falls
Canyon
Hidden Lake
2.1
2378
TRAIL
Creek
N A T I O
LAKE
DEER
3.8
Bogachiel Lake
Deer Lake
Deer Lake Shelter
P A R
5.3
3450
3500'
3000'
2500'
2000'
1500'
0 Mi. 1 2 3 4 5 6
0 0.5 1
MILE

follow the outlet stream up to the lake," the ranger told me. "It's the first stream that crosses the Lover's Lane Trail." So I took the Lover's Lane Trail to the first stream that crossed it, ignoring a dry creekbed a quarter-mile down the trail. I followed the creek uphill, battling through thickets of devil's club, over and under deadfall, moving with the speed of a pack-laden banana slug.

Thinking the jungle might be thinner above the creek, I climbed uphill away from it and stumbled out of the brush onto a trail that should not have existed. For 2 hours I had floundered around in Canyon Creek, below the Deer Lake Trail.

You'll share this trail with many hikers, but the crowds tend to thin at Deer Lake, the destination for most. Begin by walking a flat, four-lane freeway of a trail through a spruce, fir, and cedar forest to Sol Duc Falls, 0.9 mile from the trailhead. You'll cross a stream and find stadium-sized Sol Duc Shelter and a fork in the trail. Take the right fork and drop to a log bridge across Sol Duc Falls, where mist usually wets the span and cools hikers as they cross. Continue across the bridge and walk less than 200 feet to a junction with the Lover's Lane Trail.

Stay left here and follow the Deer Lake Trail as it climbs the hillside above the chattering Canyon Creek. At **2.1** miles you'll cross the Canyon Creek bridge, which provides a second cooling mist or downstream breeze. The trail continues to climb above Canyon Creek, now below on your left, rarely out of hearing distance. At about **2.9** miles the trail switches back and leaves the creek canyon along a steep sidehill.

You'll climb past several slide areas, each with its own tumbling brook, before rounding a final rock outcropping and dropping to a bridge at the outlet of Deer Lake, at **3.8** miles. The trail follows the eastern shore of the lake about 0.2 mile to cross an inlet stream, then another 0.2 mile to the end of the lake and a trail junction with the Little Divide Trail.

Stay left here and begin climbing again, contouring around a valley carved by a second Deer Lake inlet. The trail switches back at the head of the valley and, at **5.3** miles, emerges next to the first of several small tarns that mark the Potholes Meadows.

The meadows are huge, filled with clear ponds on benches and swales so that even on a crowded day, you might find your own little piece of solitude.

## Going Farther

For a real workout on one of the best day hikes in the Olympics, consider the 18.8-mile High Divide Loop (Hike 59). Hikers wishing to get an early start might consider car-camping at Sol Duc Campground, only 1.5 miles from the trailhead at the hub of most of the Sol Duc area trails. ■

# 58. Upper Sol Duc Campsite

| RATING | DISTANCE | HIKING TIME |
|---|---|---|
| ★★☆☆☆ | **10.8 miles round-trip** | **5.5 hours** |
| ELEVATION GAIN | HIGH POINT | DIFFICULTY |
| **1,300 feet** | **3,250 feet** | ◆◆◇◇◇ |
| BEST SEASON | | |
| Jan Feb Mar Apr **May Jun** Jul Aug **Sep Oct Nov** Dec | | |

## The Hike

This is a pleasant river walk through splendid forests to a picnic area beside tumbling rapids, with the chance of seeing wildlife along the way.

## Getting There

Drive 30.0 miles west on US Highway 101 from Port Angeles to the Sol Duc Hot Springs Road. Turn left and, after passing the park's fee entrance station, drive 14.0 miles on the Sol Duc Hot Springs Road to the trailhead at the end of the road, located 1,950 feet above sea level.

## The Trail

One of the nicest features of this trail is that once past Sol Duc Falls, **0.9** mile from the trailhead, the crowds thin as most hikers are headed

**PERMITS/CONTACT**
None required/Olympic National Park Wilderness Information Center,
(360) 565-3100; Olympic National Park Visitor Center, (360) 565-3130

**MAPS**
USGS Bogachiel Peak, Mount Carrie; Custom Correct Seven Lakes Basin–Hoh;
Green Trails Mount Tom

**TRAIL NOTES**
Kid-friendly

toward Deer Lake. Start by hiking to the falls and cross a footbridge just in front of the Sol Duc Shelter, then turn left at a trail junction.

The trail climbs above the shelter to the left, then angles along a green sidehill, never more than 200 feet above the river. At **1.8** miles from the trailhead, you'll turn left, away from the river and begin a gentle descent to lowland meadows separated from the Sol Duc River by a low forested hummock. The trail meanders through these lowlands, where elk can often be seen in the spring, for about a half-mile to a gurgling stream and campsite just beyond, at **2.2** miles. This would be a good turnaround point for families with small children.

Beyond the campsite, the trail begins to climb, first over a hillock away from the river. It turns toward the Sol Duc and descends back to river level at **3.1** miles, passes another campsite, then begins to climb in earnest alongside the river. The Sol Duc tumbles through a steep canyon here, with the trail climbing alongside about 50 feet above the torrent. You'll climb past a campsite at **4.0** miles, round the only switchback on the hike, and climb through deep forest away from the river, so far away that it can no longer be heard.

At **4.8** miles you'll cross a huge footlog over a raging creek and climb through the forest to a junction with the Appleton Pass Trail, 5.0 miles from the trailhead. Stay right here and climb into a sunny subalpine meadow created by winter avalanches. The view to peaks of the Upper Sol Duc across the valley opens up, and you'll see several steep avalanche chutes across the river. At **5.4** miles the trail strikes the Upper Sol Duc campsite, your turnaround spot. Turn right

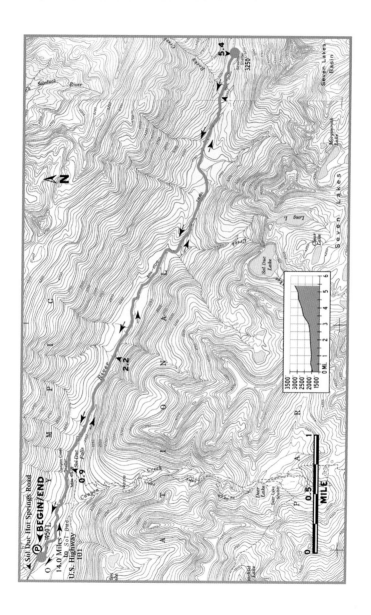

Sol Duc Hot Springs Road

**BEGIN/END**

1950'

14.0 Miles
to Sol Duc–
U.S. Highway 101

O L Y M P I C

N A T I O N A L

P A R K

Soleduck River

0.9

2.2

5.4

1250'

Canyon Creek

Sol Duc Falls

Deer Lake

Sol Duc River

Sol Duc Lake

Long L.

Clear Lake

Morganroth Lake

Seven Lakes Basin

Seven Lakes

N

MILE
0    0.5    1

0 MI.    1    2    3    4    5    6
3500'
3000'
2500'
2000'
1500'

and walk past the campsite to find picnic spots by the river. This area was the site of the Upper Sol Duc Shelter, destroyed by an avalanche in the early 1970s.

## Going Farther

From the Upper Sol Duc the trail climbs above the river, crosses it, and continues to climb in switchbacks to the high country of Lower Sol Duc Park, **6.0** miles from the trailhead and 900 feet higher. It continues to climb past Upper Sol Duc Park, at **7.2** miles, past Heart Lake, at **8.0** miles, to a junction with the High Divide Trail, **8.5** miles from the trailhead. But if you're looking to hike that far, I'd suggest the High Divide Loop (Hike 59). ■

# 59. High Divide Loop

| RATING | DISTANCE | HIKING TIME |
|---|---|---|
| ★★★★★ | 18.8 mile loop | 10 hours |

| ELEVATION GAIN | HIGH POINT | DIFFICULTY |
|---|---|---|
| 3,500 feet | 5,464 feet | ♦♦♦♦◊ |

| BEST SEASON |
|---|
| Jan Feb Mar Apr May **Jun Jul Aug Sep Oct Nov** Dec |

## The Hike

This is the best day hike in the Olympic Mountains, serving up unbeatable views, wildflowers of every color, and elk herds and black bears in the high meadows. It is a long and difficult climb, and should not be attempted as a day hike unless you're in good physical condition.

## Getting There

Drive 30.0 miles west on US Highway 101 from Port Angeles to the Sol Duc Hot Springs Road. Turn left and, after passing the park's fee

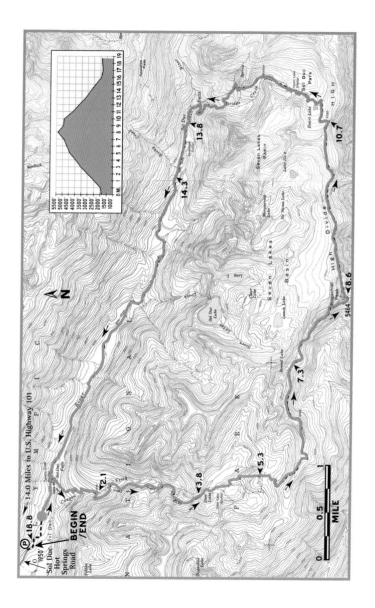

**PERMITS/CONTACT**
None required/Olympic National Park Wilderness Information Center,
(360) 565-3100; Olympic National Park Visitor Center, (360) 565-3130

**MAPS**
USGS Bogachiel Peak, Mount Carrie; Custom Correct Seven Lakes Basin–Hoh;
Green Trails Mount Tom

**TRAIL NOTES**
No dogs or bikes

entrance station, drive 14.0 miles on the Sol Duc Hot Springs Road to the trailhead at the end of the road, located 1,950 feet above sea level.

## The Trail

Take this beautiful loop hike by starting up the Deer Lake Trail and returning via the Upper Sol Duc Trail. The reason is that you gain the alpine splendor in fewer miles and thus may enjoy it longer. The two trails meet at Sol Duc Falls, 0.9 mile from the trailhead. A big reason for hiking this trail in a day is that you're not crowding the backcountry overnight campsites, leaving less of an imprint on this splendid wild country.

Begin by following the Sol Duc River Trail to Sol Duc Falls, 0.9 mile, turning right and crossing the Sol Duc Falls bridge, then climbing to Deer Lake, at **3.8** miles. Keep left at the Little Divide trail junction at the head of the lake and continue to Potholes Meadows (Hike 57), at 5.3 miles, the last certain source of water along the High Divide. The trail switches back up a ridge to the west. Once on the crest, you'll follow it southwest and, at **5.8** miles, reach an open saddle where you can look back to Deer Lake. It's one of the few spots where you can see the second, smaller Deer Lake above the trail.

From the saddle the trail enters the forested ridge above the headwaters of the North Fork of the Bogachiel River. The view opens shortly in a vast alpine basin where, at **6.8** miles, you can see almost a mile of trail ahead as it traverses toward a broad saddle to the west.

If hiking this section in the fall, look for black bear in hillside berry patches and elk in the meadows below.

At **7.3** miles you'll come to a junction with the Seven Lakes Basin Trail. You'll stay right here, but for a good view of the basin, turn left and walk fewer than 200 feet to a rock notch to look down to Lunch and Round Lakes, below. Backtrack to the junction and continue climbing as the trail heads toward Bogachiel Peak. At about **7.5** miles you'll come to a very steep, short climb in a series of switchbacks. This section can be dangerous when still covered by snow; carry an ice ax if you plan this hike before mid-July.

The trail continues to climb, just under Bogachiel Peak, to the broad saddle and a junction with the Hoh Lake Trail at **8.6** miles. The view from the saddle is nothing short of spectacular, with the silver ribbon of the Hoh River a mile below and 7,965-foot Mount Olympus seemingly close enough to hit the Blue Glacier with a rock. Keep to the left here, contouring under Bogachiel Peak for about 0.2 mile to a junction with a short trail that cuts back to the left and leads to the summit of Bogachiel Peak. The flat top of the mountain once held a World War II aircraft spotter's cabin, and the view is well worth the short walk to the summit.

You can look west and, with binoculars on a clear day, see ships on the Pacific Ocean. You can easily see the climbers' route in the snows of Mount Olympus with the naked eye, and with binoculars watch climbers on the Snow Dome of the highest peak in the Olympics. Look east across the crest of High Divide and into the rugged Bailey Range, north to Mount Appleton and Boulder Peak. Bogachiel is nearly the halfway point, but I'd suggest hiking another 2 miles to get almost all your uphill hiking out of the way before taking a break.

Once back on the High Divide Trail, you'll drop steeply to a wide meadow on the ridge crest. There's a campsite here and a shallow tarn just below the trail on the Hoh River side of the ridge. This is the only water on the High Divide, and the tarn may be dry in fall.

The trail begins climbing again and crosses a rocky, double-summited minor peak before switching back steeply down. You'll walk through meadows stretching down to timberline above the

A hiker heads along the Hoh Lake Trail from Bogachiel Peak on the High Divide Loop

Hoh River and at about **10.5** miles, reach a spot where the trail begins to drop steeply to the south.

The flat bench just above the trail at this point makes an excellent picnic spot. With two short exceptions the trail is downhill or flat all the way to the parking lot from this point.

The trail drops steeply from this meadow to a junction with the Heart Lake Trail at **10.7** miles. Turn left at this junction, which should be marked. The High Divide at this point is often covered by lingering snowfields, even into fall, so take care not to miss this junction. You'll know you're on the right path if you crest a low rise to look down at Heart Lake, 11.2 miles from the trailhead. The trail traverses the south side of the lake and begins switching back steeply down beside the outlet stream, the headwaters of the Sol Duc River.

The trail continues its rush with the river to the valley below, dropping constantly to a river crossing at Upper Sol Duc Park. The last time I was here, the footlog across the creek had broken and had not been replaced. Upper Sol Duc Park is the site of a seasonal backcountry ranger station. You'll have hiked 11.7 miles at this point.

You'll begin dropping again through subalpine forest and meadows and cross the infant Sol Duc River at **11.8** miles. Continue descending on the trail into the forest and a final meadow at Lower Sol Duc Park, where you'll cross the river once again on a footlog. Climb from the river canyon and begin a long, rocky-trailed switchbacking descent beside the tumbling Sol Duc to a high footlog crossing, at **13.8** miles from the trailhead.

It was at this very spot several years ago that a foolish, old cross-country skier (me) proceeded to break a snow step while attempting to ford the Sol Duc. I fell face-first into the icy water and—with skis and a four-day backpack to hold me down—had a devil of a time getting up. I might be there still, if it weren't for smiling Gina Binole Miller, who lifted my frozen body upright and got me moving again.

About 0.2 mile past the footlog, you'll drop to the Upper Sol Duc camp, then hike another 0.3 mile to a junction with a trail leading to Appleton Pass. Stay left at this junction and continue rolling down river with the Sol Duc.

At **16.6** miles you'll pass a campsite, cross a footlog into a lowland meadow, and hike through deep forest away from the river. The trail turns back to the river and begins a descending traverse to Sol Duc Shelter and Sol Duc Falls, closing the loop at **17.9** miles. Turn right here. I'll bet you're so pumped you can jog the last 0.9 mile to the parking lot. ■

# OTHER HIKES

The 13.0-mile loop hike over Mount Muller off US Highway 101 and Forest Road 3071 is one of the newest trails in the Olympic Mountains. It's a real workout, but the scenery might make it worthwhile.

The 6.5-mile round-trip climb from the West Snider Road off US Highway 101 takes you to the replica of the old Kloshe Nanitch lookout, also accessible by Forest Road 3040-595. The lookout, rebuilt but a few years earlier, fell in disrepair and was closed in 2011.

# COASTAL RIVERS

# 60. Bogachiel Ranger Station

| RATING | DISTANCE | HIKING TIME |
|---|---|---|
| ★★☆☆☆ | 11.2 miles round-trip | 5.5 hours |
| **ELEVATION GAIN** | **HIGH POINT** | **DIFFICULTY** |
| 170 feet | 450 feet | ◆◇◇◇◇ |

| BEST SEASON |
|---|
| Jan Feb **Mar Apr May Jun** Jul Aug Sep Oct Nov Dec |

## The Hike

This is a good, though often wet, forest walk along the wild Bogachiel River.

## Getting There

Drive west on US 101 from Forks to Bogachiel State Park and turn left on N. Bogachiel/Undi Road. Drive 5.6 miles to the trailhead, located 280 feet above sea level.

## The Trail

Water is no problem on this hike. The first time I walked this trail, I collected at least six gallons of it in my boots as it fell in buckets from the sky. No matter. This is a rain-forest hike and would hardly be complete without a little rain. If you hit it on a sunny day, consider yourself fortunate but deprived.

---

**PERMITS/CONTACT**

Parking pass required/Olympic National Park Wilderness Information Center, (360) 565-3100; Olympic National Park Visitor Center, (360) 565-3130

**MAPS**

USGS Reade Hills, Spruce Mountain; Custom Correct Bogachiel Valley; Green Trails Spruce Mountain

**TRAIL NOTES**

Leashed dogs okay; kid-friendly

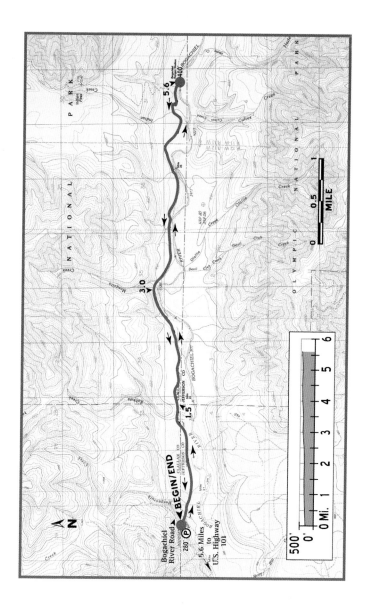

The Bogachiel Trail is one of the pathways that was hammered by storms in 2008. Fallen trees obscured the trail and Olympic National Forest crews and volunteers worked for weeks to reopen the forest path. Today a 3.0-mile nature trail forms a loop at the trailhead and much of the route is in far better condition than it was several years ago. Washington Trails Association volunteers and others continued to improve the trail in 2017.

Begin by dropping to a trail junction just before crossing Morgenroth Creek, named for early forest ranger Chris Morgenroth (often spelled "Morganroth"). Keep left on Olympic National Forest Trail 825.1 and in 1.5 miles, cross Kahkwa Creek and enter Olympic National Park, where hikers with leashed dogs must turn back.

You'll climb over a low hill and drop back to the river, crossing Mosquito Creek at **3.0** miles. The campsite by the river here might make a good turnaround point for families with small children.

Beyond Mosquito Creek, the trail meanders across meadow flatlands to Indian Creek, 5.3 miles from the trailhead. Continue through a forest of huge trees and glowing green mosses draped across vine maples. At **5.5** miles you'll strike a junction with the old Rugged Ridge Trail. Keep right and walk another 0.1 mile to the site of the old Bogachiel Ranger Station, 5.6 miles from the trailhead. The banks above the river here make a good turnaround and picnic spot.

## Going Farther

The Bogachiel River Trail continues for more than 18 miles upstream from the site of the old ranger station, eventually climbing into alpine country to join the Little Divide Trail above Mink Lake. Bogachiel State Park, just across US Highway 101 from the river road, makes a good base car camp for this hike. ∎

# 61. Happy Four Shelter

| RATING | DISTANCE | HIKING TIME |
|---|---|---|
| ★★★★☆ | 11.6 miles round-trip | 5.5 hours |
| **ELEVATION GAIN** | **HIGH POINT** | **DIFFICULTY** |
| 240 feet | 820 feet | ◆◇◇◇◇ |

| BEST SEASON |
|---|
| Jan Feb Mar Apr May Jun Jul Aug Sep Oct Nov Dec |

## The Hike

This is a great walk through the green jungle of the rain forest where you might see elk almost any time of year and almost surely in the winter, when the crowds aren't as great.

## Getting There

From US Highway 101 in Forks drive west to the Upper Hoh River Valley Road and turn left. Follow the Upper Hoh Road for 18.6 miles, past the fee booth at the Olympic National Park to the Hoh River Visitor Center. The trailhead begins next to the center, 580 feet above sea level.

## The Trail

Hikers from dry climes like Arizona or New Mexico may wish to carry snorkels on this walk through one of the wettest spots in the Lower 48. Here is the spot where Gore-Tex is about as useful at keeping you dry as a wet sponge, and an umbrella will serve you better. But that is what the rain forest is all about—rain. If you arrive on a rare sunny day, you must wait until it starts to rain before taking this gentle walk. You can be cited in Clallam County for dry pedestrianism, a gross misdemeanor, if you walk on a sunny day. Feel free to check my research on this.

After leaving the paved nature trail behind, at **0.2** mile, the steepest hill on this trail is encountered in the first mile. You'll climb above

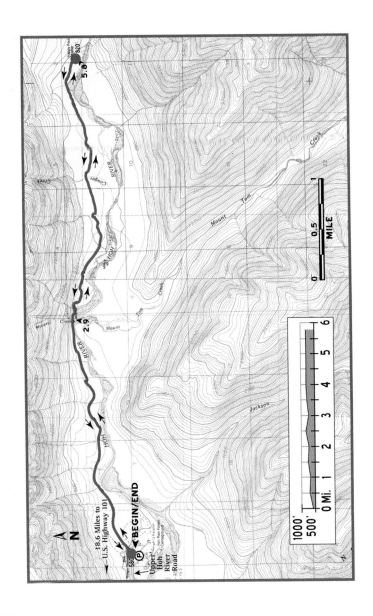

N

MILE
0     0.5     1

0 Mi.  1  2  3  4  5  6

1000'
500'

BEGIN/END

Upper Hoh River River Road

18.6 Miles to U.S. Highway 101

2.9

5.8

820'

580'

HOH RIVER

Cougar Creek

Mineral Creek

Mount Tom Creek

Mount Tom

Jackson

the Hoh River to cross a tributary creek before dropping back to a campsite by the river, 1.1 miles from the trailhead.

From here the trail meanders through bottomland in a forest of giant conifers whose tops are hidden by mists. The filtered light takes on the greenish hue of the mosses draped over bigleaf and vine maple. At **2.9** miles you'll strike a junction with the Mount Tom Trail. Stay left and continue upstream along the wet bottomland to a crossing of Cougar Creek, at **3.1** miles. This might make a good turnaround for families with small children.

Although Olympic National Park trail crews have done an excellent job of providing drainage along the path, there are some times when 1- or 2-inch rainfalls in 24 hours simply can't be accommodated, and you may find yourself skirting large puddles in some of the muddier spots. This is rather optimistic behavior, since it is impossible to walk more than 10 miles on the Hoh River Trail without getting wet. Adopt, instead, the splashing gait of a native mossback. These people simply stow dry clothes in the car and tromp through the mud and water.

Continue upstream to Five-Mile Island, where deer and elk can often be seen in the grassy flats of the river. At the east end of the island the trail climbs gently into forest away from the river and eventually emerges at Happy Four Shelter, which might better have been named Long Five Shelter, since it is **5.8** miles from the trailhead. The shelter itself isn't the best picnic spot unless it is raining hard—that is to say, when you see banana slugs on the trail wearing scuba gear.

For a picnic by the river follow the side trail to the right just before reaching the shelter.

## Going Farther

If you'd like more exercise, you can follow the Hoh River Trail another 3.4 miles to the Olympus Guard Station, which would give you a round-trip walk of 18.4 miles with an elevation gain at least equal to any interstate highway overpass in Kansas. Hoh River Campground, open all year, makes a good base for car-camping while hiking the Hoh River Trail. The visitor center offers an interesting display of plants and animals found in the rain forest. ■

# 62. Big Flat

| RATING | DISTANCE | HIKING TIME |
|---|---|---|
| ★★★★★ | 6.4 miles round-trip | 3 hours |

| ELEVATION GAIN | HIGH POINT | DIFFICULTY |
|---|---|---|
| 110 feet | 800 feet | ◆ ◇ ◇ ◇ ◇ |

| BEST SEASON |
|---|
| Jan Feb Mar Apr May Jun Jul Aug Sep Oct Nov Dec |

## The Hike

The solitude is almost palpable on this rain-forest river walk, where in the winter, elk probably outnumber people.

## Getting There

Drive west on US Highway 101 from Forks to the Clearwater Road, just opposite the Hoh Oxbow Campground. Turn left on the Clearwater Road and drive 7.0 miles to a junction and sign pointing left to the South Fork Campground. Turn left and follow the road past the South Fork Campground 10.4 miles to the end of the road at the trailhead, 800 feet above sea level.

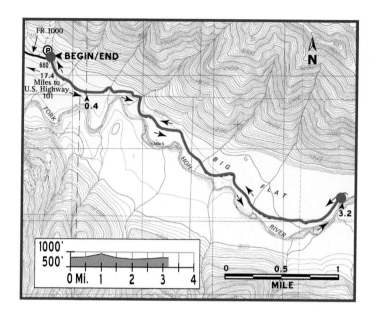

## The Trail

You'll drop from the parking area past an abandoned logging road to flats above the river, crossing the Olympic National Park boundary 0.4 mile from the trailhead. Once in the park, the trail climbs a bit to cross two creeks in a forested bench of evergreens

**PERMITS/CONTACT**
Parking pass required/Olympic National Park Wilderness Information Center,
(360) 565-3100; Olympic National Park Visitor Center, (360) 565-3130

**MAPS**
USGS Mount Tom; Custom Correct Mount Olympus Climber's Map;
Green Trail Mount Tom

**TRAIL NOTES**
Kid-friendly

The trail to the South Fork of the Hoh begins with a gentle descent through the forest

hundreds of years old. One fir next to the trail is more than 11 feet in diameter. At **1.5** miles the trail drops to a big, flat area closer to the river, curiously called Big Flat. From this point to the end of the maintained trail at **3.2** miles, you'll walk in splendid rain-forest river bottom, likely with only wildlife to keep you company. ∎

# OLYMPIC BEACHES

# 63. Cape Alava Loop

| RATING | DISTANCE | HIKING TIME |
|---|---|---|
| ★ ★ ★ ★ ★ | 9.3 miles round-trip | 5 hours |
| **ELEVATION GAIN** | **HIGH POINT** | **DIFFICULTY** |
| 140 feet | 180 feet | ◆ ◆ ◇ ◇ ◇ |

| BEST SEASON |
|---|
| Jan Feb Mar Apr May Jun Jul Aug Sep Oct Nov Dec |

## The Hike

Though I prefer the beaches of Kalaloch, the Cape Alava Loop is probably the finest wild Pacific Coast day hike that you'll find in the Lower 48.

## Getting There

Drive 38.0 miles west of Port Angeles on US Highway 101 to Sappho and turn right on US Highway 112. Follow 112 past the communities of Clallam Bay and Sekiu for 19.6 miles to the Ozette Road, turn left and follow it 20-plus miles to the end of the road. The trailhead is located about 35 feet above sea level.

## The Trail

You'll get no nosebleed from altitude on this great beach walk. Things get crowded around here in the summer, and a growing number of beach hikers brave the cold and wet in the winter. Start by crossing

**PERMITS/CONTACT**
None required/Olympic National Park Wilderness Information Center, (360) 565-3100; Olympic National Park Visitor Center, (360) 565-3130

**MAPS**
USGS Ozette; Custom Correct Ozette Beach Loop; Green Trails Ozette

**TRAIL NOTES**
Kid-friendly

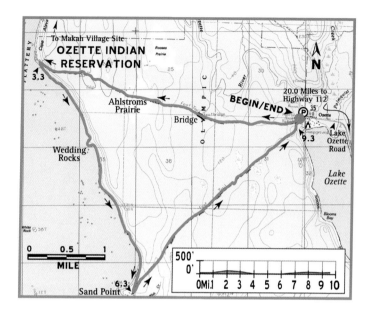

a footbridge over the Ozette River to a trail junction at **0.2** mile. Turn right on the Cape Alava Trail and follow a plank trail to the ocean, 3.3 miles away. Wooden planks on these trails have been replaced by recycled plastic ones, which may not be as slippery as the wooden ones are when wet, which is much of the time.

The big rest spot at **2.3** miles marks Ahlstrom's Prairie, named after the man who built the first plank trail and homesteaded here. Past the prairie the trail drops over a bluff onto the Pacific Ocean.

Some hikers suggest toting hiking boots for the beach section of this hike, since the beach is as much cobbles as sand. The tennis shoes adequate for the plank trail may not be as comfortable on some sections of the beach as heavier boots.

You'll turn south here and walk the beach for 3.0 miles. The beach to the north is within the Ozette Reservation and is closed to the public. After stopping at the beach, families with small children might return on the Cape Alava Trail.

Two hikers cross the Ozette River on their return from Cape Alava

Walk a mile south to Wedding Rocks, where you'll find petroglyphs on two groups of rocks above the high-tide line. High tides here and south, at **4.8** miles, could force you up and over headlands via interesting "sand ladders."

Once past the second headland, you'll walk sandy beach south to Sand Point, 6.3 miles from the trailhead. Turn left here and find the trail inland, marked by a round target.

From here it is 3.0 miles back to the trailhead via a plank pathway.

## Going Farther

You can walk the beach for more than 16 miles south from Sand Point, along a coastline that is untouched by roads. Day hikers might car camp at Ozette Campground for further exploration. ∎

# 64. Hole-in-the-Wall

| RATING ★★★★☆ | DISTANCE 5.0 miles round-trip | HIKING TIME 2.5 hours |
|---|---|---|
| ELEVATION GAIN 80 feet | HIGH POINT 80 feet | DIFFICULTY ◆◇◇◇◇ |
| BEST SEASON | | |
| Jan  Feb  Mar  Apr  May  Jun  Jul  Aug  Sep  Oct  Nov  Dec | | |

## The Hike

This beach walk follows smooth sand all the way to a big rocky headland that can be passed at low tide by walking through a natural tunnel carved by the surf.

## Getting There

From US Highway 101, just north of Forks, turn west on the La Push–Mora Road, US Highway 110, and follow the signs to Mora and Rialto Beach, turning right at Three Rivers. Drive past the Mora Campground to Rialto Beach. The trailhead is about 20 feet above sea level.

## The Trail

This walk begins on a plastic plank path that gives wheelchair hikers a chance to look out at the Pacific Ocean. After **0.2** mile you'll cross to a sandy beach on a cobblestone apron furnished by the Pacific. Once on the beach, head to the right, aiming for the big rock that marks

---

**PERMITS/CONTACT**
None required/Olympic National Park Wilderness Information Center, (360) 565-3100; Olympic National Park Visitor Center, (360) 565-3130

**MAPS**
USGS La Push

**TRAIL NOTES**
Leashed dogs okay; kid-friendly

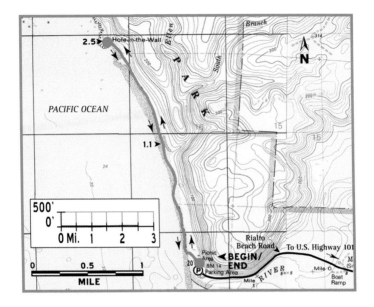

the northern end of the bay. At **0.6** mile you'll cross Ellen Creek. Leashed dogs are not allowed beyond this point.

Hole-in-the-Wall is another 1.4 miles on sandy beach. If the tide is high, look for a trail climbing steeply to the right. The trail climbs up and over the rock to drop to the beach again; if the tide is out, you can avoid this climb by walking through the Hole-in-the-Wall.

## Going Farther

The beach trail follows the wild Pacific coastline north for more than 16 miles to Cape Alava. Day hikers seeking a longer walk from Rialto Beach might make the Chilean Memorial, 1.2 miles beyond Hole-in-the-Wall, their goal. The Mora Campground makes a good car-camping base to explore other beach walks in the area. ■

## 65. Second Beach

| RATING | DISTANCE | HIKING TIME |
|---|---|---|
| ★★★☆☆ | 4.2 miles round-trip | 2.5 hours |

| ELEVATION GAIN | HIGH POINT | DIFFICULTY |
|---|---|---|
| 120 feet | 200 feet | ◆◇◇◇◇ |

| BEST SEASON |
|---|
| Jan Feb Mar Apr May Jun Jul Aug Sep Oct Nov Dec |

### The Hike

Take a short walk through dense forest to a wild Pacific beach decorated by rocky offshore spires.

### Getting There

From US Highway 101, just north of Forks, turn west on the La Push–Mora Road, US Highway 110, and follow the signs to La Push. The trailhead is located 12.7 miles from US Highway 101, just east of La Push, about 200 feet above sea level.

Spires off Second Beach

## PERMITS/CONTACT
Parking pass required/Olympic National Park Wilderness Information Center,
(360) 565-3100; Olympic National Park Visitor Center, (360) 565-3130

## MAPS
USGS La Push; Custom Correct South Olympic Coast; Green Trails La Push

## TRAIL NOTES
Kid-friendly

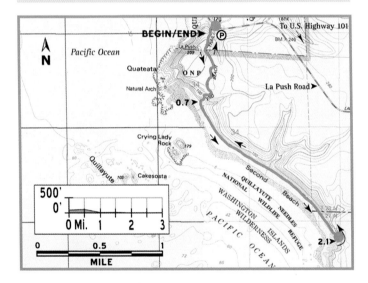

## The Trail

You'll hike through forest so thick it reduces the sound of the surf, less than a half-mile away, to a murmur. The trail drops to the beach at **0.7** mile, and if you're feeling lazy, there's really little reason to hike farther because the view here is awesome: The Quillayute Needles jab from the surf and the beach stretches to the south. You can turn left and walk down the beach for 1.4 miles before you'll have to climb over steep headlands at high tides. The way south ends at Teahwhit Head, which is impassable. ∎

## 66. Third Beach

| RATING | DISTANCE | HIKING TIME |
|---|---|---|
| ★☆☆☆☆ | 3.6 miles round-trip | 2 hours |

| ELEVATION GAIN | HIGH POINT | DIFFICULTY |
|---|---|---|
| 120 feet | 120 feet | ◆◇◇◇◇ |

| BEST SEASON |
|---|
| Jan Feb Mar Apr May Jun Jul Aug Sep Oct Nov Dec |

### The Hike

Climb down a crowded, wide trail to a plank staircase leading to a short sandy beach.

### Getting There

From US Highway 101, just north of Forks, turn west on the La Push–Mora Road, US Highway 110, and follow the signs to La Push. The trailhead is 11.3 miles from US Highway 101, about 200 feet above sea level.

### The Trail

The trail to Third Beach leads through forest dense enough to turn the brightest day dark. You'll follow a wide path for **1.4** miles to the beach before descending on a plank staircase. The sandy beach to the left

**PERMITS/CONTACT**

None required/Olympic National Park Wilderness Information Center, (360) 565-3100; Olympic National Park Visitor Center, (360) 565-3130

**MAPS**

USGS La Push; Custom Correct South Olympic Coast; Green Trails La Push

**TRAIL NOTES**

Kid-friendly

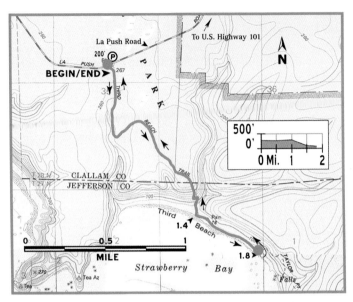

Beaches north of Kalaloch are popular with smelt fishers in late summer

extends for about 0.4 mile, the turnaround spot unless you'd like to hike another 1.2 miles on forest trail before returning to a second 0.6-mile-long beach. Third Beach is popular with backpackers who make the 17-mile trek to Oil City, climbing more than a half-dozen headlands. ■

# 67. Kalaloch North

| RATING | DISTANCE | HIKING TIME |
|---|---|---|
| ★★★★☆ | 4.8 miles round-trip | 2.5 hours |

| ELEVATION GAIN | HIGH POINT | DIFFICULTY |
|---|---|---|
| 100 feet | 100 feet | ♦◆◆◆◆ |

| BEST SEASON |
|---|
| Jan Feb Mar Apr May Jun Jul Aug Sep Oct Nov Dec |

## The Hike

The beaches north of Kalaloch are wide and sandy, and most headlands are passable at low tide. Leashed dogs are permitted on all beaches between the Hoh and Quinault Rivers.

## Getting There

Kalaloch is located on US Highway 101, 65.0 miles north of Aberdeen and 35.0 miles south of Forks. Best access to the beaches at Kalaloch is from the picnic area at Kalaloch Campground, about 80 feet above sea level. The campground is open year-round and offers garbage cans and fresh water (not available at the picnic area). It makes an excellent car-camping base for exploring Kalaloch beaches.

## The Trail

First thing: You've got to pronounce Kalaloch like a local. Say *clay lock*. The beach walk to the north of Kalaloch Campground is along uninterrupted sandy beach for 2.4 miles to rocks that can be rounded at low tide. These rocks also form tide pools that harbor

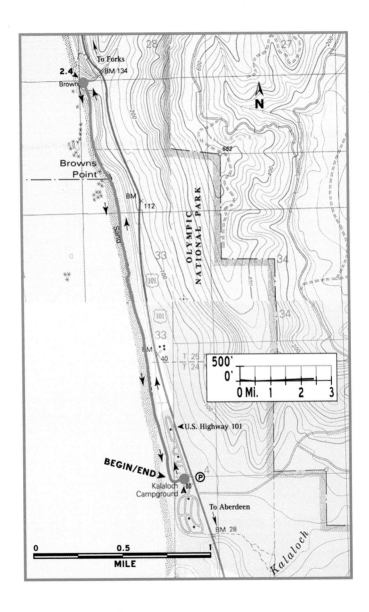

To Forks
BM 134

**2.4**
Brown

Browns
Point

BM K 112

Sand

OLYMPIC
NATIONAL PARK

682

28

27

33

101

101

33

40

T 25
T 24

**500'**
**0'**

**0 Mi.** 1 2 3

34

34

◄ U.S. Highway 101

**BEGIN/END** ►

ⓟ

Kalaloch
Campground

80'

4

To Aberdeen

BM 28

Kalaloch

0                    0.5                    1
**MILE**

a bunch of gooey but interesting intertidal marine life. Most of the beach beyond can be hiked at low tide for almost 5 miles. If you'd rather, you can get to individual beaches north of Kalaloch by parking at any of five well-marked areas along US Highway 101. Short trails lead down to the beaches. ∎

## 68. Kalaloch South

| RATING | DISTANCE | HIKING TIME |
|---|---|---|
| ★★★★ | 8.0 miles round-trip | 4 hours |
| **ELEVATION GAIN** | **HIGH POINT** | **DIFFICULTY** |
| 100 feet | 100 feet | ◆ |

| BEST SEASON |
|---|
| Jan Feb Mar Apr May Jun Jul Aug Sep Oct Nov Dec |

### The Hike
By wading the shallow Kalaloch Creek, you can hike south along wide stretches of sand for at least 4 miles, stopping to investigate the tide pools of Kalaloch Rocks. Leashed dogs are permitted on all beaches between the Hoh and Quinault Rivers.

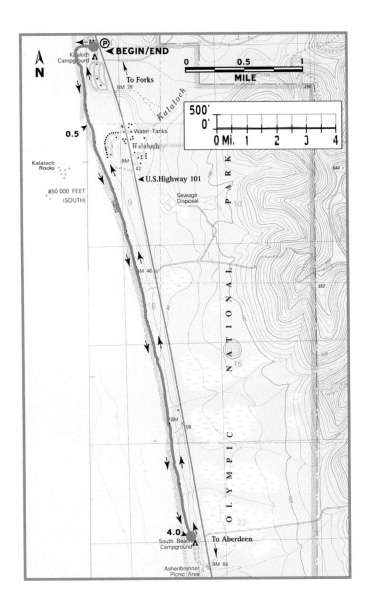

N

Kalaloch
Campground

BEGIN/END

← BM

P

To Forks

BM 28

Kalaloch

0    0.5    1
MILE

0.5

Water Tanks

Kalaloch

Kalaloch
Rocks

BM
42

850 000 FEET
(SOUTH)

U.S. Highway 101

Sewage
Disposal

500'
0'

0 Mi.  1    2    3    4

NATIONAL

PARK

BM 46

16

OLYMPIC

BM 58

4.0
South Beach
Campground

To Aberdeen

BM 64

Ashenbrenner
Picnic Area

**PERMITS/CONTACT**
None required/Olympic National Park Wilderness Information Center,
(360) 565-3100; Olympic National Park Visitor Center, (360) 565-3130

**MAPS**
USGS Destruction Island; Custom Correct South Olympic Coast

**TRAIL NOTES**
Leashed dogs okay; kid-friendly

## Getting There

Kalaloch is located on US Highway 101, 65.0 miles north of Aberdeen and 35.0 miles south of Forks. Best access to the beaches at Kalaloch is from the picnic area at Kalaloch Campground, about 80 feet above sea level. The campground is open year-round and offers garbage cans and fresh water (not available at the picnic area). It makes an excellent car-camping base for exploring Kalaloch beaches.

## The Trail

Begin by wading across ankle-deep Kalaloch Creek and walking **0.5** mile to Kalaloch Rocks, where you can find orange and purple starfishes, sea anemones, and a whole bunch of other marine life I'll bet you know better than me. The way to the south past Kalaloch Rocks is open beach for at least 4 miles to the boundary of Olympic National Park at the South Beach Campground, used in the summer for overflow camping from Kalaloch. Beaches south of Kalaloch can also be explored via two well-marked parking areas and a trail to the south of Kalaloch Resort on US Highway 101. ■

# QUINAULT RIVER

Please note, some of these trails may have been affected by recent weather patterns and repairs may be underway. Always call ahead to guarantee trail accessibility.

# 69. Colonel Bob

| RATING | DISTANCE | HIKING TIME |
|--------|----------|-------------|
| ★★☆☆☆ | **8.4 miles round-trip** | **5 hours** |
| **ELEVATION GAIN** | **HIGH POINT** | **DIFFICULTY** |
| **3,520 feet** | **4,492 feet** | ◆◆◆◆◇ |

| BEST SEASON |
|-------------|
| Jan Feb Mar Apr May **Jun Jul Aug Sep** Oct Nov Dec |

## The Hike
This is a steep climb to a spectacular viewpoint overlooking the Quinault Valley and Lake and offering a rare glimpse from the west of Mount Olympus.

## Getting There
Follow US Highway 101 for 25.0 miles north to the Donkey Creek Road, Forest Road 22, and turn right. Drive 8.0 miles to Forest Road 2204, turn left past the Humptulips Work Center and drive 12.5 miles to the Pete's Creek Trail No. 858, on the left. The trailhead is located at 970 feet above sea level.

## The Trail
This tough climb seldom gives you time to catch your breath after you cross the Colonel Bob Wilderness boundary at **0.1** mile and

---

**PERMITS/CONTACT**
Parking pass required/Quinault Ranger Station, (360) 288-2444

**MAPS**
USGS Quinault, Grisdale; Custom Correct Quinault–Colonel Bob;
Green Trails Quinault Lake, Grisdale

**TRAIL NOTES**
Leashed dogs okay

---

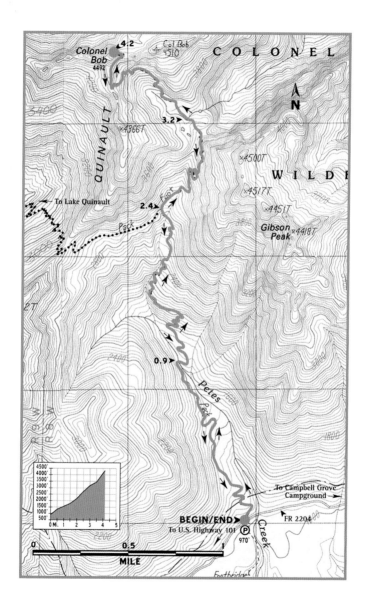

Colonel Bob 4492

4.2

Col Bob 4510

COLONEL

N

3400

×4966T

QUINAULT

3.2▸

×5007T

WILDE

×4517T

To Lake Quinault

Foot

2.4×

Pack

×4451T

Gibson Peak ×4418T

0.9▸

2400

2T

R O W . P.

Petes

Pack

4500'
4000'
3500'
3000'
2500'
2000'
1500'
1000'
500'
0 Mi. 1 2 3 4 5

To Campbell Grove Campground

FR 2204

BEGIN/END▸
To U.S. Highway 101    P
970'

Creek

1800

0

0.5

MILE

Footbridge

cross Pete's Creek at **0.9** mile. You'll continue climbing steeply along the hillside under Gibson Peak and get a glimpse of the territory crossing an avalanche path at **1.5** miles. The trail doesn't let up, climbing up another avalanche chute into open slopes to a trail junction at **2.4** miles. Bear right at the junction and continue to climb steep slopes past a silver forest before dropping slightly and crossing Moonshine Flats at **3.2** miles.

You'll begin to climb again after crossing a stream on a rocky trail to a narrow saddle south of the rocky summit, then traverse across the rock to make the final climb along a ridge from the east. The summit at **4.2** miles once held a lookout and is a good picnic spot with views in all directions.

## Going Farther

There is the possibility of a one-way trip from the Moonshine Flats area, provided you can convince a strong hiker with a second car to climb the longer, more strenuous route from the Colonel Bob trailhead on the South Shore Lake Quinault Road. A one-way hike for both parties to the trail junction, up to the summit and return, would be 10.0 miles. ■

Campbell Grove Campground is a quiet retreat among Really Big Trees, just east of Pete's Creek trailhead to Colonel Bob

## 70. Big Creek

| RATING | DISTANCE | HIKING TIME |
|:---:|:---:|:---:|
| ★★★☆☆ | 8.0 miles round-trip | 4 hours |
| **ELEVATION GAIN** | **HIGH POINT** | **DIFFICULTY** |
| 840 feet | 1,340 feet | ♦♦◇◇◇ |

| BEST SEASON |
|:---:|
| Jan Feb Mar Apr May Jun Jul Aug Sep Oct Nov Dec |

## The Hike

Climb into the fringes of one of the most remote regions of Olympic National Park—the rugged Skyline Trail—to a tumbling mountain stream or, 2.0 miles farther, a really big Alaska cedar.

## Getting There

Turn east of US Highway 101 onto South Shore Road, located just north of Neilton. Drive 12.8 miles to a bridge spanning the Quinault River, cross the bridge and turn right on the North Shore Road. Drive 3.3 miles to the trailhead, 519 feet above sea level. The trailhead can also be reached via the rough, narrow North Shore Road, which is posted with signs warning it is unsuitable for RVs and trailers.

## The Trail

A startling scene awaited me as I stopped at the trailhead to Big Creek: where once a shady forested canopy welcomed hikers headed

**PERMITS/CONTACT**
None required/Olympic National Park Wilderness Information Center,
(360) 565-3100; Olympic National Park Visitor Center, (360) 565-3130

**MAPS**
USGS Mount Christie; Custom Correct Colonel Bob; Green Trails Mount Christie

**TRAIL NOTES**
Kid-friendly

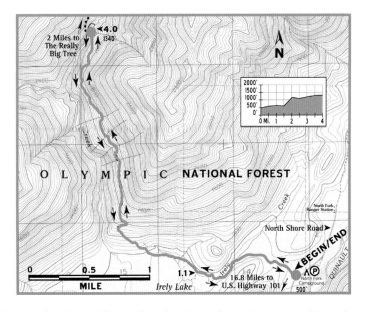

to Irely Lake and beyond, today the trail is a dusty or muddy path through a brushy maze of broken spruce and cedar. The trail is one of the victims brutalized by coastal winter storms and the rain forest is no longer—at least on several sections of the trail. The North Fork of the Quinault River and the mountains that hunker above are some of the wildest territory remaining on the Olympic Peninsula. The Skyline Trail follows a rugged ridge above the river to its headwaters at Low Divide.

Start by hiking the flat turnpike trail for 0.7 mile to Irely Creek and, in another 0.4 mile, to a junction with a side trail leading to Irely Lake. At **1.1** miles, this lowland lake contains trout and might be the best turnaround point for families with small children. Bugs are not as great a problem in the fall, and the red huckleberries and thimbleberries around the lake are easy pickings. Irely is also the first likely spot to see wildlife around here, including beaver in the lake and giant osprey above.

Hikers bound for Big Creek should keep right and begin to climb steeply above the creek for another 2.9 miles before crossing the stream. At **4.0** miles, this is a good turnaround for most day hikers.

## Going Farther
Pedestrians seeking a longer walk to a wet subalpine basin can cross the creek and begin climbing in steep switchbacks for 1.8 miles. Here the trail makes a more gentle entrance into the basin, where it passes the largest recorded Alaska cedar in the world, 6.0 miles from the trailhead. Beyond, the Skyline Trail continues to climb steeply another mile to a camp below Three Lakes, then turns along the ridge and alternately climbs and drops for another 22.0 miles to Low Divide. ■

# 71. Halfway House

| RATING | DISTANCE | HIKING TIME |
|---|---|---|
| ★★★☆☆ | 10.2 miles round-trip | 5 hours |

| ELEVATION GAIN | HIGH POINT | DIFFICULTY |
|---|---|---|
| 430 feet | 950 feet | ♦ ◇ ◇ ◇ ◇ |

| BEST SEASON |
|---|
| Jan Feb Mar Apr May Jun Jul Aug Sep Oct Nov Dec |

## The Hike
This is a rain-forest walk past massive, moss-laden trees along a clear mountain river, with options for both shorter and longer hikes to destinations along the river.

## Getting There
Turn east of US Highway 101 onto the South Shore Road, located just north of Neilton. Drive 12.8 miles to a bridge spanning the Quinault River, cross the bridge and turn right on the North Shore Road. Drive 3.3 miles to the trailhead, 519 feet above sea level. The trailhead can

also be reached via the rough, narrow North Shore Road, which is posted with signs warning it is unsuitable for RVs and trailers.

## The Trail

This is a good trail for wildlife watching, especially in late fall or early spring. It's also a trail where you should consider yourself lucky if you walk it on a day without some rain.

Begin by following an abandoned road as it climbs from the parking area to cross a stream at **0.2** mile then following a bench above the river before dropping to meander along a green floodplain above the river. The trail crosses two dry watercourses along the way where a really stupid hiker could get completely turned around in the dark at 4 a.m. and begin walking the wrong direction—but I caught my mistake shortly thereafter.

At **2.5** miles the trail strikes a junction with a side path leading to Wolf Bar. This grassy meadow beside the river makes an excellent picnic spot and turnaround point for families with small children. Beyond Wolf Bar, the trail alternately climbs and descends forests along a hillside away from the river. You'll hear the rushing Quinault, but it is sometimes difficult to see through the thick forest.

The North Fork Quinault Trail seems more rocky to me than most Olympic trails, and I'm always footsore and stone-bruised when I return. This is a river trail where sturdy boots might serve hikers best. You'll cross several wide footbridges over a couple of creeks that drop in steep canyons to the river. The last bridge spans Wild Rose Creek, at **4.9** miles from the trailhead.

---

**PERMITS/CONTACT**
None required/Olympic National Park Wilderness Information Center,
(360) 565-3100; Olympic National Park Visitor Center, (360) 565-3130

**MAPS**
USGS Mount Christie; Custom Correct Colonel Bob; Green Trails Mount Christie

**TRAIL NOTES**
Kid-friendly

---

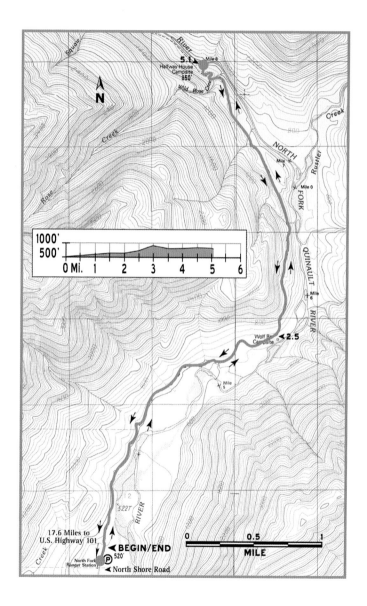

River

5.1

Mile 8

Halfway House
Campsite
850'

Wild Rose Creek

Shale

Creek

Rose

Creek

NORTH

Mile 7

Rustler

Creek

FORK

Mile 6

QUINAULT

RIVER

Mile 5

Wolf Bar
Campsite ◀2.5

Mile 5

1000'
500'

0 Mi.  1   2   3   4   5   6

5227

RIVER

17.6 Miles to
U.S. Highway 101

◀BEGIN/END

Ⓟ 520'

North Fork
Ranger Station

◀North Shore Road

Creek

0                    0.5                    1

MILE

Here the trail drops to green bottomland beside the river again, offering a number of great picnic spots 5.1 miles from the trailhead. This was the site of Halfway House, a commercial lodge operated in the 1920s for hikers bound for Low Divide, long since disappeared.

## Going Farther
The North Fork Quinault Trail continues another 11.0 miles upstream to Low Divide, alternately climbing and dropping along the river to a spot 12.2 miles from the trailhead, where it fords the river and begins to climb steeply to the divide. Beyond Halfway House, turnaround destinations might include Elip Creek Camp, 6.4 miles from the trailhead; Kimta Creek, 7.7 miles from the trailhead; and Trapper Shelter, 8.2 miles from the trailhead. ■

# 72. Pony Bridge

| RATING | DISTANCE | HIKING TIME |
|--------|----------|-------------|
| ★★☆☆☆ | 5.0 miles round-trip | 2.5 hours |
| ELEVATION GAIN | HIGH POINT | DIFFICULTY |
| 575 feet | 1,175 feet | ♦♦◇◇◇ |
| BEST SEASON | | |
| Jan Feb Mar Apr May Jun Jul Aug Sep Oct Nov Dec | | |

## The Hike
Walk up an abandoned road through forest to a picnic spot above the river, then switchback down to a high log bridge crossing the East Fork of the Quinault River.

## Getting There
Turn east of US Highway 101 onto South Shore Road, located just north of Neilton. Drive 19.1 miles to the end of Graves Creek Road, 600 feet above sea level.

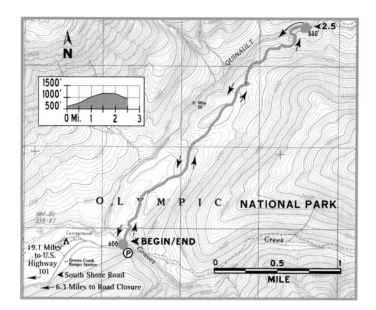

## The Trail

Start by crossing Graves Creek and begin a long, gentle uphill grade along the abandoned road, climbing left past a junction with the Graves Creek Trail at **0.1** mile. The wide, cobbled path climbs in a broad curve along a hillside away from the river.

**PERMITS/CONTACT**
None required/Olympic National Park Wilderness Information Center, (360) 565-3100; Olympic National Park Visitor Center, (360) 565-3130

**MAPS**
USGS Mount Christie, Mount Steel; Custom Correct Enchanted Valley–Skokomish; Green Trails Mount Christie, Mount Steel

**TRAIL NOTES**
Kid-friendly

The trail reaches a high point as it turns back toward the Quinault at **2.4** miles. There's a picnic table and wide bench overlooking the narrow river canyon below at the end of the abandoned road. If you wish, follow the trail another 0.2 mile from this point as it switches back to a log bridge above the steep-walled canyon. This is the turn-around point for most day hikers.

## Going Farther

You can walk up this fork of the Quinault for more than 18 miles to Anderson Pass, but day hikers might choose Fire Creek, 3.5 miles from the trailhead, as a saner alternative. Beyond Fire Creek the trail climbs over a forested hump and returns to a spot above the river at 4.3 miles. Several picnic spots might be found at campsites along the river past here to O'Neil Creek, 6.7 miles from the trailhead. ■

The East Fork of the Quinault River carves through a rocky gorge under the Pony Bridge

# 73. Low Divide–Elwha

| RATING | DISTANCE | HIKING TIME |
|---|---|---|
| ★★★★☆ | 44.5 miles point-to-point | 17 hours |
| ELEVATION GAIN | HIGH POINT | DIFFICULTY |
| 3,800 feet | 3,600 feet | ◆◆◆◆◆ |

| BEST SEASON |
|---|
| Jan Feb Mar Apr May Jun **Jul Aug** Sep Oct Nov Dec |

Unless the Olympic Hot Springs and Whiskey Bend Roads are not open—tentatively scheduled for October 2023—this hike would be about 53 miles.

## The Hike

This is the ultimate day hike, an extreme one-way challenge that follows the North Fork Quinault Trail to Low Divide, then follows the Elwha Trail to the Elwha trailhead, a total of 44.5 miles.

## Getting There

This one-way hike requires two cars or a pickup at the Elwha River trailhead, 1,100 feet above sea level. The Elwha River trailhead is located at the end of Whiskey Bend Road, 9.0 miles up the Olympic Hot Spring and Whiskey Bend Roads from US Highway 101, 7.5 miles west of Port Angeles. The North Fork trailhead is located at the

### PERMITS/CONTACT
None required/Olympic National Park Wilderness Information Center, (360) 565-3100; Olympic National Park Visitor Center, (360) 565-3130

### MAPS
USGS Mount Christie, Mount Steel, Mount Angeles, Hurricane Hill; Custom Correct Quinault–Colonel Bob, Elwha Valley; Green Trails Mount Christie, Mount Steel, Mount Angeles, Hurricane Hill

### TRAIL NOTES
No dogs or bikes

end of North Shore Road, reached by following South Shore Road off US Highway 101 for 12.8 miles to a bridge and turning right on North Shore Road, driving 3.3 miles to the trailhead, 520 feet above sea level.

## The Trail

Now, before you have me committed, let me assure you that any adult in very good physical condition can make this hike in a single day. Although you must maintain a 3.0-mile-per-hour pace for fifteen hours, it isn't the length of this hike that can stop you. A more likely difficulty would be bruised feet, blisters, or perhaps pulled or strained muscles.

Why bother inflicting this kind of pain on yourself? Two main reasons come to mind:

- You can see beautiful parts of Olympic National Park that you likely will never see unless you have time for a seven- to nine-day backpack.
- You'll gain the confidence and knowledge that no matter what lies on the trail ahead, you can handle it. You will have accomplished something many nonhikers might regard as impossible.

Begin by parking a car at the Elwha trailhead or arranging for a pickup there, then drive to the North Fork Quinault trailhead. The primitive campground 0.5 mile from the trailhead is now closed, but you won't likely be hassled by sleeping in your car or tenting next to the seasonal ranger station at the trailhead. You'll need to start hiking at 4 a.m. in order to leave a margin of daylight at the end of the trail. I've done this hike twice, first in my fiftieth year and second in my fifty-first, when forty others accompanied me. I'm telling you this not to brag, but to let you know that if it can be done by an old fart like me, you won't have the problems you're imagining you'll have right now.

I had hoped to try this hike again with a group of hardy Scouts from Bremerton's Troop 1549 in 2004, at age 62. I trained hard and felt strong, but the farthest I could hike without crippling foot pain was 24 miles, so I chickened out. Four of the Scouts and leaders

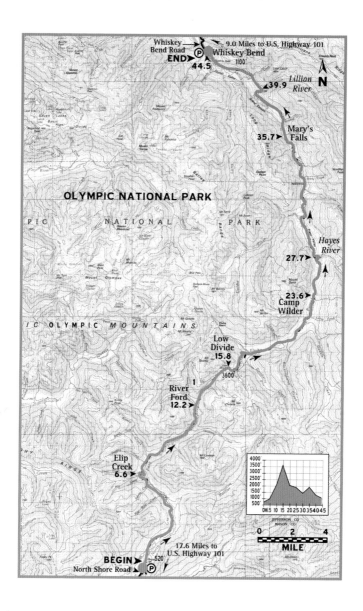

Whiskey —
Bend Road ▶
**END** ⓟ
**44.5**
◀ 9.0 Miles to U.S. Highway 101
Whiskey Bend
1100'

**N**

▶**39.9**
*Lillian
River*

**35.7**▶
*Mary's
Falls*

**OLYMPIC NATIONAL PARK**

P I C        N A T I O N A L        P A R K

*Hayes
River*

**27.7**▶

**23.6**▶
Camp
Wilder

I C   O L Y M P I C   M O U N T A I N S

Low
Divide
▶**15.8**
3600'

River
Ford
**12.2**▶

1

Elip
Creek
**6.6**▶

4000'
3500'
3000'
2500'
2000'
1500'
1000'
500'
0MI.5 10 15 20 25 30 35 40 45

JEFFERSON CO.
MASON CO.

0        2        4
**MILE**

17.6 Miles to
U.S. Highway 101
**BEGIN** ▶
North Shore Road ▶
520'

made the trek, the remaining eleven Scouts bivouacked at the Lillian River bridge, after hiking more than 40 miles.

Take a look at the map: You start at 520 feet above sea level and climb to the high point at Low Divide, 3,600 feet above sea level, in 15.8 miles. With one major exception it's all downhill or flat from this point—28.7 miles of essentially excellent trail along the Elwha River. When I planned my hikes, I allowed 2 hours for rest stops consisting of 5 minutes every hour and two 20-minute breaks for meals. The hourly stops are essential for marathon walks like this. That means you'll spend 17 hours on the trail. Here's a brief trail log and schedule to consider:

**4:00 a.m.**—Leave North Fork Quinault Trail by flashlight. Sunrise in midsummer here is about 4:30 a.m. It was in dry creekbeds in a fog less than a mile from the trailhead that I somehow got turned around 180 degrees and nearly walked back to the parking lot before I discovered the mistake. Keep right at all trail junctions from the trailhead to Low Divide.

**8:30 a.m.**—Ford the Quinault River, 12.2 miles from the trailhead. The ford is usually calf-deep in midsummer. A second creek must be forded about 2.0 miles farther.

**10:30 a.m.**—Arrive at Low Divide for a 20-minute rest stop. This is the point of no return, 15.8 miles from the trailhead, because if you turn back beyond this point, you'll face 3.0 miles of steep killer uphill and a rocky, rootbound trail back to the trailhead. Follow the trail to Lake Margaret, where you descend on a steep, rocky trail to Chicago Camp on the Elwha River, 3.0 miles below.

**Noon**—Ford the Elwha River to Chicago Camp and follow the Elwha Trail downriver, keeping right at the junction with the Elwha Basin Trail at Chicago Camp. The Elwha Trail from Chicago Camp to the Elwha trailhead is generally smooth and well-maintained; many of the forty hikers with me wore running shoes on this section. A final ford of the Elwha is necessary about 1.5 miles below Chicago Camp.

**3:00 p.m.**—Arrive at Hayes River, 27.7 miles from the trailhead. The last half-mile to a junction with the Hayden Pass Trail above Hayes River is up a gradual grade. Turn left at the trail junction and drop to the Hayes River Guard Station on the Elwha River.

**4:15 p.m.**—Arrive at Remann's Cabin on the Elwha River Trail for a 20-minute break, 31.5 miles from the trailhead. You've only 13.0 miles to go!

**6:00 p.m.**—Arrive at Mary's Falls on the Elwha River Trail, 35.7 miles from the trailhead. The trail begins a 2.0-mile climb over a hill above the Elwha River.

**7:30 p.m.**—Begin the short but steep switchback climb from the Lillian Bridge 0.6 mile to a junction with the Lillian Trail. Keep left.

**8:30 p.m.**—Pass Michael's Cabin, 42.8 miles from the trailhead. Keep right at all trail junctions from this point to the Elwha trailhead.

**9:00 p.m.**—Arrive at the Elwha trailhead at 44.5 miles. Consume ibuprofen. Find a hot tub.

High fives. Hugs. ■

# BEYOND THE TRAILS

Most off-trail hiking in the Olympic Mountains is beyond the reach of day hikers. That is a shame because finding your own path through the Olympic wilds is possibly the only true means of gaining the solitude and primitive wilderness the first white exploring parties found little more than a hundred years ago. Strong, experienced day hikers in excellent physical condition, however, will find several off-trail routes that can be navigated in a long summer or early autumn day. These hikes are reserved for those who can find the way without relying on those who have gone before them, that is, those who can read topographic maps and navigate with a compass.

If you choose to try one of the three hikes that follow, you should be comfortable traveling on steep, exposed snow and scree or rock fields. You should be prepared to do battle with brush and be able to stop yourself with an ice ax in the event of a slide on steep snow. You can expect to encounter obstacles such as deadfall in forests, steep cliffs that must be bypassed, and snowfields to be climbed. Day hikers planning to try one of these hikes would certainly benefit from a basic mountaineering class—not necessarily from the climbing skills they learn, but from the confidence they gain by hiking beyond the trails. Perhaps the only gear you'll want to add to your day pack— assuming you're carrying the Ten Essentials (see Introduction)—is an ice ax. Although the routes outlined here can be safely traversed without adding any gear to your day pack, carrying and knowing how to use an ice ax for self-arrest can greatly improve your comfort level on short passages of these routes.

Sections of road closed in the past three decades makes the Boulder Lake to Appleton Pass hike longer and more difficult than it once was. Taking these hikes will require covering those added miles of road and established trail quickly, leaving enough time to traverse the off-trail portion. Before attempting them, you should be able to maintain a 3-mile-per-hour pace on established trails—regardless of their steepness or condition. For the off-trail portion of these hikes, I'm assuming you should be able to move an average of about a mile every hour. In wide-open alpine terrain you'll undoubtedly move faster.

I'd heartily recommend planning these walks only when there's an excellent chance of clear, sunny weather. After all, there's little point in wandering around in fog and sleet when the spectacular vistas are the major reasons for the hike. Navigating with poor visibility could also slow your pace so much that you'll end up finishing by flashlight. Finally, although these routes involve some sort of loop hike, keep in mind that you needn't follow the entire route. You can turn around at any point and still enjoy a day hike beyond the trails. The walks take you past alpine lakes or along scenic ridges that make ideal places to stop short of the halfway point.

## Obstruction Point to Gladys Lake

Here's a great alpine hike that involves scrambling over the tops of several 6,700-foot peaks with splendid views of the Grand Valley below and a choice of returning via established trail. It is the easiest hike of the three mentioned here and makes a great introduction to off-trail adventure. The total distance on-trail is 6.0 miles; off-trail hiking is about 2.5 miles, with perhaps 2,500 feet of elevation gain.

Begin by hiking the trail to Moose Lake (Hike 39). The trail first climbs, then drops, then climbs south from the parking lot to a 6,450-foot high point 1.5 miles from the trailhead. Here, at the point where the trail rounds the shoulder of a ridge and begins a long descending traverse to Grand Valley, is where you leave the trail. Follow a faint side-trail that turns right as the main trail rounds the ridge to the left. This trail drops about 20 feet to a flat saddle and fades out as it begins to climb a sharp ridge leading to the peak immediately south of the established trail.

Climb to the summit ridge of this peak, which is broad and flat, and follow the ridge through alpine evergreens to the south. You'll emerge from the brush as the ridge drops to another saddle. Descend and cross to a second peak and look for a faint way trail that traverses under the east side of this peak. Follow the trail or climb over the second peak, staying on the crest of the ridge, which will now grow increasingly steep on both sides. From the low point on the ridge, an obvious notch marked by reddish rock on either side, two routes are possible.

The first route follows a rocky, steep gully that descends to a flat alpine basin to the northeast, to the left. Then traverse scree and talus slopes before climbing back to the ridge and over the 6,701-foot peak via its distinctive permanent snowfield along its west-facing shoulder. Once over the peak, you'll drop along the ridgeline to a wide, flat saddle that overlooks the trail to Grand Pass less than a quarter-mile above Gladys Lake.

The second route from the low point on the ridge descends about 250 feet into subalpine forest to the southeast, or right. Then begin a climbing traverse on scree and broken rock under the 6,701-foot peak to the flat saddle overlooking the trail to Grand Pass.

Once at the saddle, you can drop about 200 vertical feet to the established trail by following a wide, descending ledge across a crumbling cliff of rock and scree. Follow the established trail to the left past Gladys and Moose Lakes to return to Obstruction Point—remembering the 1,100-foot climb that begins just past Moose Lake. Hikers can also return via the off-trail route, avoiding the descent into the Moose Lake basin.

## Appleton Pass to High Divide

This is a historic high alpine traverse pioneered by Herb Crisler, the last mountain man of the Olympics and the cinematographer responsible for Disney's nature film, *The Olympic Elk*. It follows an indefinite way trail for about 5 miles around the Cat Creek basin, where the Blue Glacier on Mount Olympus seems so close you can count crevasses creasing its white cloak. The total trail distance is 16.6 miles; off-trail hiking is 4.5 miles. You'll gain and lose about 3,800 feet on this hike.

Begin by following the trail to Upper Sol Duc Campsite (Hike 58). You'll strike the Appleton Pass Trail junction 5.0 miles up the trail. Turn left at this junction, marked by a sign, and begin climbing 2.6 miles on established trail to Appleton Pass. You'll leave the established trail at 5,100-foot Appleton Pass and climb past Oyster Lake over a low, flat summit to the south.

Cross the summit and begin a descending traverse along the west shoulder of the peak, aiming toward an obvious low saddle to the south. The late Robert L. Wood named the pass "Spread Eagle," for the snowfield on the north side. This saddle marks the divide in the ridge that separates the Cat Creek drainage, to the south, from the Sol Duc River drainage, to the north. You may see a way trail climbing to the saddle; in any event, climb to the saddle. You'll get a good view of the Cat Creek basin below, and two small tarns in the flat meadows 500 feet below to the south.

Once at the saddle, turn right and follow way trails and game trails as they traverse to the west underneath the crest of the ridge. Try to maintain your elevation at about 5,000 feet. You'll round a sharp ridge descending to Cat Creek basin into a second cirque. Stay high here, maintaining as much elevation as the terrain will permit. After crossing the second cirque, you'll round a second sharp ridge into a third cirque, where you'll encounter the steepest sidehill. You should find a number of elk trails traversing the steep meadows above Cat Creek basin. Stay high if possible, but if you need to drop into the Cat Creek basin below, follow meadows and forested ridges west to find the Cat Creek Basin Trail. If you stay high, you'll cross into a high, flat basin that holds Cat Lake, also called Swimming Bear Lake from an opening scene in Crisler's movie.

From Cat Lake climb several hundred feet up the swale to the west, round a final ridge and traverse a final cirque to join the established trail leading up to High Divide a few hundred feet below the divide. Turn right, or west, on the trail and follow it for about 1.3 miles to its junction with the trail heading downhill to Heart Lake and Upper Sol Duc Park. Turn right on this trail and follow it from Heart Lake for 8.0 miles, as described in the High Divide Loop (Hike 59). You'll pass the Appleton Pass Trail 5.0 miles from the trailhead.

## Boulder Lake to Appleton Pass

Here's a long, very difficult alpine traverse that entails just about every kind of off-trail walking: forest side-hilling, climbing steep snowfields and rock fields, and walking broad alpine benches carpeted by heather and a kaleidoscope of wildflowers. The total distance on the trail is 13.4 miles; the off-trail distance is about 4.5 miles. You'll climb and descend 3,800 feet. You can shorten the trail distance by about 5 miles if you backpack 2.5 miles to the old auto campground at Olympic Hot Springs, then get an early start the following morning.

The Olympic Hot Springs Road is expected to be open by October 2023, but it is always wise to check with the Olympic National Park Visitor Center, (360) 565-3130, before planning this hike. Since removal of the Elwha dams, the river has been a bit unpredictable and lower portions of the road could be impassable from time to time.

Begin by following the trail to Boulder Lake (Hike 49). Cross the outlet stream and follow the way trail around the south shore of the lake. This trail climbs above the lake through alpine forest and soon turns up a steep gully to the south. Climb the gully to a rock overlook, where you can see a small tarn to the east. From here you may be able to follow a faint way trail as it traverses south through the forest, about 100 feet above benches below. Continue through the forest for about a half-mile to the point where the sharp ridge above you on your right drops steeply down to the east. From the ridge crest you should be able to see Three Horse Lake about 300 feet below the ridge, to the south.

A rough way trail drops steeply down the east side of the ridge through subalpine forest, then turns south to a flat bench above Three Horse Lake, 4,150 feet above sea level. Stay on the north shore around the lake to a campsite just across the inlet stream.

The lake is a shallow, clear tarn that holds a rare sustaining population of rainbow trout, which spawn in the inlet creek. It makes an excellent destination for hikers looking for a shorter off-trail adventure.

To continue, follow the inlet stream from the campsite along the south side of the stream about a quarter-mile, climbing through an avalanche path marked by Alaska cedar about 100 feet above the inlet stream to a cliff and waterfall on the left, or south. Look for a way trail leading up the rocky ridge just east of the waterfall, and follow that way trail into a gully leading south. The way trail climbs the gully for several hundred vertical feet, then switches back abruptly to cross to the ridge crest to the west, following the ridge crest to a flat basin just below 5,100-foot Everett Peak. Here you'll find a clear, shallow alpine tarn just below the ridge crest.

Climb around the tarn and up to the crest of the ridge, a broad, open saddle that overlooks Blue Lake, your next destination. You'll find a faint way trail or game trail that drops steeply down the open meadow into Alaska cedar groves before turning to drop and cross the outlet stream at Blue Lake, 4,750 feet above sea level. Blue Lake is another good turnaround spot for hikers who aren't looking for a full day of hiking, although you'll definitely deserve a soak in Olympic Hot Springs and several bottles of ibuprofen if you return via Boulder Lake by retracing your route. The lake is probably the point of no return; once past here, it's likely quicker to return by pressing on to Appleton Pass.

Follow the east shore around Blue Lake, then climb a swale to the south, emerging on a broad ridge of glacier-polished rock. Climb this ridge to the west to tiny Mud Lake, a beautiful alpine tarn about 5,100 feet above sea level that is not shown on any USGS map. Circle the lake on the south side and climb a steep 30-degree snowfield to an obvious, tree-topped notch to the west. This notch was named Passout Pass by the late Robert L. Wood, which may well describe your physical condition upon reaching it—as it did ours.

Push through the trees at the pass and descend the steep west side from the notch, following traces of a way trail leading southwesterly into the basin below Mount Appleton. Stay as high as possible around the basin to gain the rocky, rounded ridge to the west.

Once there, turn south again and after dropping about 100 feet through alpine forest, traverse underneath the unnamed peak just south of Mount Appleton. You'll cross two gullies on a descending traverse before emerging into steep alpine meadows leading down to the trail at Appleton Pass.

Turn east, or left, on the established trail and begin the 7.6-mile trek downhill to the trailhead.

# INDEX